Advanced Data Analytics with AWS

Explore Data Analysis Concepts in the Cloud to Gain Meaningful Insights and Build Robust Data Engineering Workflows Across Diverse Data Sources

Joseph Conley

www.orangeava.com

First published: April 2024

Published by: Orange Education Pvt Ltd, AVA™

Address: 9, Daryaganj, Delhi, 110002, India

275 New North Road Islington Suite 1314 London,

N1 7AA, United Kingdom

ISBN: 978-81-97081-89-7

www.orangeava.com

Dedicated To

Joey, Brendan, Jack, and Luke

For Keeping me Young and Curious

About the Author

Joseph Conley holds a Master of Science in Computer Science from Drexel University and a Bachelor of Science in Mathematics and Economics from the University of Scranton. He has developed large-scale, data-centric platforms for various companies and startups in the Greater Philadelphia area. Joe holds a patent for creating a system for anti-monotony detection in new home construction for master-planned communities and has also earned his AWS certificate for Data Analytics - Specialty (DAS-C01).

Joe enjoys working on side projects and has contributed to several open-source projects. He shares his knowledge through various blogs, seminars, and online posts on social media. You can find him on Twitter/X at @jpc2_ and on his blog at jpc2.org. Beyond his tech pursuits, Joe is an avid investor and enjoys spending time researching companies and business models.

When not working on technical projects, Joe enjoys reading, golfing, and is a lifelong Philadelphia sports fan. He enjoys spending his summers at the Jersey Shore with his wife Janine and four young boys.

About the Technical Reviewer

Gaurav H Kankaria, with nearly a decade of experience in Data and Analytics, specializes in driving business growth for retail and financial clients. His expertise lies in architecting data-intensive solutions and leveraging AI/ML technologies to solve complex challenges.

Gaurav has a proven track record of delivering impactful results, from designing scalable data architectures to implementing predictive analytics solutions. He has served a diverse range of clients, spanning retail and financial sectors, where he has led projects to drive top-line and bottom-line improvements.

Gaurav holds an MBA in Finance from the Indian School of Business and a Bachelor of Technology in Electrical, Electronics, and Communications Engineering from Vellore Institute of Technology. He is also certified in AWS Cloud Practitioner, AWS Solutions Architect - Professional, AWS Data Analytics - Specialty, and AWS Security - Specialty.

As a technical reviewer for the book, Gaurav has contributed his expertise to ensure its quality and accuracy. Passionate about sharing his knowledge, he looks forward to the book's launch, aiming to empower professionals with actionable insights and expertise.

Acknowledgements

I have truly enjoyed the journey of writing *Advanced Data Analytics with* AWS, and I am deeply grateful to everyone who has played a crucial role in bringing this book to fruition. This endeavor would not have been possible without the support, guidance, and expertise generously shared by many.

Firstly, I have had the privilege to work with and learn from some of the smartest people in the world. Thank you to all current and past coworkers who have inspired me to take risks and push myself to keep learning.

To everyone at the publication house who has contributed in various capacities, your collective efforts have greatly helped me in this endeavor. I appreciate the collaborative spirit that has fueled the creation of *Advanced Data Analytics with* AWS. Special gratitude is extended to the technical reviewers who provided insightful feedback and guidance. Their expertise has been invaluable in refining the content and ensuring its accuracy.

To my family, thank you for your unwavering support. I especially want to thank my wife, Janine, for being a constant source of inspiration and strength throughout this process. We make a great team!

Finally, to the readers, thank you for choosing this book as a trusted guide in your quest for knowledge. I hope it proves to be a valuable companion on your journey to learning data analytics and inspires you to keep learning these cutting-edge technologies.

Preface

Our world is awash in data, and arming yourself with the tools to manage and understand this data will be a key differentiator for your career. *Advanced Data Analytics with* AWS seeks to give you a broad introduction to the skills needed to find data-driven insights and effectively present that information to important stakeholders.

This book comprises 10 chapters, with each module designed to cover a specific core concept of data analytics. Topics range from basic introductions and exercises to more comprehensive explorations and advanced topics.

Chapter 1. Introduction to Data Analytics and AWS: This chapter provides an introduction to data analytics, covering key concepts such as the types of analytics, real-world applications across industries, tools and platforms, and the benefits and limitations. Readers will gain a foundational understanding of what data analytics is, why it matters, and how AWS enables scalable and secure analytics capabilities.

Chapter 2. Getting Started with AWS: This chapter provides an introduction to using Amazon Web Services (AWS) for data analytics. Readers will learn foundational concepts like EC2, S3, and IAM, as well as best practices around account setup, security, pricing, and assembling basic analytics pipelines using services like Athena and QuickSight.

Chapter 3. Collecting Data with AWS: This chapter covers strategies and tools for efficiently collecting and storing different types of data using AWS services. Readers will learn best practices for pulling data from APIs and databases, receiving pushed data streams, running large batch jobs, choosing optimal data formats, and leveraging AWS tools like S3, Glue, and Lambda to build robust and automated data pipelines.

Chapter 4. Processing Data on AWS: This chapter explains how to process data on AWS using Glue, a visual data preparation tool, walking through key concepts such as automatically crawling data sources, leveraging a centralized data catalog, and transforming data via graphical no-code workflows or Spark scripts. Readers will learn hands-on skills to prepare raw data for analysis, including ingesting, cleansing, reshaping, and enriching it using Glue's intuitive interface and managed Apache Spark environment.

Chapter 5. Descriptive Analytics on AWS: This chapter explores descriptive data analytics techniques, such as measures of central tendency and variability, using Amazon Athena to query datasets stored on AWS, and following best practices to optimize performance, cost, and security. Readers will learn fundamental descriptive statistics concepts and how to apply them at scale to uncover insights from data using Athena's SQL capabilities.

Chapter 6. Advanced Data Analysis on AWS: This chapter provides an in-depth overview of advanced data analysis capabilities on AWS through the machine learning service Amazon SageMaker. Readers will learn core concepts of machine learning, different approaches and real-world use cases, a step-by-step introduction to SageMaker including no-code options, and examples of building models for tasks like predictions, recommendations, classification, and decision-making.

Chapter 7. Additional Use Cases for Data Analysis: This chapter explores additional advanced use cases for leveraging *Advanced Data Analytics with* AWS, including time series forecasting with Amazon Forecast, text analytics using Amazon Comprehend, graph database analytics with Amazon Neptune, and analyzing IoT data with AWS IoT Analytics. Readers will learn how these specialized AWS services can help transform diverse data types like time series, text, graphs, and IoT data into meaningful business insights tailored to different needs.

Chapter 8. Data Virtualization and Interaction on AWS: This chapter provides a comprehensive overview of data visualization and interaction capabilities on AWS, guiding readers through foundations like Amazon QuickSight for building stunning, interactive dashboards fueled by real-time data to uncover actionable insights. Readers will learn best practices for choosing optimal chart types, implementing effective visual design, and leveraging machine learning to take their data exploration to the next level.

Chapter 9. The Future of Data Analytics: This chapter explores several cutting-edge innovations that are shaping the future of data analytics, including generative AI, blockchain, edge computing, quantum computing, and sustainability. Readers will learn about the tremendous new capabilities these technologies can enable for gathering insights from data as well as perspectives on how to navigate the rapid pace of change in the data analytics landscape.

Chapter 10. Conclusion and Next Steps: This chapter provides a conclusion to the book by reviewing why data analytics is important for business, potential career paths, additional compatible frameworks, AWS certification options, and extra learning resources. Readers will learn key reasons to invest in data analytics capabilities and skills, obtain advice on specializing and advancing their careers, discover complementary open-source tools, evaluate certification choices, and find recommendations for further developing their data analytics acumen.

This book is a hands-on guide filled with practical examples, real-world scenarios, and best practices. I hope this journey of learning Data Analytics through the lens of AWS sparks ideas for how to build and analyze your own data applications. Enjoy!

Get a Free eBook

We hope you are enjoying your recently purchased book! Your feedback is incredibly valuable to us, and to all other readers looking for great books.

If you found this book helpful or enjoyable, we would truly appreciate it, if you could take a moment to leave a short review with a 5 star rating on Amazon. It helps us grow, and lets other readers discover our books.

As a thank you, we would love to send you a free digital copy of this book, and a **30%** discount code on your next cart value on our official websites:

www.orangeava.com

www.orangeava.in (For Indian Subcontinent)

☑ **Here's how:**

Leave a review for the book on Amazon.

Take a screenshot of your review, and send an email to **info@orangeava.com** (it can be just the confirmation screen).

Once, we receive your screenshot, we will send you the digital file, within 24 hours.

Thank you so much for your support – it means a lot to us!

Downloading the code bundles and colored images

Please follow the links or scan the QR codes to download the **_Code Bundles and Images_** of the book:

https://github.com/ava-orange-education/Advanced-Data-Analytics-with-AWS

The code bundles and images of the book are also hosted on **_https://rebrand.ly/gywa23f_**

In case there's an update to the code, it will be updated on the existing GitHub repository.

Errata

We take immense pride in our work at **Orange Education Pvt Ltd,** and follow best practices to ensure the accuracy of our content to provide an indulging reading experience to our subscribers. Our readers are our mirrors, and we use their inputs to reflect and improve upon human errors, if any, that may have occurred during the publishing processes involved. To let us maintain the quality and help us reach out to any readers who might be having difficulties due to any unforeseen errors, please write to us at :

errata@orangeava.com

Your support, suggestions, and feedback are highly appreciated.

DID YOU KNOW

Did you know that Orange Education Pvt Ltd offers eBook versions of every book published, with PDF and ePub files available? You can upgrade to the eBook version at **www.orangeava.com** and as a print book customer, you are entitled to a discount on the eBook copy. Get in touch with us at: **info@orangeava.com** for more details.

At **www.orangeava.com**, you can also read a collection of free technical articles, sign up for a range of free newsletters, and receive exclusive discounts and offers on AVA™ Books and eBooks.

PIRACY

If you come across any illegal copies of our works in any form on the internet, we would be grateful if you would provide us with the location address or website name. Please contact us at **info@orangeava.com** with a link to the material.

ARE YOU INTERESTED IN AUTHORING WITH US?

If there is a topic that you have expertise in, and you are interested in either writing or contributing to a book, please write to us at **business@orangeava.com**. We are on a journey to help developers and tech professionals to gain insights on the present technological advancements and innovations happening across the globe and build a community that believes Knowledge is best acquired by sharing and learning with others. Please reach out to us to learn what our audience demands and how you can be part of this educational reform. We also welcome ideas from tech experts and help them build learning and development content for their domains.

REVIEWS

Please leave a review. Once you have read and used this book, why not leave a review on the site that you purchased it from? Potential readers can then see and use your unbiased opinion to make purchase decisions. We at Orange Education would love to know what you think about our products, and our authors can learn from your feedback. Thank you!

For more information about Orange Education, please visit **www.orangeava.com**.

Table of Contents

CHAPTER 1

Introduction to Data Analytics and AWS

Introduction

This chapter introduces the fundamentals of data analytics and reviews the most important concepts to keep in mind as you learn the art and science of data analytics. We will learn about the four different types of data analytics, and how and why they are used.

This chapter will also introduce you to **Amazon Web Services (AWS),** briefly describing its history and evolution and why it is an appropriate choice for any data analytics project, both now and in the future.

Structure

In this chapter, we will discuss the following topics:

- What is Data Analytics? Why is It Important?
- Types of Data Analytics: Descriptive, Diagnostic, Predictive, Prescriptive
- Tools of Data Analytics: Going Beyond Spreadsheets
- Data Analytics in the Real World
- What is AWS? Why Should We Use It for Data Analytics?
- What is Cloud Computing, and What are Its Benefits?
- Case Studies of Successful Data Analytics Projects

Navigating the World of Data

Data! Data! Data! I can't make bricks without clay.

- *Sherlock Holmes, "The Adventure of the Copper Beeches"* (1892)

Our world is awash in data! Recent advancements in technologies like the internet, personal computing, and now cloud infrastructure have lowered the cost of generating, storing, and using data. Tools like spreadsheets and relational databases have made it easy to share and analyze data. And more recently, the advent of Generative AI has further democratized the analysis of data, allowing users to make simple text-based queries of data to generate insights. The IDC estimates that our world will generate 163 zettabytes (one zettabyte = 1021 bytes = a trillion GB) of data by 2025 [1]:

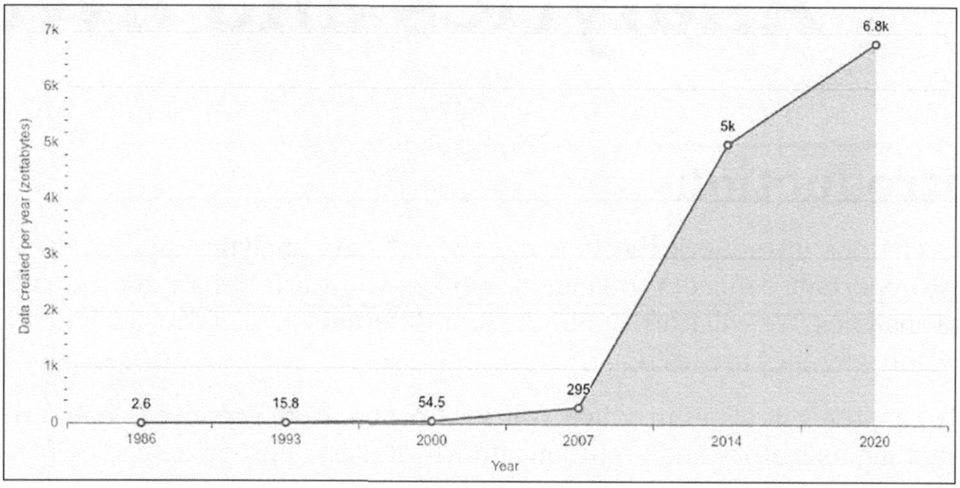

Figure 1.1: *Data Created Per Year (zettabytes) - IDC Global Report*

Luckily, this exponential growth of data has been accompanied by the rapid advancement of tools to help make sense of the data. Such tooling can be daunting, especially for people who think they might lack the ability to analyze such large volumes of data. This book will dispel that notion by providing simple yet effective strategies for analyzing data and empowering you, dear reader, to navigate the tides of these massive oceans of data.

Welcome to Data Analytics

As we embark on our journey, let's start with the basics: what is data analytics? It is **the process of collecting and investigating data to find insights**. Sounds simple? If we break this process down to its core functions, it can be. Let's walk through the steps:

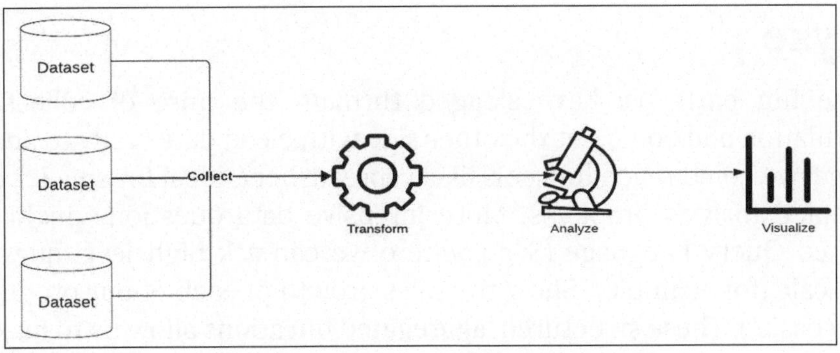

Figure 1.2: *Data Analytics Pipeline*

Collect

This part seems easy; can't we just grab the data wherever it lives? Easier said than done. Collecting data involves gaining access to the target system by managing an authentication flow (for example, OAuth to get API access), streaming data from a high-volume source (for example, imagine drinking from the firehose of Twitter tweets), and/or querying relational data from multiple source systems. This traditionally required having some basic knowledge of a programming language (Python is considered the *lingua franca* of working with data, and is definitely useful!), but as we will see, modern tooling has become much more user-friendly and has greatly reduced the technical barriers to making sense of data.

Transform

Collecting data is only part of the battle. Data can be encoded in various structured formats (CSV, JSON, XML), or unstructured formats like plain text or audio/video media. Data usually requires some level of cleaning (that is, normalizing state names or converting a string-based field to numeric). Combining multiple datasets usually requires some level of transformation to a common data model and implementing domain-specific business logic (for example, applying invoicing logic to determine if a customer is overdue and needs to go to a collection agency). Finally, we might want to format our final dataset into a specific format for use in another source system, like structuring data for an analytics database or preparing text data for a natural language pipeline. This might seem like low-level plumbing work, but doing this step well ensures that we have high-quality, accurate data to analyze. "*Garbage in, garbage out*" readily applies here, so make sure your data stays clean!

Analyze

Now the fun part! We have slogged through the mire of collection and transformation and come out the other side with clean data ready to analyze. At this stage, we could reach for tools like a spreadsheet, ideal for smaller datasets and simpler analysis problems. More intensive data questions might require Structured Query Language (SQL), where we can ask high-level questions of data at scale (for example, "Show the sales growth of each of our products on a monthly basis"). These structured, aggregated questions allow us to make sense of our data across several dimensions. For more advanced queries, we could also turn to Machine Learning to detect regression patterns and make predictive forecasts.

Visualize

At this stage, we have hopefully gotten some basic answers, and now we need to present that information in a useful way, either through a static data-driven presentation or a real-time data dashboard, to help decision-makers understand reality and make decisions. As management guru Peter Drucker said, "What gets measured, gets managed". Visualization is a core part of understanding how to use data to manage your business, and it's critical that these visualizations use up-to-date, high-quality data to empower decision-makers.

While you are likely familiar with tools like PowerPoint for presentation, there are more data-centric visualization tools like Tableau and Quicksight, which connect directly with your datasets and help you shape and visualize your data across many dimensions. These tools not only offer an extensive library of visualization types but also the ability to show data in real-time, especially in situations where real-time data is critical (for example, in financial markets).

Example - Land Grab

Let's walk through a simple example. You work for a real estate development company and you want to build a brand new residential community targeting the 55 and over population. You want to ask questions about the U.S. Census data and local property transactions to get insights on demographics and price trends. The preceding process could be executed by doing the following:

1. **Collect**: Download the Census data from data.census.gov [2] (you can use the filter controls on the left to filter by specific geographic areas and postal codes). Find a source for recent real estate transactions (for

example, Redfin's monthly housing market data [3]) to get the latest pricing data. Integrate with mortgage rate providers like FRED [4] to see how rates have changed over time.

2. **Transform**: Clean the data (these sources are typically pristine, so this step might be minimal) and model the data into a smaller, simpler set of fields that you want to analyze:

	A	B	C	D	E	F
1	**period_begin**	**period_end**	**region**	**state_code**	**property_type**	**median_sale_price**
2	2023-08-01	2023-08-31	Washington	WA	All Residential	614800
3	2023-03-01	2023-03-31	North Dakota	ND	Single Family Residential	279500
4	2023-02-01	2023-02-28	Hawaii	HI	Single Family Residential	809100
5	2023-06-01	2023-06-30	Oregon	OR	Multi-Family (2-4 Unit)	535600
6	2023-05-01	2023-05-31	Oklahoma	OK	Multi-Family (2-4 Unit)	243500
7	2023-03-01	2023-03-31	Texas	TX	Condo/Co-op	274000
8	2023-07-01	2023-07-31	Illinois	IL	All Residential	287500
9	2023-03-01	2023-03-31	Kentucky	KY	Multi-Family (2-4 Unit)	209500
10	2023-06-01	2023-06-30	Virginia	VA	Townhouse	461800
11	2023-05-01	2023-05-31	Washington	WA	Condo/Co-op	439400
12	2023-02-01	2023-02-28	Kentucky	KY	Condo/Co-op	182300
13	2023-05-01	2023-05-31	South Dakota	SD	All Residential	318900
14	2023-04-01	2023-04-30	Hawaii	HI	Condo/Co-op	576200
15	2023-04-01	2023-04-30	Delaware	DE	Townhouse	252900
16	2023-02-01	2023-02-28	Montana	MT	Condo/Co-op	746100
17	2023-05-01	2023-05-31	South Carolina	SC	Multi-Family (2-4 Unit)	359300
18	2023-03-01	2023-03-31	Illinois	IL	All Residential	259100
19	2023-07-01	2023-07-31	Tennessee	TN	All Residential	383900
20	2023-07-01	2023-07-31	New Jersey	NJ	Multi-Family (2-4 Unit)	593900

Figure 1.3: *Sample Monthly Real Estate Pricing Data. Source: Redfin https://www.redfin.com/*

3. **Analyze**: Write queries to see how the demographic and price data correlate. Which states/zip codes show an increasing 55+ population? Have land/home prices appreciated at a reasonable level, or are certain areas too expensive and pricing out potential homebuyers?

4. **Visualize**: Generate charts to show the answers to your questions and to show a simple linear regression of the most important variables. You can use popular data visualization tools like Tableau, PowerBI, or even Google Sheets for simpler visuals. We will show how to build dashboards in later chapters using Amazon Quicksight:

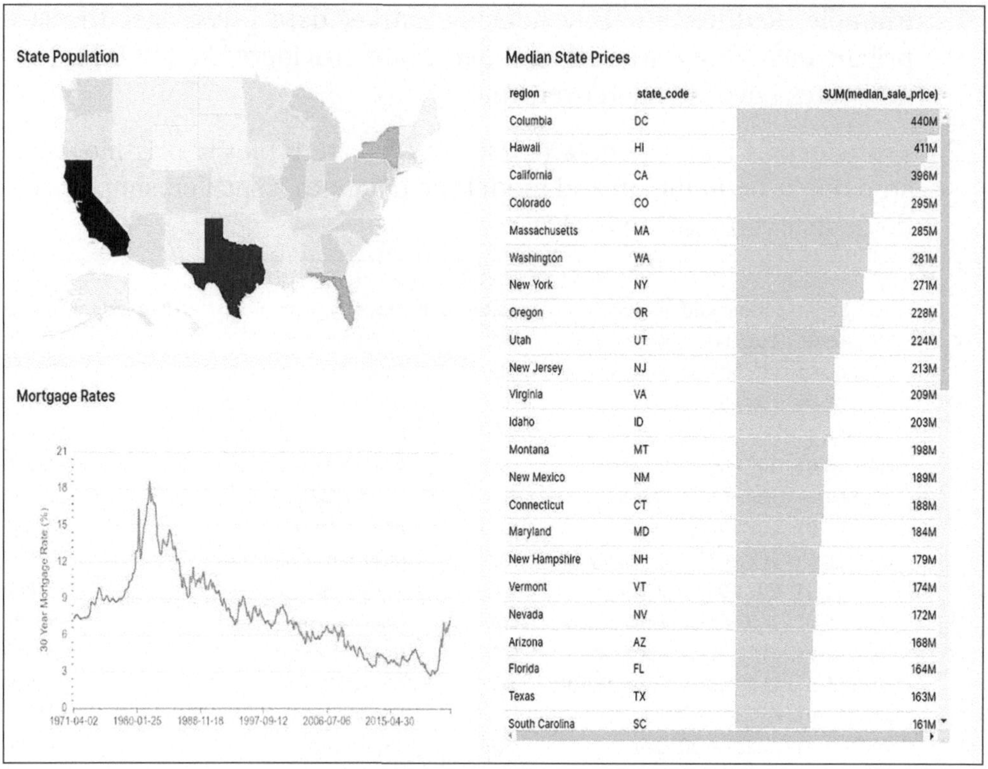

Figure 1.4: *Sample Real Estate Data Dashboard*

You can see how powerful the Data Analytics toolbox can be, and why the field is growing in popularity. Universities now offer over 1,000 degrees and specializations related to data science [5], ranging in focus from high-level decision-making to technical mastery of the preceding steps. It can be daunting to wrap your head around all aspects of Data Analytics, but luckily modern tools greatly simplify this process, allowing you to focus on the unique challenges of your business.

As we will soon learn, AWS provides a variety of tools to reduce the complexity involved in collecting, transforming, analyzing, and visualizing data. Most tools rely on tried-and-true languages like SQL, which have simple yet powerful techniques to ask questions of your data.

The Purpose of Data Analytics

If you're going to live a long time, you have to keep learning…if you don't adapt, you're like a one-legged man at an ass-kicking contest.

-Charlie Munger, legendary investor

This process may still seem overwhelming - is all of this really necessary? Are the insights we find from data really worth the cost of setting up all this data analytics infrastructure? In a word, yes!

Data analytics turns the ocean of raw data into actionable insights. Businesses collect vast amounts of data, but without analytics, this data remains untapped and underutilized. Through various types of analytics – descriptive, diagnostic, predictive, and prescriptive – we will learn techniques to understand past performance, diagnose issues, forecast future trends, and make informed decisions. Whether it's optimizing operations, enhancing customer experience, or identifying new market opportunities, data analytics provides the tools to make sense of complex data landscapes.

Another key reason is to gain a competitive advantage. In today's data-driven world, businesses that leverage analytics effectively outperform those that don't. A recent McKinsey study shows that companies who use data analytics in their operations realize 5-6% more productivity and profitability than their peers who don't [6].

By acting on these insights, businesses can stay ahead of competitors, adapt to market changes more quickly, and ultimately drive greater profitability.

Efficiency and cost reduction also rank high among the reasons for using data analytics. By analyzing operational data, companies can identify bottlenecks, inefficiencies, or areas where resources are underutilized. This leads to better resource allocation, streamlined processes, and reduced operational costs. For example, predictive maintenance analytics can forecast when a machine is likely to fail, allowing for timely repairs and avoiding costly downtime. In essence, data analytics enables businesses to do more with less, maximizing both performance and profitability.

Data Analytics is a powerful tool and can give any business an edge by improving how they serve their customers. Ignore this tool at your own peril!

Types of Data Analytics

There are four main types of data analytics: descriptive, diagnostic, predictive, and prescriptive. Each type focuses on a different goal with respect to data and requires different tools and techniques to realize these goals.

Descriptive Analytics - The What

Descriptive analytics serves as the foundation of data analysis by summarizing raw data and converting it into a form that is easy to understand. It employs statistical techniques to present a clear picture of what has happened in the past by focusing on providing insights into existing data. It uses measures such as mean, median, and standard deviation, as well as data visualization tools like charts, histograms, and dashboards, to make the data comprehensible:

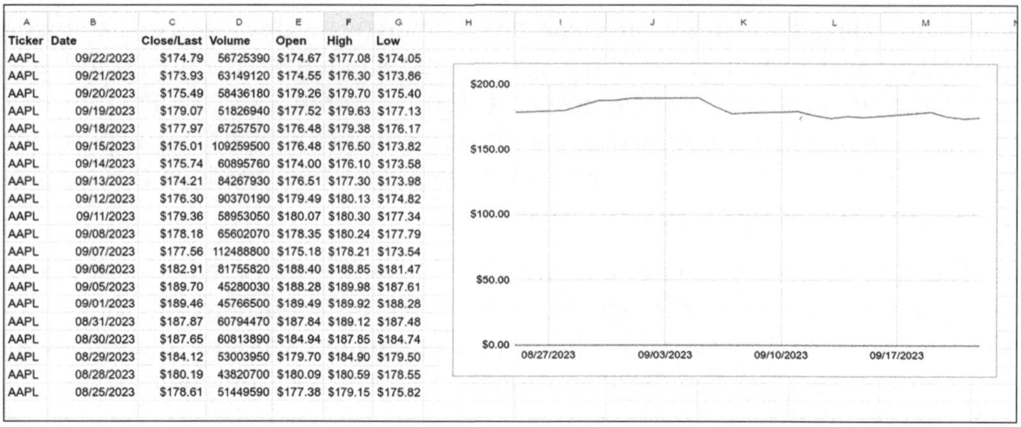

Ticker	Date	Close/Last	Volume	Open	High	Low
AAPL	09/22/2023	$174.79	56725390	$174.67	$177.08	$174.05
AAPL	09/21/2023	$173.93	63149120	$174.55	$176.30	$173.86
AAPL	09/20/2023	$175.49	58436180	$179.26	$179.70	$175.40
AAPL	09/19/2023	$179.07	51826940	$177.52	$179.63	$177.13
AAPL	09/18/2023	$177.97	67257570	$176.48	$179.38	$176.17
AAPL	09/15/2023	$175.01	109259500	$176.48	$176.50	$173.82
AAPL	09/14/2023	$175.74	60895760	$174.00	$176.10	$173.58
AAPL	09/13/2023	$174.21	84267930	$176.51	$177.30	$173.98
AAPL	09/12/2023	$176.30	90370190	$179.49	$180.13	$174.82
AAPL	09/11/2023	$179.36	58953050	$180.07	$180.30	$177.34
AAPL	09/08/2023	$178.18	65602070	$178.35	$180.24	$177.79
AAPL	09/07/2023	$177.56	112488800	$175.18	$178.21	$173.54
AAPL	09/06/2023	$182.91	81755820	$188.40	$188.85	$181.47
AAPL	09/05/2023	$189.70	45280030	$188.28	$189.98	$187.61
AAPL	09/01/2023	$189.46	45766500	$189.49	$189.92	$188.28
AAPL	08/31/2023	$187.87	60794470	$187.84	$189.12	$187.48
AAPL	08/30/2023	$187.65	60813890	$184.94	$187.85	$184.74
AAPL	08/29/2023	$184.12	53003950	$179.70	$184.90	$179.50
AAPL	08/28/2023	$180.19	43820700	$180.09	$180.59	$178.55
AAPL	08/25/2023	$178.61	51449590	$177.38	$179.15	$175.82

***Figure 1.5**: Spreadsheet with Chart - AAPL Daily Stock Prices*

Why should you care about descriptive analytics? It sets the stage for informed decision-making. By offering a snapshot of key metrics, it helps you understand your organization's strengths and weaknesses. Whether you are looking at customer behavior, sales performance, or operational efficiency, descriptive analytics gives you the baseline data you need. Without it, you are essentially flying blind, unable to move on to more advanced analytics or make data-driven decisions.

You will find descriptive analytics at work in various sectors. Retailers use it to monitor sales, inventory, and customer traffic. Healthcare providers rely on it to summarize patient histories and treatment outcomes. Financial firms track trading volumes and market prices with it. Even sports teams use descriptive analytics to evaluate player performance and strategize for games. These examples highlight how descriptive analytics serves as an indispensable tool in our data-driven world.

These data summaries can typically be represented as simple metrics that can be tracked over time. They can also lead to deeper investigations of portions of the data, leading to diagnostic analytics.

Diagnostic Analytics - The Why

Diagnostic analytics digs deeper into data to go beyond "what" questions to ask "why". This form of analytics often involves more complex statistical tools and data mining techniques, such as regression analysis, drill-down, and data discovery. By dissecting historical data, diagnostic analytics helps you identify patterns, anomalies, and relationships that might not be immediately obvious:

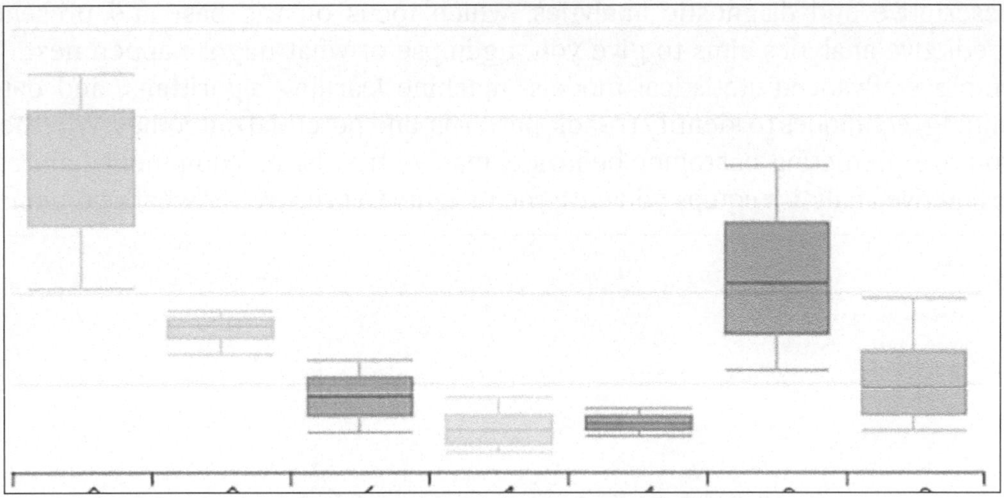

Figure 1.6: *Box Plot - Diagnosing Outliers*

The importance of diagnostic analytics lies in its problem-solving capabilities. Once you know the "why" behind the data, you can take targeted actions to address issues or capitalize on opportunities. For instance, if a business notices a sudden drop in sales, diagnostic analytics can help pinpoint whether the cause is a change in consumer behavior, a new competitor, or a flawed marketing strategy. This level of insight is crucial for making informed decisions and strategizing effectively for the future.

Examples of diagnostic analytics are plentiful across industries. In healthcare, it can help analyze why a particular treatment is more effective for a certain demographic. In marketing, it can dissect why a specific campaign outperformed others, breaking down variables like audience targeting, messaging, and timing. Manufacturing companies often use diagnostic analytics to identify bottlenecks in their production processes or to understand the causes of equipment failures. By providing a deeper understanding of the factors influencing outcomes, diagnostic analytics plays a critical role in shaping smarter, more effective strategies.

Investigations might include:

- Why did a large number of customers churn last quarter?
- Why did a specific drug treatment have success in our latest trials?
- Why did energy consumption increase significantly during a specific time period?

Predictive Analytics - The Future

Predictive analytics uses historical data to forecast future events. Unlike descriptive and diagnostic analytics, which focus on the past and present, predictive analytics aims to give you a glimpse of what might happen next. It employs advanced statistical models, machine learning algorithms, and data mining techniques to identify trends, patterns, and potential outcomes. Whether you are predicting customer behavior, market trends, or equipment failures, predictive analytics equips you with the insights to prepare for what's coming:

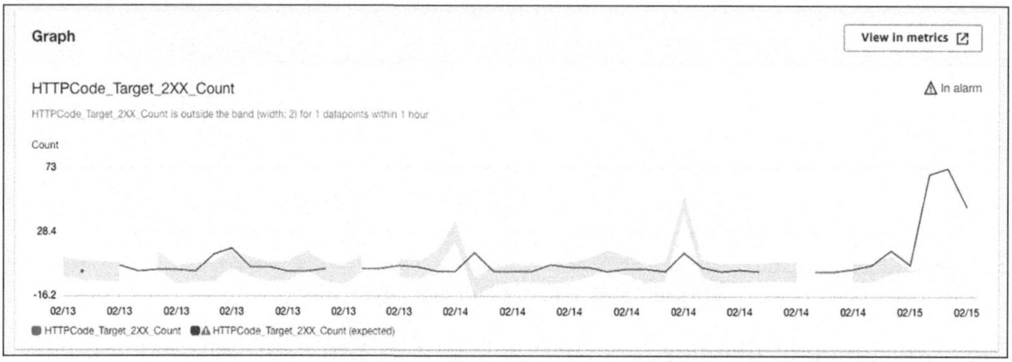

***Figure 1.7**: CloudWatch Predictions with Anomaly Detection*

Why does predictive analytics matter? It gives you a competitive edge. By anticipating future events, you can make proactive decisions rather than reactive ones. Imagine knowing which products will likely become bestsellers, which marketing strategies will resonate with your audience, or when a machine on your production line is likely to fail. Armed with these insights, you can allocate resources more efficiently, improve customer satisfaction, and even prevent costly problems before they occur.

You will find predictive analytics in action across various sectors. Retailers use it to forecast demand and manage inventory. Financial institutions employ it to assess credit risk and detect fraudulent activities. Healthcare providers use predictive models to identify patients at high risk of readmission or to anticipate the spread of infectious diseases. Even weather forecasting relies on predictive analytics to anticipate climatic conditions. These examples show how predictive analytics not only informs better decision-making but also drives innovation and efficiency across industries.

Prescriptive Analytics - The Should

Prescriptive analytics goes beyond telling you what will likely happen; it recommends specific actions to achieve desired outcomes. Building on insights from descriptive, diagnostic, and predictive analytics, prescriptive analytics uses advanced algorithms and simulations to suggest the best course of action. It answers the question, "What should we do?" Whether you are optimizing supply chain routes, personalizing marketing campaigns, or managing energy consumption, prescriptive analytics provides actionable recommendations:

Figure 1.8: *Funnel Chart - Narrow Down Sales Focus*

So why pay attention to prescriptive analytics? It's your decision-making powerhouse. While predictive analytics can forecast potential future scenarios, prescriptive analytics tells you how to steer toward the best possible outcome. It eliminates guesswork and subjectivity, allowing you to make data-driven decisions that align with your goals. In a world where timing is everything, the ability to make quick, informed decisions can be your competitive advantage.

Examples of prescriptive analytics are abundant and growing. In logistics, companies use it to determine the most efficient delivery routes, saving both time and fuel. In healthcare, prescriptive models can recommend personalized treatment plans for patients, improving outcomes and reducing costs. Energy companies use it to optimize power grid distribution, while online retailers employ prescriptive analytics to personalize shopping experiences, from product recommendations to promotional offers. These applications demonstrate the transformative power of prescriptive analytics in driving operational excellence and strategic decision-making.

Tools of Data Analytics

Data analytics tools include several options, such as spreadsheets for basic data handling, SQL for structured queries, and machine learning for predicting outcomes.

Spreadsheets

Spreadsheets serve as the go-to tool for quick and easy data manipulation and visualization. You enter data into rows and columns, making it visually easy to identify trends, outliers, or interesting patterns. Standard functions for basic statistical analyses, such as mean, median, and standard deviation, are right at your fingertips. You can also employ more complex functions to manipulate data, perform lookups, or even run basic simulations. Need a quick chart or graph? Spreadsheets have you covered with just a couple of clicks.

Spreadsheets don't just offer ease; they also serve as the gateway to more advanced data analytics tools. Many professionals begin their data journey with spreadsheets, learning essential skills like data cleaning, sorting, and basic calculations. This foundational experience creates a smooth transition into more complex platforms and programming languages like SQL or Python. In summary, spreadsheets may not be the most powerful or flashy tool in the data analytics toolbox, but they offer a critical starting point and continue to provide value for tasks requiring quick and straightforward analyses.

Structured Query Language (SQL)

SQL stands as a cornerstone for any serious data analytics effort, especially when dealing with large, complex datasets housed in relational databases. With SQL, you can execute well-defined queries to create custom views on data, conduct joins across multiple tables, and carry out aggregations like sums and averages. Need to analyze quarterly sales data across various regions and product categories? SQL enables you to pull that information efficiently, filter it based on specific criteria, and even perform time-based analyses. It's the go-to tool for turning raw data into actionable insights:

```sql
SELECT year, month, page, COUNT(website_visits) as page_count
FROM user_visits
WHERE year > 2020
GROUP BY year, month, page
ORDER BY page_count DESC;
```

Figure 1.9: *Example SQL Query - Monthly Website Visits by Page*

The importance of SQL in data analytics can't be overstated. While spreadsheets offer a good starting point for smaller data tasks, SQL provides the scalability and complexity needed for real-world applications. The sample query in *Figure 1.9* could be applied across hundreds of GBs of data to answer this question in seconds.

Data analysts, data engineers, and database administrators use SQL daily to manipulate and query data, making it a universal skill in the field. Mastering SQL not only opens the door to in-depth data analysis but also makes you a valuable asset in today's data-driven world. It gives you the ability to interact directly with databases, providing a level of flexibility and power that other tools often can't match.

Machine Learning

Machine learning algorithms sift through large volumes of data to identify patterns, make predictions, or categorize information. Where traditional analytics methods hit a ceiling, machine learning algorithms excel. For example, you can use machine learning to forecast sales based on historical data, identify fraudulent transactions in real-time, or even predict disease outbreaks based on various health indicators. The scope is virtually limitless: from natural language processing in chatbots to recommendation systems that personalize your online shopping experience, machine learning brings a predictive and automated layer to data analytics.

The role of machine learning in data analytics is monumental and continues to grow. Traditional data analytics tools provide a retrospective view of data, helping you understand what has happened. Machine learning, on the other hand, focuses on what could happen in the future, based on existing data. It's like having a crystal ball powered by data points and algorithms. This predictive capability makes machine learning essential for any organization looking to leverage data for competitive advantage. As we generate more and more data, the ability to analyze it in complex ways becomes increasingly crucial, and machine learning stands as the tool that makes this high level of analysis possible.

Data Analytics in the Real World

We have talked at length about what Data Analytics is, why it's important, and what some of the fundamental components are of any good data analysis. Now let's take a deeper look at how specific industries use data analytics.

Healthcare

Data analytics revolutionizes patient care by enabling healthcare workers to make more informed decisions. Advanced analytics tools can analyze a patient's medical history, current condition, and even genetic makeup to recommend personalized treatment plans. These insights help doctors and nurses identify the most effective interventions, predict patient responses, and minimize adverse effects. Real-time monitoring of vital signs and other health metrics also allows for immediate adjustments to treatment, improving patient outcomes:

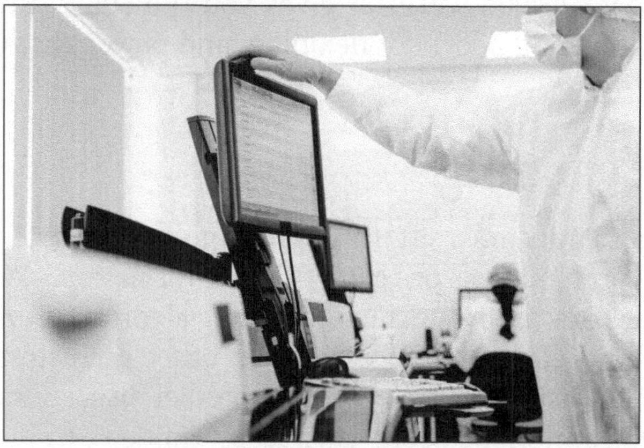

Figure 1.10: *Reviewing Patient Data*

In the realm of medical research, data analytics accelerates the discovery of new treatments and medical technologies. Researchers can sift through vast amounts of clinical data, academic papers, and patient records to identify patterns or correlations that might lead to breakthroughs. Analytics can also optimize clinical trials by predicting outcomes and identifying the most suitable candidates. This speeds up the research process, making it more cost-effective and increasing the likelihood of finding effective treatments for various conditions.

When it comes to hospital management, data analytics streamlines operations and enhances efficiency. By analyzing data on patient flow, staff allocation, and resource utilization, administrators can identify bottlenecks and areas for improvement. Predictive analytics can also forecast patient admissions, helping hospitals to allocate resources more effectively. This ensures that the right staff and equipment are available when needed, reducing wait times and improving the overall quality of care.

Retail

Data analytics transforms inventory management in the retail sector. By analyzing sales data, seasonal trends, and customer behavior, retailers can accurately forecast demand for various products. This allows them to stock the right amount of inventory, reducing carrying costs and avoiding understock or overstock situations. Real-time analytics can also trigger automatic reordering of products, ensuring that popular items are always available for customers.

Customer satisfaction gets a significant boost from data analytics as well. Retailers can track customer interactions across multiple channels, from in-store visits to online browsing. This data helps in personalizing marketing messages, recommending products, and even optimizing store layouts based on customer preferences. Analytics can also identify pain points in the customer journey, such as long checkout lines or difficult website navigation, allowing retailers to address these issues proactively.

In terms of market strategy, data analytics provides invaluable insights. Retailers can analyze market trends, competitor performance, and consumer sentiment to make informed decisions. Whether it's choosing the location for a new store, launching a promotional campaign, or entering a new market, analytics offers the data needed to minimize risk and maximize return on investment. By understanding what drives customer behavior and market trends, retailers can craft strategies that resonate with their target audience, ultimately driving sales and increasing market share.

Finance

Data analytics plays a pivotal role in fraud detection within the financial sector. By analyzing transaction patterns, user behavior, and other relevant data, financial professionals can identify suspicious activities that deviate from the norm. Machine learning algorithms can even adapt over time, becoming more effective at flagging potential fraud. Immediate alerts allow for quick action, minimizing losses and protecting both the institution and its customers.

For crafting investment strategies, data analytics serves as a powerful tool. Financial analysts can sift through vast amounts of market data, historical trends, and economic indicators to identify lucrative investment opportunities. Algorithms can simulate various scenarios to predict how different assets will perform under specific conditions. This data-driven approach enables professionals to make more accurate forecasts, optimize portfolios, and provide better advice to clients.

Risk assessment also benefits immensely from data analytics. Financial institutions can evaluate the creditworthiness of individuals or businesses by analyzing income, spending habits, and past financial behavior. For larger investments, like mergers or acquisitions, analytics can assess the potential risks and returns by examining market conditions, competitor data, and regulatory implications. This comprehensive analysis allows financial professionals to make informed decisions, manage risks effectively, and ensure the long-term stability of their portfolios and institutions.

Life in the Clouds - Introduction to AWS

Now that we have reviewed the nature of data analytics and why it's used, let's explore the innovation that made performing data analytics at scale possible - cloud computing:

Figure 1.11: *Data in the Cloud*

Cloud computing, like personal computing and the internet before it, created an entire category of new businesses and enabled businesses to scale by several orders of magnitude. Before cloud computing, businesses that wished to host software applications or store large amounts of data had to buy and configure physical servers themselves. This often required hiring specialized resources in-house to set up and maintain these servers. Moreover, companies who built applications that had highly variable workloads would have to over-provision their platforms by buying enough servers to cover peak usage, with excess compute capacity sitting idle (incurring unnecessary overhead cost).

Amazon.com struggled with this very issue and devised a unique solution to this problem (initially an internal solution) by centralizing all of their computing and infrastructure needs. Rather than having different teams independently scale up their own resource usage, they built out a common set of infrastructure services that teams could consume. They soon realized how this idea could scale as its own external offering to customers, and soon after, AWS was born.

AWS heralded this new approach, soon to be dubbed "cloud computing", and allowed external companies to rent computing power and storage, scaling their needs up or down with unprecedented flexibility. AWS continued to expand its virtual offerings to object storage (S3), networking (EC2/VPC), databases (RDS/ Aurora), monitoring (CloudWatch), and more in-depth offerings like machine learning, artificial intelligence, Internet of Things (IoT), and even satellite data processing. Each new service aimed to solve specific problems for different types of businesses, making AWS a one-stop-shop for cloud computing needs. This extensive suite of services attracted a diverse clientele, from startups to Fortune 500 companies, all seeking to leverage the power of the cloud.

One of the key ingredients to the success of AWS is how all of their services integrate seamlessly with one another. AWS Step Functions alone can integrate with over 200 different AWS services [7]! Anyone who has built and deployed software will tell you the amount of work it takes to integrate various systems effectively (and conversely the reluctance to move to a different vendor once your platform is launched and serving customers in production):

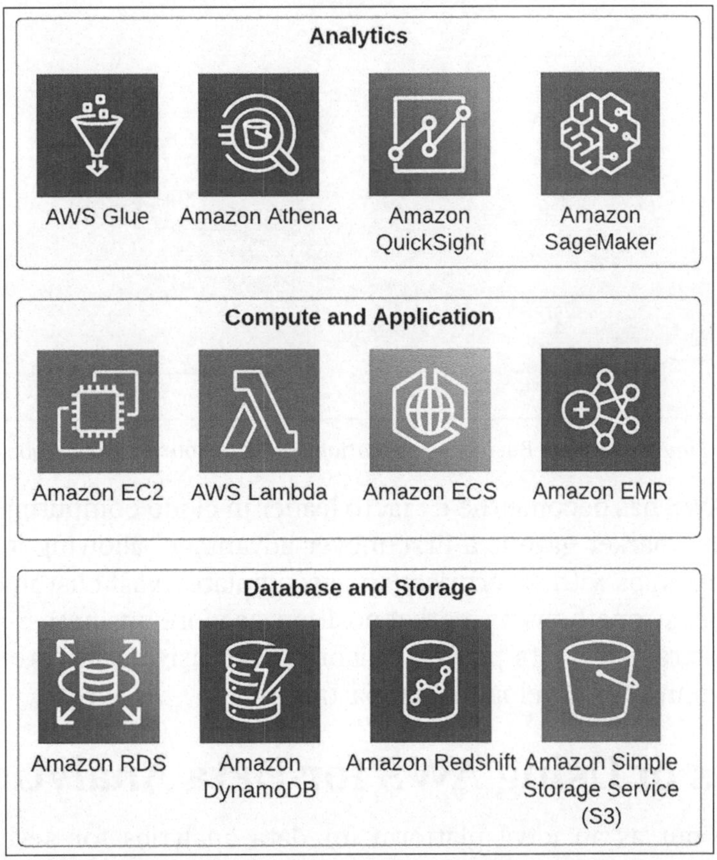

Figure 1.12: *Overview of Core AWS Services for Data Analytics*

The success of AWS has had a massive ripple effect on the broader technology landscape. By giving birth to the cloud computing industry, it inspired competitors like Microsoft (Azure) and Google (GCP) to build similar platforms. As a result, the cloud became an integral part of modern business strategy, offering cost-effective, scalable, and secure solutions. AWS remains a dominant force in the industry, setting trends and pushing the boundaries of what cloud computing can achieve.

Another result of this democratization of computing power is the explosion of startup companies forming over the past decade. Nascent software companies with minimal budgets can now build proof-of-concept or minimalistic versions of their app and only pay for the resources they need by renting compute power that scales up and down based on user demand:

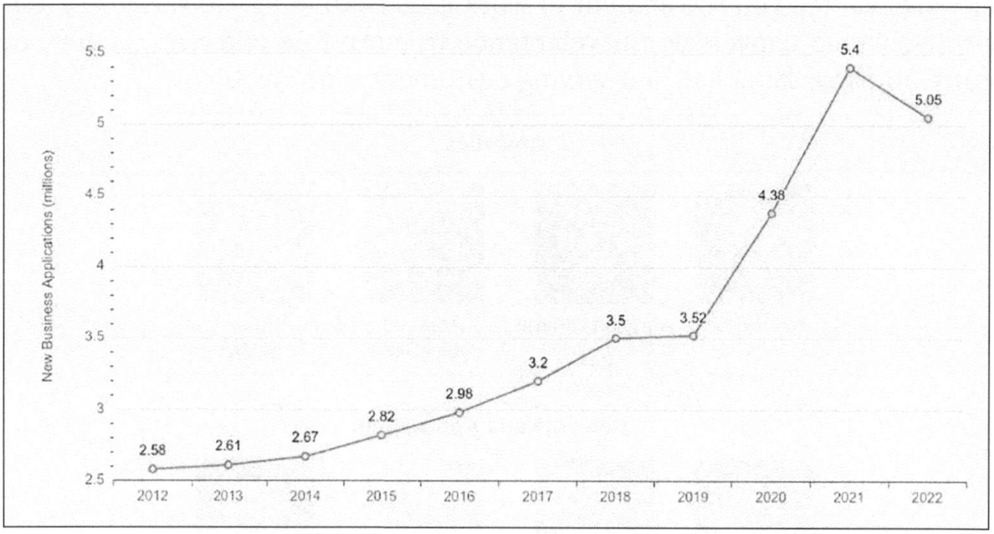

Figure 1.13: *New Business Applications by Year. Source: Census.gov*

As a result, AWS has become the de facto leader in cloud computing. Their early entry into the market gave it a first-mover advantage, allowing it to establish strong relationships with enterprises and accumulate a vast customer base. This network effect strengthens its market position, as more businesses join the AWS ecosystem, attracted by its proven reliability, extensive service offerings, and vibrant community of developers and partners.

Benefits of Using AWS for Data Analytics

AWS stands out as an ideal platform for data analytics for several reasons, starting with its extensive suite of analytics services. Whether you are interested in real-time analytics, big data processing, or even machine learning, AWS has specialized tools like Amazon Kinesis, Amazon EMR, and Amazon SageMaker to meet those needs. These services integrate seamlessly, allowing you to build end-to-end analytics pipelines without the hassle of managing interoperability between different tools. This lets you focus on deriving insights rather than wrestling with infrastructure.

Scalability is another strong suit of AWS. Data analytics often involves processing large volumes of data, and AWS allows you to scale your resources up or down as your needs change. You can start small and then expand your computing power and storage capacity with just a few clicks. This flexibility is not only cost-effective but also ensures that you can adapt to the ever-changing demands of data analytics projects, from data ingestion to processing and visualization.

Security and compliance also make AWS a go-to choice for data analytics. AWS offers robust security features like data encryption, identity and access management, and network firewalls, ensuring that your sensitive data remains protected. Additionally, AWS complies with various industry standards and regulations, making it easier for businesses in heavily regulated sectors like healthcare, finance, and government to maintain compliance while still using best-in-breed analytics capabilities. These features collectively make AWS a comprehensive, scalable, and secure platform for any data analytics endeavor.

Benefits of Cloud Computing in Data Analytics

Cloud computing revolutionizes the way businesses execute data analytics, offering scalability as one of its most compelling benefits. Traditional on-premises solutions often struggle to manage fluctuating data volumes, requiring companies to over-provision resources to avoid performance issues. Cloud computing eliminates this problem. With the cloud, you can easily scale your analytics operations up or down based on real-time needs, ensuring that you neither waste resources nor suffer from limited capacity. This scalability is particularly crucial for businesses that experience seasonal fluctuations or are in rapid growth phases.

Another significant advantage is cost-effectiveness. Running a data analytics operation in-house involves substantial upfront costs for hardware, software, and manpower. Cloud computing services operate on a pay-as-you-go model, allowing businesses to only pay for the resources they actually use. This approach not only reduces initial capital expenditure but also lowers ongoing operational costs. You can allocate your budget more efficiently, directing funds toward innovation and other strategic initiatives.

Speed and agility also come into play when you opt for cloud-based analytics. Traditional analytics setups can take weeks or even months to deploy, hindering your ability to make timely decisions. Cloud services, on the other hand, enable quick deployment and configuration of analytics tools. You can get your analytics operations up and running in a matter of hours, allowing you to start drawing insights and making data-driven decisions almost immediately. This speed is invaluable in today's fast-paced business environment, where delays can result in missed opportunities.

Finally, cloud computing enhances collaboration and accessibility. With data stored in the cloud, team members can access analytics tools and insights from anywhere, using any device with an internet connection. This remote accessibility fosters better collaboration among teams spread across different locations, making it easier to share insights and make collective decisions. In a world where remote work is becoming the norm, the ability to collaborate effectively on analytics projects from anywhere is a game-changer.

Limitations of Data Analytics

Data analytics, while powerful, confronts several limitations that often obstruct the seamless extraction of insights. One of the most prevalent challenges is data quality. Dirty or inconsistent data can distort outcomes, making any analysis unreliable. To solve this issue, analysts spend a significant amount of time cleansing and preparing data, which can delay the actual analytical process.

Another hurdle that analysts face is data complexity. With the advent of Big Data, analysts now grapple with huge datasets that are both varied and fast-changing. Traditional analytics tools often fall short when dealing with this level of complexity, forcing organizations to invest in more sophisticated systems. Yet, even with advanced tools, analysts still struggle to navigate the intricacies of multi-dimensional datasets.

Cost poses yet another challenge. The machinery for data analytics – software, hardware, and human expertise – doesn't come cheap. Small businesses often find the overhead costs prohibitive, restricting access to high-quality analytics to larger corporations with deeper pockets. This economic disparity creates an imbalance, making it difficult for small entities to compete with large ones, particularly when analytics play a crucial role in strategic decisions.

Lastly, the ethical considerations tied to data analytics cannot go unnoticed. Issues around data privacy and security are escalating as analytics become more prevalent. Failure to maintain confidentiality can not only harm an organization's reputation but also result in legal repercussions. Hence, analysts must walk a fine line, balancing the drive to uncover insights against the need to respect privacy and ethical boundaries.

Despite these challenges, the field of data analytics continues to evolve, offering new methods and tools to overcome these obstacles. However, awareness of these limitations is essential for any data professional, as acknowledging them is the first step towards finding solutions.

Case Studies of Data Analytics

Let's explore some of the captivating case studies of data analytics, shedding light on how data-driven decisions can revolutionize industries.

Moneyball and the Rise of Sports Analytics

The story of "Moneyball," Michael Lewis's book that has now become synonymous with applying data analytics to sports, provides a groundbreaking example of how data analytics disrupted traditional practices; specifically, how players are valued in Major League Baseball (MLB). The Oakland Athletics and General Manager Billy Beane, dealing with one of the smallest budgets in the league, turned to data analytics in 2002 to identify undervalued players. Scouting methods often focused on a player's physical attributes (the "eye test") and traditional power statistics like batting average, home runs, and runs batted in. Beane and his team used techniques pioneered by Bill James called sabermetrics – a specialized analysis of baseball through objective evidence – to look at less celebrated metrics such as On-Base Percentage (OBP):

	A	B	C	D	E	F	G	H	I	J	K	L	M	N	O
1	Team	League	Year	RS	RA	W	OBP	SLG	BA	Playoffs	RankSeason	RankPlayoffs	G	OOBP	OSLG
2	ARI	NL	2012	734	688	81	0.328	0.418	0.259	0			162	0.317	0.415
3	ATL	NL	2012	700	600	94	0.32	0.389	0.247	1	4	5	162	0.306	0.378
4	BAL	AL	2012	712	705	93	0.311	0.417	0.247	1	5	4	162	0.315	0.403
5	BOS	AL	2012	734	806	69	0.315	0.415	0.26	0			162	0.331	0.428
6	CHC	NL	2012	613	759	61	0.302	0.378	0.24	0			162	0.335	0.424
7	CHW	AL	2012	748	676	85	0.318	0.422	0.255	0			162	0.319	0.405
8	CIN	NL	2012	669	588	97	0.315	0.411	0.251	1	2	4	162	0.305	0.39
9	CLE	AL	2012	667	845	68	0.324	0.381	0.251	0			162	0.336	0.43
10	COL	NL	2012	758	890	64	0.33	0.436	0.274	0			162	0.357	0.47
11	DET	AL	2012	726	670	88	0.335	0.422	0.268	1	6	2	162	0.314	0.402
12	HOU	NL	2012	583	794	55	0.302	0.371	0.236	0			162	0.337	0.427
13	KCR	AL	2012	676	746	72	0.317	0.4	0.265	0			162	0.339	0.423
14	LAA	AL	2012	767	699	89	0.332	0.433	0.274	0			162	0.31	0.403
15	LAD	NL	2012	637	597	86	0.317	0.374	0.252	0			162	0.31	0.364
16	MIA	NL	2012	609	724	69	0.308	0.382	0.244	0			162	0.327	0.399
17	MIL	NL	2012	776	733	83	0.325	0.437	0.259	0			162	0.326	0.414
18	MIN	AL	2012	701	832	66	0.325	0.39	0.26	0			162	0.333	0.442
19	NYM	NL	2012	650	709	74	0.316	0.386	0.249	0			162	0.315	0.401
20	NYY	AL	2012	804	668	95	0.337	0.453	0.265	1	3	3	162	0.311	0.419
21	OAK	AL	2012	713	614	94	0.31	0.404	0.238	1	4	4	162	0.306	0.378
22	PHI	NL	2012	684	680	81	0.317	0.4	0.255	0			162	0.306	0.407

Figure 1.14: *Sample MLB Data Used in the "Moneyball" Analytics Process. Source: kaggle.com*

This analytical approach allowed the Athletics to find players who were undervalued by the rest of the league but still contributed significantly to producing wins over a 162-game season. By identifying and exploiting these price/value inefficiencies, the A's assembled a winning team and even strung together a 20-game winning streak en route to winning their division. They proved that committing to a smart analytical strategy, despite the risk of failure, could outshine traditional methods of baseball player analysis. While their approach didn't earn them a World Series title, the entire league soon adopted similar strategies, and just two years after the A's magical season, the Boston Red Sox won the World Series using methods similar to Beane's.

Netflix and the $100 Million Gamble

One of the most famous examples of how Netflix used data analytics to improve its business is the creation of the original series "House of Cards." Netflix invested $100 million in the show without even seeing a pilot, a decision driven largely by data analytics [8]. They analyzed their user data and found that a significant number of subscribers had watched entire seasons of the original 1990 BBC series. They also noticed that films directed by David Fincher and starring Kevin Spacey had high ratings on their platform. By combining these data points,

Netflix concluded that a remake of "House of Cards" directed by Fincher and starring Spacey would be a hit.

The gamble paid off. "House of Cards" became an enormous success, both critically and commercially. It won several awards and attracted a large viewership, validating Netflix's data-driven approach. The show's success also paved the way for additional original content on Netflix, transforming the company from a simple streaming service to a content-producing powerhouse. This approach not only increased subscription volume but also reduced Netflix's dependence on external content providers, a pattern that other streaming services would soon imitate.

The "House of Cards" example showcases the power of data analytics in making informed business decisions. Netflix didn't just use data for content recommendations; they used it to shape their content strategy, which has been a significant factor in their growth. This data-driven approach has become a case study for how companies can leverage big data to drive decision-making and innovation.

By leveraging data analytics, Netflix didn't just create a hit show; they revolutionized the way content gets produced and consumed, setting a precedent for the entire industry.

Hold the Mayo

The Mayo Clinic has been using advanced analytics and machine learning to predict which patients are at risk of developing heart failure. The clinic uses an algorithm that analyzes electronic health records, including medical history, lab results, and other vital statistics, to identify early signs of heart failure. This predictive model allows doctors to intervene before the condition worsens, thereby improving patient outcomes.

The Mayo Clinic's algorithm doesn't just identify at-risk patients; it also helps customize individual treatment plans. By analyzing a patient's data, the algorithm can recommend specific medications or lifestyle changes that are most likely to be effective for that individual. This personalized approach has led to better patient compliance and, consequently, improved health outcomes.

The impact of this data-driven approach extends beyond individual patient care. The Mayo Clinic uses the insights gained from their analytics to continually refine their treatment protocols. This iterative process ensures that the healthcare provider stays at the forefront of medical best practices, setting a standard for the industry.

In summary, the Mayo Clinic's use of data analytics for predicting heart failure serves as a compelling example of how data can improve healthcare outcomes. By leveraging predictive analytics, the clinic not only enhances patient care but also drives operational efficiencies. Their work serves as a blueprint for how data can transform healthcare, making it more proactive rather than reactive.

Conclusion

As we have seen, data analytics is a powerful tool that is revolutionizing industries and driving competitive advantage. This chapter provided an overview of the fundamentals of data analytics, from the types of analytics to real-world applications. With the right strategy and tools, anyone can tap into the insights hidden within data. With the rise of cloud computing and advanced analytics services like those on AWS, implementing data analytics has become more accessible than ever. By starting with small steps like tracking key business metrics, you can begin uncovering insights to drive growth. The data analytics journey requires commitment but pays dividends to those willing to embrace it.

In the next chapter, we will take a more practical look at implementing data analytics through the lens of the world's most popular cloud computing platform, AWS. Mastering the basics of AWS will give us a solid foundation for our journey, empowering us to be masters of data!

Points to Remember

- Data analytics is the process of collecting, transforming, analyzing, and visualizing data to find valuable insights and enable data-driven decision-making. It is critical for businesses seeking a competitive edge.
- There are four main types of analytics: descriptive (summarizing what happened), diagnostic (understanding why it happened), predictive (forecasting what could happen), and prescriptive (recommending what should be done).
- Spreadsheets, SQL, and machine learning are essential tools for performing data analytics at any scale. Cloud computing via platforms like AWS has also been a game-changer.
- Data analytics delivers tangible business benefits across industries like healthcare, retail, and finance by optimizing operations, reducing costs, improving customer experience, and identifying new opportunities.
- However, data analytics has limitations like poor data quality, high costs, and ethical concerns around privacy that must be acknowledged and mitigated.

References

1. "Data Age 2025: The Evolution of Data to Life-Critica". IDC Group. https://www.seagate.com/files/www-content/our-story/trends/files/Seagate-WP-DataAge2025-March-2017.pdf
2. Total Population, https://data.census.gov/table/ACSDT1Y2022.B01003?q=Population%20Total
3. Downloadable Housing Market Data From Redfin, https://www.redfin.com/news/data-center/
4. Mortgage Rates, https://fred.stlouisfed.org/categories/114
5. DataScience Programs, https://www.datascienceprograms.org
6. McKinsey and Co., 2015. Big Data, Analytics, and the Future of Marketing & Sales.
7. AWS Step Functions Developer Guide, https://docs.aws.amazon.com/step-functions/latest/dg/connect-to-services.html
8. "How Netflix built a House of Cards with big data", 2017 https://www.idginsiderpro.com/article/3207670/how-netflix-built-a-house-of-cards-with-big-data.html

CHAPTER 2

Getting Started with AWS

Introduction

The cloud has opened up exciting new possibilities for organizations to harness the power of data analytics. However, navigating the vast array of services can be daunting for beginners. This chapter serves as a simple introduction to using Amazon Web Services (AWS) for data analytics. We demystify core concepts and provide practical advice on getting started on your journey. From setting up your AWS account to exploring essential services, this chapter equips you with the knowledge to hit the ground running. Your journey into data analytics on AWS starts now!

Structure

In this chapter, we will cover the following topics:

- Core Concepts and Terminology
- Setting Up Your AWS Account
- Navigating the AWS Management Console
- Introduction to the AWS Command Line (CLI)
- Exploring AWS Services with an Example Pipeline
- Security Practices on AWS
- Understanding AWS Pricing

Core Concepts and Terminology

The limits of my language are the limits of my world.

-*Ludwig Wittgenstein, Tractatus Logico-Philosphicus* (1922)

Setting sail in this brave new world of the cloud and AWS for the first time can be challenging. You will see a plethora of different terminology, concepts, and ideas that might seem daunting. So, let's walk before we run, and focus on the most important terms and concepts that we can use as a foundation for building our knowledge of AWS.

Computing Your Data

A good place to start, and one of the first places AWS started, is compute. Compute is one of the most common capabilities that AWS provides and allows users to rent server space to run any application they desire. Here are the most common compute services:

Amazon EC2

Amazon Elastic Compute Cloud (**EC2**) forms the backbone of cloud computing on AWS. Imagine it as your personal computer in the cloud, where you have the freedom to install and run any software, talk to data, and host websites. EC2 provides virtual machines, known as **instances**, that you can create and customize based on your memory, processing, and storage needs. You can turn these shared servers on and off based on your needs, paying only for what you use, or configure several instances to scale up and down in response to application demands. Features like these make EC2 a good fit for data analytics projects that may require heavy computation at times and little to no processing time at others.

For more advanced analytics use cases, like machine learning projects, AWS offers GPU-backed compute instances that are optimized to work with machine learning frameworks. These frameworks can train models using massive datasets and high-performance techniques like parallel processing.

Another great feature of EC2 is the deep library of **Application Machine Images** (**AMI**) available to choose from. Users can avoid the hassle of configuring servers from scratch and instead choose pre-configured images from AWS or the public marketplace to start their projects quickly:

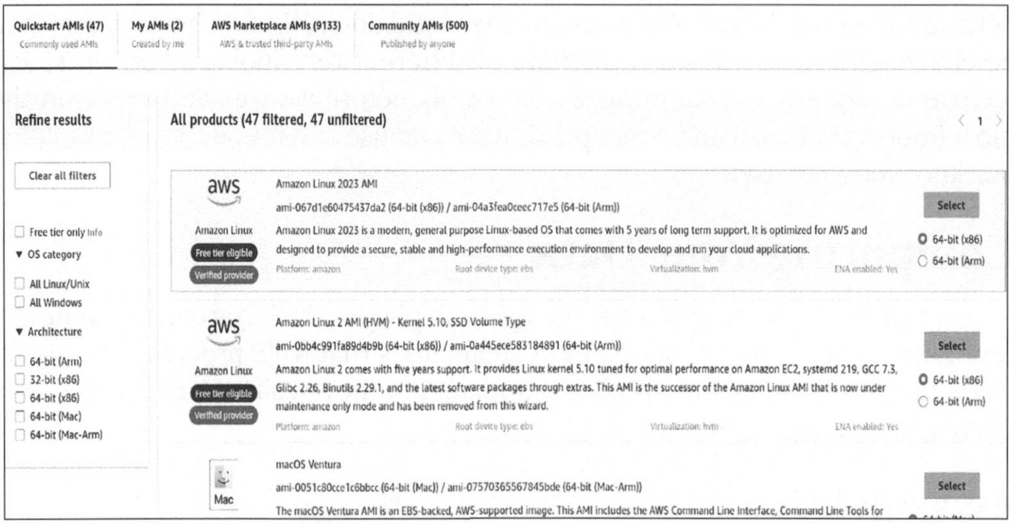

Figure 2.1: *AWS Marketplace for AMIs*

It's also important to understand how instances are deployed geographically. AWS has a global network of data centers grouped into what they call **Regions**. As of this writing, there are 32 regions around the world [1]. While not all regions support all AWS services, the most basic AWS offerings should be available in all regions, giving you the power to run and deploy your applications wherever you want (ideally as close to your customers as possible):

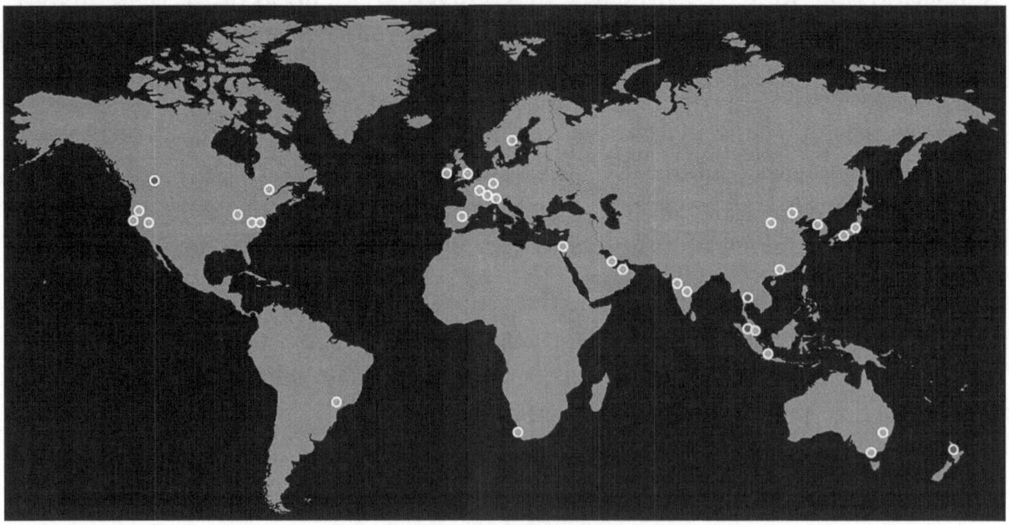

Figure 2.2: *AWS Regions Worldwide, as of November 2023. Source: amazon.com*

Within each Region are one or more **Availability Zones** (**AZ**), which provide isolated locations that offer redundancy and failover protection. There are currently 102 Availability Zones worldwide. While spreading your computing needs across multiple availability zones might not be required for data analytics projects, it's important to note how your projects will be deployed and to be prepared in case an AZ goes down.

Amazon ECS and Amazon EMR

Working directly with EC2 instances can be challenging and might be unnecessary if you have a simple workload that you want to extend across one or more machines. **Docker** provides a framework to allow you to define the configuration of a virtual machine in a **container**. A container definition file (Dockerfile) defines your application dependencies and commands and should run the same regardless of where it's deployed. AWS allows you to run these containers across multiple machines using **Amazon Elastic Container Service** (**ECS**).

Using ECS, you can deploy, manage, and scale your Docker containers with ease, without having to worry about the underlying infrastructure. ECS will monitor the health of your cluster, handle failures, and scale up and down to meet your application needs.

Another similar service relevant to data analytics is **Elastic Map Reduce (EMR)**. EMR allows you to scale up a cluster of EC2 instances to execute Hadoop (or more recently Spark) jobs, which are designed to execute highly parallelized transformations across data stored at large scale (in the order of petabytes). Spark then collects the results of the parallel transformations to generate a consolidated result set for storage.

AWS Lambda

Our final stop on this tour of computing power is with **AWS Lambda.** Imagine you have a much simpler task to execute (say a simple function), and you don't want the overhead of managing EC2 instances or a cluster of machines. Lambda provides **serverless** computing (eliminating the need to configure an operating system), allowing you to execute a single function of code in your favorite coding language. It is ideal for quick, event-driven tasks in your data analytics workflow, such as data cleaning, transformation, or real-time analytics. Simply upload your code, define triggers tied to specific events, and let Lambda handle the rest.

Lambda supports multiple programming languages, including Python, Node.js, and Java, and integrates smoothly with other AWS services. This makes it easy to plug into your existing data analytics pipeline, offering a quick way to automate tasks and data workflows.

Storing Your Data

Compute services can help you process your data, but storing it is one of the most important aspects of a successful data analytics pipeline. Here are some efficient data storage options:

Amazon Simple Storage Service (S3)

The **Amazon Simple Storage Service** (**S3**) was another early service pioneered by AWS to enable scalable, reliable storage in the cloud. Think of S3 as an endless filing cabinet where you can store anything - photos, documents, videos, and even backups of your entire website. It's based on some very simple concepts. All files uploaded to S3 are known as **objects.** Each object can be identified by a unique **key,** which mimics the folder structure convention of your computer's file system by using the "/" delimiter to define keys. All of these objects are stored in a specific **bucket**. As you create buckets and keyed objects, you can define **metadata** properties that determine who can access these objects, how they should be served to clients, and other metadata relevant to operations and storage tiers:

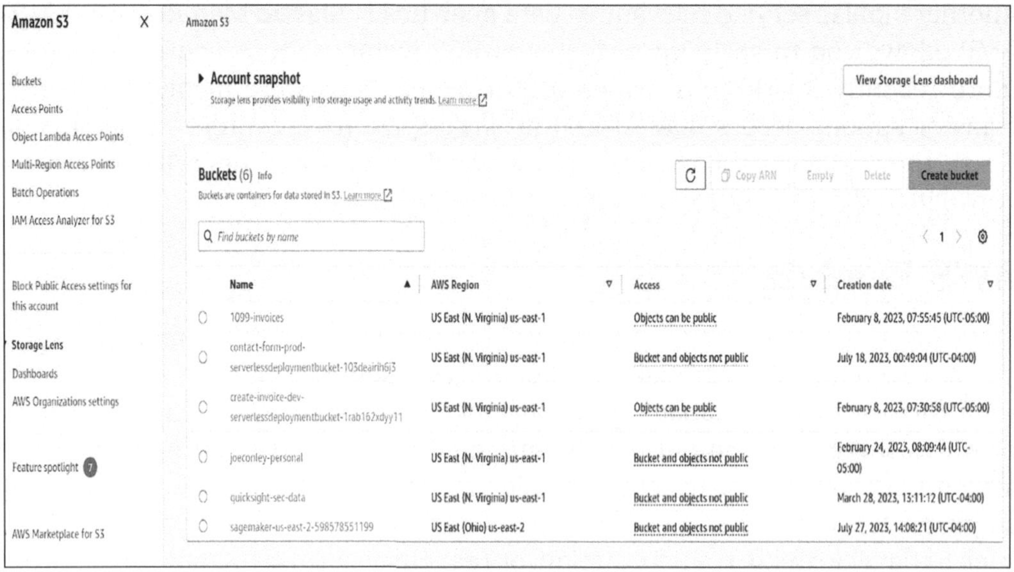

***Figure 2.3**: S3 Dashboard*

S3 is a popular solution for data analytics tasks because you can quickly dump raw data into an S3 bucket without having to worry about managing disk space as you would on a normal server. Moreover, S3 integrates with many AWS services to allow for simpler processing. It scales automatically and provides features like versioning, where S3 keeps multiple versions of an object, and data lifecycle policies, which allow you to move less frequently accessed data to cheaper storage, making S3 both flexible and cost-effective. S3 has become the de facto cloud storage system, so much so that competing services even maintain S3-compatible interfaces.

Amazon RDS

If you are looking to analyze your data using SQL queries, and you plan on storing highly relational data at reasonable volumes (say at the hundreds of GB level), then the **Amazon Relational Database Service** (**RDS**) is an excellent fit for you. RDS manages the complexity of database administration, making it easy to create and scale instances, monitor performance, and manage user access. It also provides features to handle backups and versioning and performs basic administration tasks, such as applying security patches and replication, which formerly required hiring a **database administrator** (**DBA**).

RDS supports several types of relational databases, like MySQL, PostgreSQL, and even commercial databases like Oracle. It also has its own innovative engines like Aurora, which provide MySQL- and Postgres-compatible instances but with a better performance and cost profile. Moreover, RDS recently pioneered the use of a serverless instance, which is ideal for use cases where your workload patterns are more erratic or if you only need database access during testing and want to shut it down the rest of the time.

Amazon DynamoDB

Traditional software platforms rely heavily on relational databases to store data. To store this data, you create a well-defined schema of tables with columns that have rigid data types. The database engine uses this information and other metadata to ensure the shape and consistency of your data.

While these types of databases are still popular, a recent trend of **NoSQL databases** emerged in the late 2000s [2]. As computing power became more readily available and features like high performance and speed of development became paramount, these NoSQL databases allowed users to store data without defining rigid schemas, typically in a key-value format similar to **JavaScript Object Notation (JSON)**:

```
{
  "id": 1,
  "username": "JohnDoe",
  "email": "john.doe@example.com",
  "profile": {
    "firstName": "John",
    "lastName": "Doe",
    "age": 30,
    "address": {
      "street": "123 Main St",
      "city": "Anytown",
      "state": "CA",
      "postalCode": "12345"
    }
  },
  "orders": [
    {
      "orderId": "1234",
      "status": "shipped",
      "items": [
        {
          "productId": "001",
          "quantity": 2
        },
        {
          "productId": "002",
          "quantity": 1
        }
      ]
    }
  ]
}
```

***Figure 2.4**: JSON Object - NoSQL Database Example Record*

One of the early pioneers of this movement was AWS. Their paper in 2007 [3] on their in-house key-value store Dynamo led the way for developing their high-performing, low-latency key-value store known as **Amazon DynamoDB**. Similar to other managed services, DynamoDB handles the complexity of managing and scaling key-value datastores at scale. Similarly to RDS, DynamoDB also recently announced its own Serverless offering, making it even easier to configure a DynamoDB instance without having to provision dedicated capacity for workloads that might have erratic traffic patterns.

Processing Your Data

This final set of concepts outlines how AWS provides services to help you transform, query, and visualize your data. Here are some key services for these tasks:

Transform with AWS Glue

The aptly-named **AWS Glue** service provides a key transformation step in the data pipeline, gluing together various data sources, performing transformational logic, and presenting ready-made datasets for analysis. Imagine having to manually collect and aggregate data scattered across various formats and locations like Excel spreadsheets, remote databases, and structured data files on the cloud. Glue discovers, catalogs, and prepares data for analysis, making it easy for you to get insights from your data. It can automatically discover both structured and semi-structured data and store the metadata in a centralized Glue Data Catalog.

The best part about AWS Glue is that you don't need to write code to move data between different storage and database services. Using visual tools like Glue Studio allows you to automate and monitor transformation tasks. Another added benefit is that it works seamlessly with other AWS data analytics services like S3 and RDS, making it a great choice for managing a data transformation pipeline with minimal overhead:

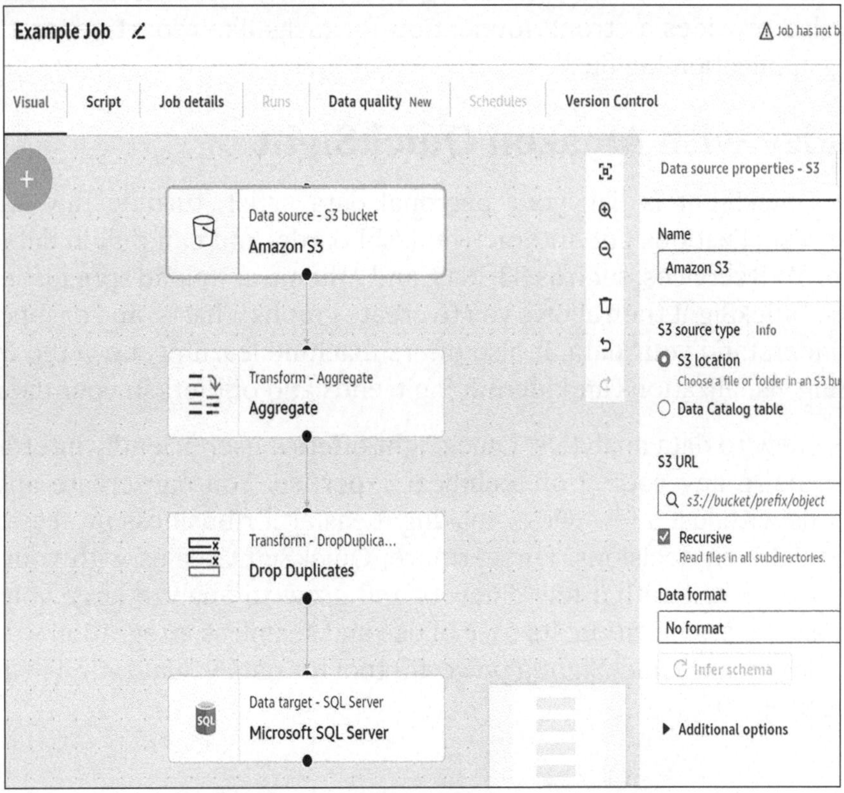

***Figure 2.5**: AWS Glue Studio Example ETL Job*

Query with Amazon Athena

Amazon launched **Amazon Athena** in 2016, giving users the power to directly query their structured data stored on S3. Before Athena, users would need to manually transform and push their data into a traditional relational database to perform SQL queries. Athena gives users the ability to analyze data in various formats, such as CSV, Parquet, or JSON, and as with most AWS services, you pay only for the queries you run, making it a cost-effective solution for ad-hoc data exploration and analysis.

Athena relies on Presto, an open-source distributed SQL query engine, for its underlying technology. Facebook originally developed Presto to query large datasets quickly and efficiently [4]. Athena's integration with Presto allows users to perform ad-hoc queries on structured and semi-structured data stored in Amazon S3.

Athena is particularly useful for ad-hoc data exploration as you can quickly run queries on your data stored in S3 and get real-time results across petabytes of data. It also provides a strong foundation for tasks like report generation and querying application log files.

Visualize with Amazon QuickSight

Amazon QuickSight is like your personal data artist, turning raw data into beautiful visualizations and interactive dashboards. You can pull in data from a variety of AWS services, such as S3, RDS, and Athena, or upload spreadsheets and CSV files. QuickSight then allows you to create graphs, charts, and dashboards to better understand your data. It also offers machine learning-powered insights, suggesting visualizations and identifying trends and outliers in your data.

For those new to data analytics, QuickSight offers a user-friendly interface that doesn't require any coding or technical expertise. You can create and share dashboards with just a few clicks, making it easier for business professionals to make data-driven decisions. Furthermore, QuickSight scales with your needs. You can start small with a few datasets and grow to analyze large volumes of data across the organization. Its ease of use and seamless integration with other AWS services make QuickSight a powerful tool for data visualization in any data analytics project:

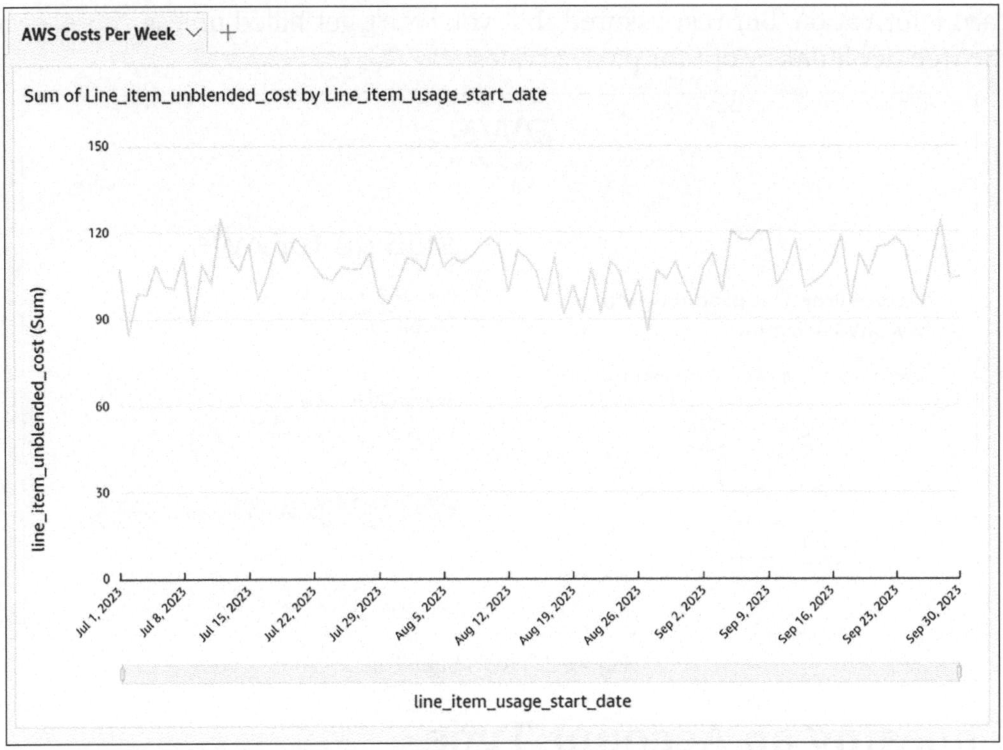

Figure 2.6: *Amazon QuickSight - Visualizing Weekly AWS Costs*

Setting Up Your AWS Account

Now that we have a basic understanding of AWS, let's take concrete steps to set up an account.

Requirements for Creating an Account

First and foremost, you will need a valid email address, credit or debit card for billing purposes, and a phone number for account verification. AWS uses the phone number to send a verification code during the sign-up process and charges a nominal amount to verify your account, which is typically refunded within a few days.

Sign-Up Process

Navigate to the AWS homepage and click `Create a Free Account` button. You will then go through a series of forms where you enter your email, desired password, and an AWS account name. Follow the on-screen instructions and proceed to the next step, which usually involves providing billing details. Fill out your credit card information, but rest assured that you won't get billed unless you exceed the free tier limits or opt for paid services:

Figure 2.7: *AWS Sign-Up*

Choosing an Account Type

During the sign-up process, AWS will ask you to select an account type: Individual or Professional. For personal use, the Individual account type is usually sufficient. If you are configuring a company account, you will likely want to pick the Professional account type, and you can nominate an admin team member to be the point person for managing the company AWS account. This choice doesn't limit your access to any services but helps AWS tailor recommendations and resources more appropriately to your needs.

Selecting Your Region

AWS allows you to select a geographical region closest to you or your target audience. The region you select impacts data latency and cost. For data analytics, choosing a region close to where the bulk of your data originates can reduce data transfer times and costs. You can change your region later, but it's a good idea to think this through during account setup.

Confirming Your Account

After entering all the required information, AWS will prompt you to verify your account via a phone call or text message. Once you enter the verification code you receive, your account moves into a pending status for up to 24 hours, although activation usually occurs much more quickly. After AWS approves your account, you gain access to the AWS Management Console, where your journey into data analytics truly begins.

Navigating the AWS Management Console

The AWS Management Console provides the graphical interface you will use to interact with AWS services. Consider it the cockpit from which you control your cloud resources. Understanding how to navigate this interface is essential for using AWS effectively, especially for data analytics tasks. Even if you are a beginner, a few key tips can make your journey much smoother:

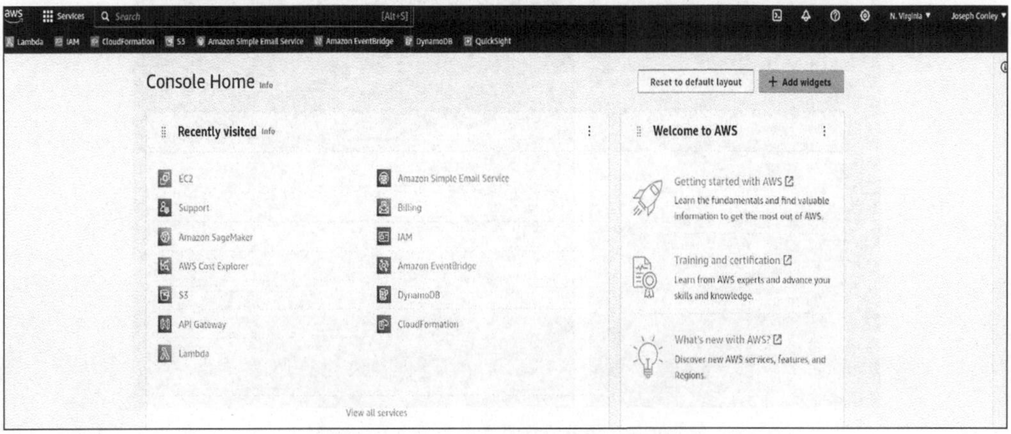

Figure 2.8: *AWS Management Console*

Understanding the Dashboard

After logging in for the first time, you will land on the dashboard. Here, you will find several controls to help you navigate the various AWS services:

- A search bar at the top for locating services quickly.
- A navigation pane on the left for exploring services by categories.
- A central area that shows recently accessed services or provides recommendations.

It can be a bit overwhelming at first but spending a few minutes to familiarize yourself with the layout will pay off. In addition, you can bookmark services for quick access.

Using the Services Menu

At the top of the dashboard, you will see the `Services` menu, which provides a dropdown list of all available AWS services categorized by domain, such as `Compute`, `Storage`, and `Database`. If you are focusing on data analytics, you will likely frequent the `Analytics` section. Clicking on any service takes you to that service's console, where you can create, manage, and configure resources related to that service:

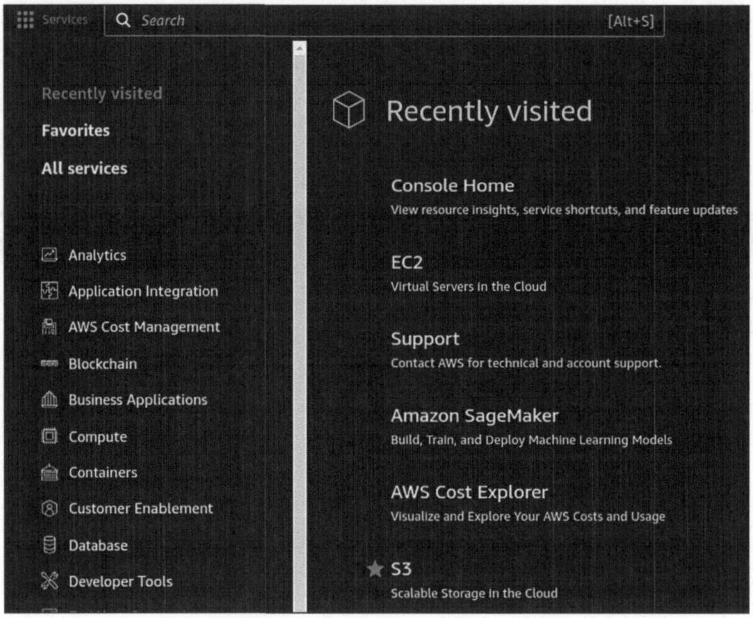

Figure 2.9: *AWS Services Menu*

Finding Essential Features and Settings

The AWS Management Console also has utility features like the account settings located at the top right corner. Here, you can access billing information, manage security credentials, or sign out of the console. Many services have their specific settings or features typically located under a Settings tab within that service's console. Make it a habit to explore these settings each time you start using a new service.

Using the Search Bar Effectively

The search bar at the top allows you to quickly locate services, features, and even AWS Marketplace products. It's a powerful tool that can save you time, especially when you know exactly what you are looking for. Simply start typing the name or acronym of a service, and a dropdown will appear with matching results. Select the one you need, and you will jump straight to that service's console.

Accessing Shortcuts and Recently Used Services

The dashboard also has a `Recently visited services` section that provides quick access to the services you have used recently. This feature is particularly handy as you will likely find yourself using a set of core services frequently for your data analytics projects. You can also pin your most-used services to the navigation pane for quicker access.

By becoming proficient in navigating the AWS Management Console, you set the stage for a more efficient and streamlined experience in managing your data analytics projects. It's worth investing the time upfront to understand the console's layout and features, as this will enable you to focus on building and optimizing your data analytics pipelines rather than grappling with the user interface.

Introduction to the AWS Command-Line Tool (CLI)

Using the AWS Management Console is the easiest way to start building your data analytics pipeline. However, you might have use cases where you want to write code and automate interactions with your AWS services. One common way to do this is to use the **AWS Command Line Interface** (**CLI**). The CLI lets you interact with AWS services directly from your terminal. You can define commands or scripts using CLI commands to configure services, load data, and execute data pipelines. Another nice feature is that the underlying API that handles CLI commands can also be encoded in any popular programming language, allowing you to further automate AWS API interactions.

Getting Started with the AWS CLI

Before you can start using the AWS CLI, you will need to install it on your machine. AWS supports installation on multiple operating systems, including Windows, macOS, and Linux. The installation process varies by OS, but it's generally straightforward. For example, on a macOS, you can install the AWS CLI using Homebrew by running the command `brew install awscli`. Detailed installation instructions are available on the AWS website and usually involve downloading a package and following the setup steps.

After installation, the next step is configuration. You will need to provide your AWS credentials, specify a default region, and choose the output format for the CLI responses. You can set up these configurations by running *aws configure* in the terminal. It will prompt you for the necessary information, which you can find in the `Access keys` section of your AWS IAM dashboard.

Basic Commands for Data Analytics Tasks

When it comes to data analytics, a few basic AWS CLI commands can help you manage your resources effectively. For example, to list all the S3 buckets (which may contain your raw or processed data), you can use `aws s3 ls`. If you are dealing with EC2 instances to run analytics jobs, `aws ec2 describe-instances` will provide details of all your running instances. You can inspect Glue tables using `aws glue get-tables`, and query S3 data using Athena by calling `aws athena start-query-execution`. These are just a few of the commands at your disposal when managing data pipelines on AWS.

Data Transfer and Synchronization

Transferring data is a common task in analytics projects. The AWS CLI makes this easy with commands like `aws s3 cp` to copy data from your local machine to an S3 bucket or vice versa. If you need to synchronize a local directory with an S3 bucket, you can use `aws s3 sync`. These commands are especially useful when dealing with large datasets that need to be moved to AWS for processing.

Scripting and Automation

One of the major advantages of the CLI is its ability to automate repetitive tasks through scripting. For example, you could write a script to automatically launch EC2 instances, run a Spark job for data processing, and then terminate the instances once the job is complete. This can save both time and money, particularly for large-scale analytics projects.

The AWS CLI is a versatile tool that can greatly enhance your efficiency and capabilities when working with AWS services for data analytics. By familiarizing yourself with basic commands and taking advantage of CLI's scripting capabilities, you can streamline your analytics workflows, optimize resource management, and automate repetitive tasks, so that you can focus on deriving insights from your data.

Exploring AWS with an Example Pipeline

Now that we have taken a quick tour of AWS and its services, let's walk through a simple example of an end-to-end data analytics pipeline:

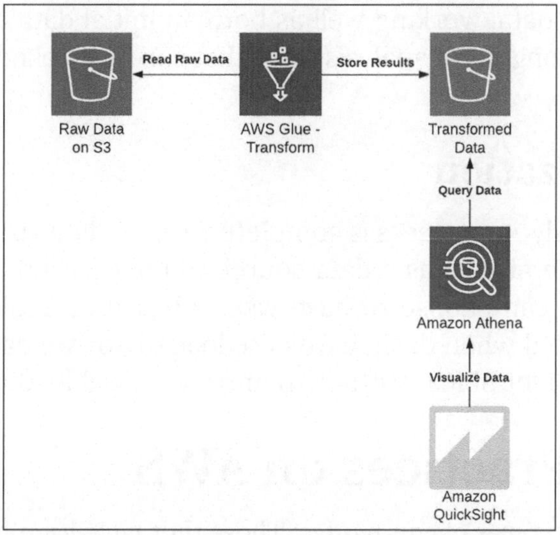

Figure 2.10: *Sample AWS Data Analytics Pipeline*

Data Storage and Ingestion

While most use cases would involve building a script to extract data from a data source, in this example, let's assume we have already done the hard work of extraction and have saved our raw data directly onto S3. Having it on S3 makes it accessible to a Glue job, as S3 is one of the many sources of data compatible with Glue.

Data Processing and Transformation

Once in Glue, we can apply a variety of different kinds of transformations to prepare our data for analysis:

- **Cleaning functions:** These functions will drop bad data, impute new values, and drop fields not relevant to our analysis.
- **Enriching functions:** These functions perform aggregations, impute data, and add other useful information for downstream queries.

- **Restructuring functions:** These functions map and join records, perform normalization and flattening of objects, and additional filtering/sorting capabilities to organize data into a final target structure.

Data Query

Once the data has been thoroughly cleaned, we can persist it back to S3 and make it available to Athena for querying. Athena can execute SQL-like queries on any structured data, working well as both an initial data exploration engine and for managing long-term analysis tasks that can be invoked by many different AWS services.

Data Visualization

Finally, no data analytics process is complete without data visualization. Amazon QuickSight can use Athena as a data source to build dashboards based on our cleaned data. We can choose to have visuals based on real-time data (where queries are executed when dashboards are loaded), or we can optionally cache our data in QuickSight SPICE storage to improve visual loading times.

Security Practices on AWS

"There are only two types of companies: Those that have been hacked and those that will be hacked."

– Robert S. Mueller, III, former Director of the FBI

Security remains a paramount concern for any organization, regardless of where they deploy their data infrastructure. According to the Privacy Rights Clearinghouse reports, there have been over 35k data breaches since 2002, resulting in over 17.5 billion compromised records [5].

Luckily, AWS takes security seriously. Ensuring the integrity, confidentiality, and availability of your data is crucial, especially when dealing with and storing sensitive customer information. A data breach or unauthorized access can result in financial loss and irreparable damage to a company's reputation. Therefore, understanding AWS's approach to security and implementing best practices is essential for safeguarding your resources.

Shared Responsibility Model

AWS operates on a shared responsibility model, a concept that dictates who is responsible for what in the security landscape. AWS assumes responsibility for the security of the cloud, such as the infrastructure that runs AWS services, including the hardware and software. You, on the other hand, are responsible for security in the cloud. This means you manage the security configurations, data encryption, and access control for the resources you deploy on AWS.

Infrastructure Security by AWS

To protect its global data centers, AWS employs multiple layers of security. Physical data centers are fortified with stringent access controls and surveillance to prevent unauthorized entry. On the network level, AWS uses firewalls, encryption, and intrusion detection systems to monitor and protect data as it travels across the network. This robust security protocol provides a strong foundation on which you can build your applications and store data.

IAM for Access Control

Identity and Access Management (**IAM**) is a critical component of AWS security. IAM allows you to control who has access to which services within your AWS environment. You can create users, groups, and roles with specific permissions to restrict or grant access to certain AWS resources and use wildcard patterns to enable broader access. You can also enforce MFA and token rotation to ensure users keep their credentials secure. IAM also works with services like AWS CloudTrail to audit account actions and understand how users are executing AWS services. Using IAM effectively helps give you complete control over your environment.

Data Encryption

AWS provides several methods for encrypting data at rest and in transit. Services like Amazon S3 and Amazon RDS offer built-in encryption features that you can enable with just a few clicks. For more advanced encryption needs, AWS **Key Management Service** (**KMS**) allows you to create and manage cryptographic keys. Encryption adds an extra layer of security that can protect your data even if other security measures fail.

Monitoring and Auditing

AWS offers tools like CloudWatch and CloudTrail for monitoring activity and auditing your environment. CloudWatch provides real-time monitoring and alerts for resource utilization and performance, while CloudTrail keeps a log of all API calls and changes to resources, providing clear visibility on who invoked the calls. These tools can alert you to suspicious activity, helping you respond to potential security incidents more rapidly.

By understanding AWS's approach to security and employing best practices, you can build a secure environment for your data analytics projects. Leveraging tools like IAM, encryption, and monitoring services can significantly bolster your security posture. A commitment to security is not a one-time effort but an ongoing process that involves staying updated with the latest security features and continuously auditing and improving your environment configuration.

Understanding AWS Pricing and Budgeting

Understanding AWS pricing is crucial for managing your cloud-based data analytics projects effectively. The cost of using AWS services can quickly escalate if you don't have a clear picture of how AWS charges for its services. With various pricing models and numerous services, it's easy to get overwhelmed. However, a basic grasp of how AWS pricing works can help you predict costs, manage your budget, and decide which services best suit your needs.

Different Pricing Models

AWS offers several pricing models, including **On-Demand**, **Reserved**, and **Spot** Instances. **On-Demand** pricing allows you to pay for compute capacity per hour or per second, with no long-term commitments, providing the most flexibility, especially for situations where you can't predict your workload ahead of time. However, if you can commit to a specific amount of usage, then **Reserved** Instances provide a discounted rate of usage in exchange for a commitment over a term, usually one or three years.

While Reserved Instances can be ideal for production workloads, you might have some testing workloads where uptime isn't as critical. **Spot** Instances lets you use spare AWS computing capacity at significant discounts, but these instances can be terminated at any time if the capacity is needed elsewhere. Understanding these models will help you choose the most cost-effective approach for your specific use case.

Billing Cycles and Payment Methods

AWS billing cycles run on a monthly basis. At the end of each month, AWS generates an invoice detailing your usage and charges. Payment methods include credit cards, bank transfers, and even AWS-specific credits. It's essential to review your bills regularly to understand your spending patterns and catch any unexpected charges.

AWS Budgets for Cost Management

AWS Budgets is a powerful tool that can help you manage your spending. You can set custom budgets that alert you when your costs or usage exceed a pre-set threshold. AWS Budgets can also forecast future costs based on your historical usage patterns. It's an excellent way to proactively manage your AWS spending and avoid surprises at the end of the billing cycle:

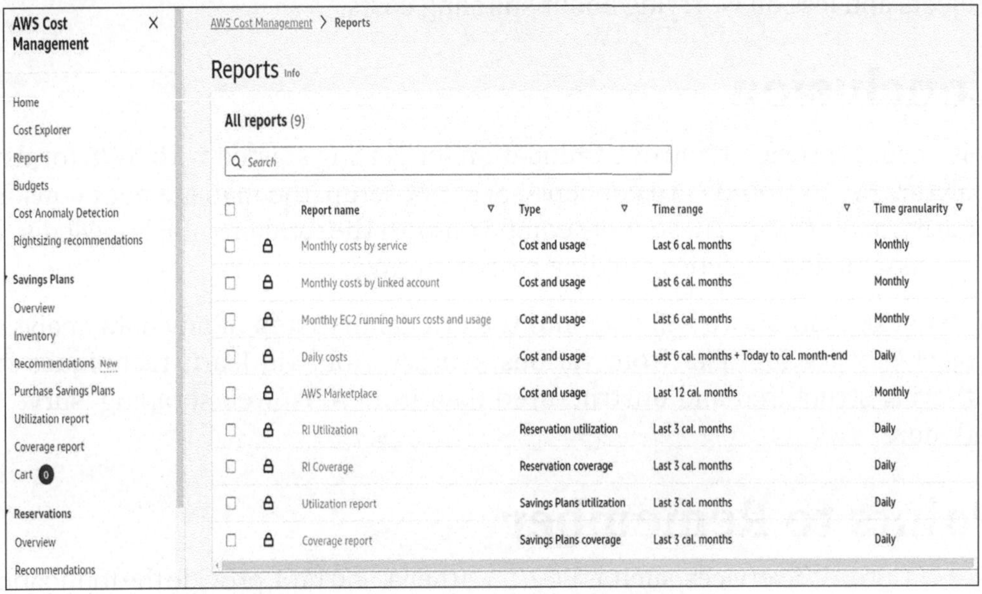

***Figure 2.11**: AWS Budget Reports*

Cost Explorer for Analysis

For a more in-depth look at your costs and usage, AWS Cost Explorer provides detailed reports and charts. This tool allows you to analyze your spending by service, region, or even specific tags you have assigned to your resources. By using Cost Explorer, you can identify trends, pinpoint cost drivers, and get recommendations for reducing your costs.

Free Tier and Special Offers

AWS offers a Free Tier for new customers, which includes a limited number of free resources each month for the first 12 months. This allows you to experiment with certain AWS services without incurring any significant costs. After the Free Tier expires, or if you exceed the Free Tier limits, standard charges apply. Occasionally, AWS also provides special offers or credits that can further offset costs, like the AWS Activate program, which provides credits to early-stage startups [6].

Navigating AWS pricing may seem daunting, but armed with the right knowledge and tools, you can effectively manage your costs. By understanding the different pricing models, keeping an eye on your billing cycles, and leveraging budgeting and analysis tools, you can gain better control over your AWS expenses. This will enable you to focus more on maximizing the value of your data analytics projects and less on worrying about spiraling costs.

Conclusion

This chapter provided a strong foundation for getting started with AWS for data analytics. We explored core concepts, account setup, the management console, security, and pricing. These tools equip you with the fundamental knowledge to begin assembling analytics building blocks on AWS.

In the next chapter, we will dive into the critical first step of any data analytics project - collecting data from various sources. You will learn techniques for gathering structured and unstructured data from APIs, web scraping, surveys, and more.

Points to Remember

- Core AWS services, such as EC2, S3, Athena, and IAM, provide the foundation for building analytics pipelines. Understanding these basic building blocks is essential to building data analytics platforms in the cloud.
- AWS offers a broad range of integrated services purpose-built for data analytics. You can mix and match these services to create customized pipelines.
- The AWS Management Console provides a user-friendly graphical interface to manage services and resources. It's important to become proficient in navigating this interface.
- Employing security best practices such as access control, encryption, and monitoring is crucial when working with sensitive data on AWS.
- AWS Budget and Cost Explorer can give you peace of mind and help you manage your costs as you take advantage of all of the different AWS services.

References

1. AWS Global Infrastructure, https://aws.amazon.com/about-aws/global-infrastructure/
2. "What is NoSQL? NoSQL Databases Explained", https://www.mongodb.com/nosql-explained
3. Dynamo: Amazon's Highly Available Key-value Store, 2007. https://assets.amazon.science/ac/1d/eb50c4064c538c8ac440ce6a1d91/dynamo-amazons-highly-available-key-value-store.pdf
4. Presto: SQL on Everything, 2019. https://research.facebook.com/publications/presto-sql-on-everything/
5. "Data Breach Chronology", 1/1/2002 - 9/30/2023. Privacy Rights Clearinghouse. https://privacyrights.org/data-breaches
6. Build Your Startup - AWS Startups, https://aws.amazon.com/startups

CHAPTER 3

Collecting Data with AWS

Introduction

This chapter will guide you through the basics of data collection and strategies for collecting and storing data from public sources like Zillow and Census.gov. You will learn about other common tools for data manipulation and how to use AWS services to manage this process.

Structure

In this chapter, we will cover the following topics:

- Data Types and Formats
- Data Collection Tools
- Data Collection Strategies
- Data Storage Strategies
- Applying Lessons to Real Estate Data Collection

Understanding Data Types and Formats

Let's take a closer look at some of the most common data types you will work with when collecting data on AWS or any other platform.

Data Types

First up is **text data**, also known as string data. Text data is alphanumeric and can represent simple text fields, categories, or descriptions. You will find this data type prevalent in name fields, product descriptions, or any form of textual data:

	A	B	C	D
1	**Company Name**	**City**	**State**	**Description**
2	Tech Innovate Inc.	Innovatown	CA	Develops cutting-edge software solutions for businesses.
3	Green Future Solutions	Greenfield	OR	Provides sustainable energy solutions and consulting.
4	Prime Health Ltd.	Healthville	NY	Offers healthcare services and products for wellness.
5	Global Finance Group	Finance City	TX	Specializes in investment and financial advisory services.
6	EduBright Academy	Educationburg	MA	Educational institution focusing on innovative learning methods.

Figure 3.1: *Simple Dataset with Text Data Fields*

In data analytics, text data often undergoes processes like text mining or natural language processing to derive insights. For example, customer reviews on an e-commerce platform would typically be stored as text data and could be analyzed for sentiment.

Next is **numerical data**, which encompasses integers and floating-point numbers. This data type commonly appears in finance, engineering, and scientific contexts. Numerical data plays a significant role when you need to perform mathematical calculations or when you are developing statistical models. For example, a sales database would contain numerical data such as the cost of items sold, quantities, and sales figures.

"Time is what we want most, but what we use worst."

- William Penn

Time-series data consists of metrics collected or recorded at a time interval. Whether it's stock prices recorded every millisecond or temperature readings taken every hour, time-series data offers a temporal dimension that is crucial for trend analysis and forecasting. AWS services like Kinesis can handle time-series data well, allowing you to stream this kind of data in real-time:

	A	B
1	Date	Price
2	2023-01-02	100.4967142
3	2023-01-03	100.3584499
4	2023-01-04	101.0061384
5	2023-01-05	102.5291682
6	2023-01-06	102.2950149
7	2023-01-09	102.0608779
8	2023-01-10	103.6400907
9	2023-01-11	104.4075255
10	2023-01-12	103.9380511
11	2023-01-13	104.4806111
12	2023-01-16	104.0171934
13	2023-01-17	103.5514637
14	2023-01-18	103.7934259

Figure 3.2: *Simple Time-Series Dataset*

Geospatial data refers to any data that has a geographical or spatial component. This could be as simple as latitude and longitude coordinates or as complex as a geographical shape defined by multiple points. Applications that use geospatial data include location-based services, mapping software, and environmental studies. For instance, a food delivery app would use geospatial data to locate restaurants and customers, optimizing delivery routes:

	A	B	C
1	City	Latitude	Longitude
2	New York	40.7128	-74.006
3	London	51.5074	-0.1278
4	Tokyo	35.6895	139.6917
5	Paris	48.8566	2.3522
6	Sydney	-33.8688	151.2093
7	Cairo	30.0444	31.2357
8	Rio de Janeiro	-22.9068	-43.1729
9	Cape Town	-33.9249	18.4241
10	Moscow	55.7558	37.6173
11	Beijing	39.9042	116.4074

***Figure 3.3**: Geospatial Dataset Measuring Latitude and Longitude of Cities*

Each of these data types has its own specialized uses, and you may often find them combined in complex datasets. Knowing what type of data you are dealing with helps you choose the appropriate AWS services and data storage formats, setting the stage for effective data collection and subsequent analysis.

Data Formats

Different data formats come with various advantages and drawbacks, depending on what you aim to achieve. Let's explore some of the most commonly used data formats in data collection efforts:

- **JSON**, or **JavaScript Object Notation**, is a lightweight data-interchange format that is easy to read and write and is one of the most common data formats in modern data integration. It's highly flexible, allowing for hierarchical structures, and it supports all the basic data types like strings, numbers, and Booleans. JSON is often used in web applications for asynchronous browser/server communication. AWS services like Kinesis and Lambda work seamlessly with JSON-formatted data, making it a convenient choice for real-time data streaming and transformation tasks.

- **XML,** or **eXtensible Markup Language**, is another text-based format used for storing and transporting data. Unlike JSON, XML does not use arrays or objects, but it allows for nested elements. This can be both an advantage and a drawback, depending on the complexity of your data. XML files are often larger than comparable JSON files, which can be a concern for storage and transmission costs. However, XML is still widely used in various domains, including healthcare, finance, and online publishing:

```
<?xml version="1.0" ?>
<Students>
    <Student id="1">
        <Name>Alice Johnson</Name>
        <Age>21</Age>
        <Major>Mathematics</Major>
    </Student>
    <Student id="2">
        <Name>Bob Smith</Name>
        <Age>23</Age>
        <Major>Literature</Major>
    </Student>
    <Student id="3">
        <Name>Catherine Lee</Name>
        <Age>22</Age>
        <Major>Computer Science</Major>
    </Student>
    <Student id="4">
        <Name>David Brown</Name>
        <Age>18</Age>
        <Major>Mathematics</Major>
    </Student>
</Students>
```

***Figure 3.4**: Sample XML Dataset of a Student Roster*

- **CSV**, or **Comma-Separated Values**, is another common data format that is structured in a tabular format, not hierarchical like JSON or XML. As the name suggests, data fields are separated by commas (or other delimiters like tabs or spaces). CSV files are highly efficient in terms of storage space and are easy to process, making them ideal for tabular data without complex relationships. This format is commonly used in spreadsheet applications and databases. AWS services like S3 and RDS can readily import and export CSV files.

While these are the most common data formats, there are also more advanced data types that focus on optimizing data storage for analytics use cases:

- One such format is **Parquet**, a columnar storage file format often used with big data processing frameworks. It is particularly useful when dealing with data warehouses or large-scale data lakes due to its efficient read and write operations. Parquet also supports complex nested data structures and offers excellent data compression. It integrates well with big data processing frameworks like Hadoop and Spark, as well as AWS analytics services like Amazon Redshift and Athena. A 2016 case study [1] demonstrated that by simply switching from Parquet to other similar optimized storage formats, Spark processing jobs were able to execute **3.5x more efficiently.**

- **ORC**, or **Optimized Row Columnar**, is another columnar storage format designed for big data workloads. It offers benefits similar to Parquet, including high compression and efficient columnar storage. However, ORC tends to offer better performance when reading, writing, and searching data. It's often used in conjunction with Hadoop-based big data ecosystems and integrates well with AWS services geared for big data analytics.

In summary, the choice of data format can impact storage costs, read/write speed, and the complexity of the data you can handle. Understanding these formats will enable you to choose the most appropriate AWS services and configurations for your data collection efforts.

Choosing the Right Data Type and Format

Choosing the right data types and formats is pivotal to your data analytics projects, affecting everything from storage costs to processing speed and analytic capabilities. Understanding the use cases for each can guide you toward the most effective and efficient solutions.

For text-based data like logs, customer reviews, or natural language inputs, the string or text data type is often the most suitable. JSON is a widely used format for storing such text-based, semi-structured data. It is lightweight and works well for real-time data exchange, particularly in web-based applications or APIs. If your project involves real-time data streaming or web scraping, JSON coupled with text data types can be a solid choice. AWS services like Kinesis and Lambda offer native support for JSON, making the ingestion and transformation of this data straightforward.

Numerical data is generally best stored in integer or floating-point data types. For use cases like financial calculations, scientific modeling, or statistical analysis, the choice of numerical data types is crucial for preserving data integrity. When it comes to formats for numerical data, CSV can often be sufficient and efficient, particularly for smaller datasets. However, for large datasets with millions of rows and multiple numerical columns, columnar formats like Parquet or ORC are better suited because they offer excellent compression and fast read/write operations.

Time-series data is usually numerical but with a critical time component. For instance, if you are tracking stock market prices or sensor data over time, then time-series data is what you will work with. Formats like Parquet or ORC are highly efficient for storing time-series data because they allow for optimized reads of large time spans of data. AWS services like Amazon Timestream are specifically designed for managing time-series data at scale.

For geospatial data, which often consists of latitude and longitude coordinates or even more complex polygons, the data type could be either text (for GeoJSON, WKT formats) or numerical (for raw coordinates). Storage formats like Parquet and ORC can efficiently store geospatial data due to their support for complex nested data structures. AWS offers geospatial support through services like Amazon Location Service, which can integrate with your data storage solutions.

XML is often the format of choice for applications requiring data with complex relationships, or for industries like healthcare and insurance, where XML is often a mandated standard. If you are dealing with hierarchical data models or metadata-rich information, XML can be an appropriate format despite its relatively larger file size compared to JSON or CSV.

In conclusion, your use case should dictate your choice of data types and formats. Evaluate the nature of your data, the requirements of your application, and the capabilities of your analytics services to make an informed decision. AWS offers a broad range of services that can accommodate various data types and formats, giving you the flexibility to tailor your data collection strategy to meet specific needs.

Strategies for Data Collection on AWS

In the realm of data collection, two primary methodologies exist: push and pull. We will review the nuances of each as we look to build out the first part of our data pipeline, and how to handle each type of data collection with both simple and large-scale use cases.

Fetch Your Data - The Pull Approach

Here, your centralized system actively requests, or **pulls**, data from various data sources. Think of it like visiting multiple grocery stores to collect different types of foods, rather than having them delivered to your doorstep. The pull methodology suits scenarios where you need to aggregate data from disparate sources at specific intervals, like scraping web pages for information or pulling data from APIs.

Before diving into data collection, you should identify where you are going to pull the data from. This could be public APIs, databases, or web pages. Once you know your sources, determine the frequency of your data pulls. Will you pull data every hour, once a day, or on a trigger like a stock price hitting a certain threshold? Your answer will depend on the nature of your project and the volume of data you are handling.

AWS provides a plethora of tools to facilitate the pull methodology. AWS Lambda functions, for instance, can run code that pulls data from an API at scheduled intervals. You can use AWS Glue for more complex **ETL (Extract, Transform, Load**) tasks. If you are pulling data from a database, AWS Data Migration Service supports a continuous data replication feature that essentially pulls data from source databases to AWS storage solutions.

While the pull methodology provides flexibility, it comes with its set of challenges. These include rate-limiting issues with APIs, the risk of overloading source systems, and ensuring data consistency. To mitigate these, always adhere to best practices like respecting API rate limits and using incremental pulls to avoid system overload. Additionally, ensure you pull only the data you need – unnecessary data adds to storage costs and complicates analytics.

Receive Your Data - The Push Methodology

In contrast to the pull methodology, where your system actively fetches data, the push methodology allows data sources to send data directly to your storage or processing hub. Imagine a mailbox that receives letters from various locations; you simply open it to find all the mail collected for you. This approach is particularly beneficial for real-time analytics or when the data sources are designed to broadcast data instantaneously, such as IoT sensors, application logs, or user activity streams.

Getting AWS ready to receive pushed data involves configuring storage or stream services to accept incoming data. AWS Kinesis is excellent for handling real-time data streams. Kinesis receives data from multiple data **producers** with low latency, buffers that data, and then pushes that data out to one or more **consumers** (typically data stores) like S3 or DynamoDB. If you are working with structured relational data, AWS RDS provides easy access to relational databases. AWS also provides many popular **Software Development Kits (SDK**) and APIs to integrate these services directly into your applications or devices, enabling them to push data seamlessly:

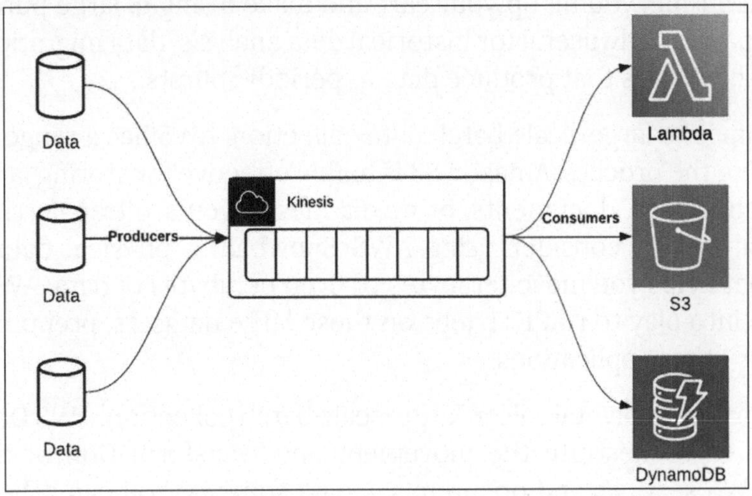

Figure 3.5: *Example of an Amazon Kinesis Flow with Data Producers and Consumers*

Other AWS services, such as AWS IoT Core, allow IoT devices to push data securely to the cloud. **Amazon Simple Notification Service (SNS)** can act as a mediator to push data and notifications to various AWS services. Even databases in AWS RDS can be configured to push changes using triggers or stored procedures. These services make it easier to build a comprehensive and integrated push-based data collection system.

The push methodology, while effective for real-time data collection, also has its challenges. These range from handling high data throughput to ensuring data security during the transmission. AWS solves some of these challenges by offering auto-scaling features and built-in encryption. However, you must also be cautious about setting proper permissions and validation steps to prevent unauthorized data injection. Additionally, proper monitoring should be in place to track any bottlenecks or failures in the data pipeline.

By effectively configuring AWS to handle push-based data collection, you build a robust and real-time data pipeline that fuels your analytics efforts. Not only does this enable quicker decision-making, but it also enhances the overall quality and freshness of the data you are analyzing.

Batch - Fetching Data at Scale

In scenarios involving massive volumes of data, real-time or continuous data collection may not always be feasible or cost-effective. Batch collection offers a solution by gathering large sets of data at specific intervals for processing or analysis. Imagine this approach as similar to bulk shopping: instead of buying one item at a time, you fill up your cart and make a single, large purchase. This method is particularly useful for historical data analysis, data migration, or when dealing with sources that produce data in periodic bursts.

When it comes to large-scale batch data collection, AWS has a range of services to streamline the process. Amazon S3 is highly effective for storing large batches of data such as logs, documents, or media files. If you are transferring gigantic datasets into AWS, consider using AWS Snowball, a physical data transport solution that helps you move terabytes or even petabytes of data. AWS Glue can then come into play to run ETL jobs on these large datasets, prepping them for analytics or other applications.

Automation plays a pivotal role in large-scale batch collection. AWS Data Pipeline allows you to orchestrate the movement and transformation of data across different AWS services and on-premises data sources. You can schedule batch jobs to run at specific intervals, collect data from various sources, and push it to the desired AWS storage or database service. AWS Lambda also supports scheduled execution, enabling you to run custom scripts for batch collection tasks at predefined times.

Batch collection at scale introduces challenges related to data integrity, latency, and resource management. Due to the large volumes of data being transferred, any hiccup could result in data loss or corruption. AWS helps mitigate these issues by offering robust data validation and integrity checks. Also, always plan your resource allocation wisely. Large batch processes could hog resources, affecting other operations. Therefore, use services like AWS Auto Scaling to dynamically adjust resources based on demand.

By mastering the batch collection approach on AWS, you gain the ability to handle large volumes of data efficiently. This approach provides you with the raw material needed for deep and comprehensive analytics. Moreover, by leveraging AWS's powerful toolset for batch collection, you can automate, optimize, and scale your data pipelines to meet the evolving needs of your analytics projects.

Streaming - Consuming Data at Scale

Understanding the distinction between batch and streaming data collection is crucial for designing an effective data pipeline. Each method has its benefits and limitations, and the choice often depends on the specific needs of your project. Let's delve into the differences between the two.

Batch data collection involves gathering data over a specific period and then processing it all at once. This approach is well-suited for scenarios where real-time analysis is not essential, and the focus is on comprehensive, large-scale analytics. For instance, if you are generating daily sales reports or analyzing user behavior on a website over a month, batch processing is often the most straightforward and cost-effective method. AWS services like AWS Glue or Amazon EMR are commonly used for batch data processing tasks.

Streaming data collection, on the other hand, is designed for real-time data ingestion and processing. As data flows in, it gets processed and analyzed immediately, allowing for real-time insights and actions. Streaming is ideal for applications that require instant data analysis and responsiveness, such as fraud detection, live dashboards, or monitoring systems. AWS Kinesis and AWS Lambda are popular choices for implementing real-time data pipelines on AWS.

The choice between batch and streaming also impacts data storage solutions. Batch processes often use data lakes or traditional databases where large volumes of data are stored and then queried. In contrast, streaming solutions frequently use data stores optimized for a quick read and write operations, sometimes employing in-memory databases like Amazon DynamoDB or time-series databases like Amazon Timestream for immediate data retrieval.

Cost factors also play a significant role in the decision-making process. Batch processing can be more cost-effective because it allows for the optimization of computational resources. You can schedule batch jobs during off-peak hours to save costs, for instance. Streaming, while offering real-time capabilities, may require more computational power and thus could be more expensive, especially if you have to maintain a continuous stream 24/7.

Error handling and data quality assurance practices also differ between the two methods. Batch processing provides the luxury of time, allowing for more elaborate data quality checks and error correction steps. In contrast, streaming data pipelines often require more robust, immediate error-handling mechanisms to ensure that real-time analytics aren't compromised.

In summary, the choice between batch and streaming data collection will largely depend on the specific requirements of your project, such as the need for real-time analytics, the volume of data, and the available budget. AWS offers a variety of services tailored for both batch and streaming data collection methods, enabling you to build a data pipeline that best fits your needs.

Open-Source Tools for Data Collection

While AWS provides some great functionality out-of-the-box to quickly consume and work with data, there are some additional tools you should be aware of to help make your life much easier when collecting data. These tools complement your AWS toolbox and provide a more targeted inspection of your data as you build out your pipeline.

Working with APIs Using Postman

Postman is a popular tool that developers and data professionals use to test, develop, and document APIs. Initially designed as a simple HTTP client for testing web services, Postman has evolved into a robust platform that supports multiple aspects of API development and testing. With a user-friendly interface, it enables users to send requests to web servers and get responses back, simplifying the process of interacting with APIs. This tool supports a wide array of HTTP methods such as `GET`, `POST`, `PUT`, and `DELETE`, as well as various authentication protocols, making it a versatile option for API testing:

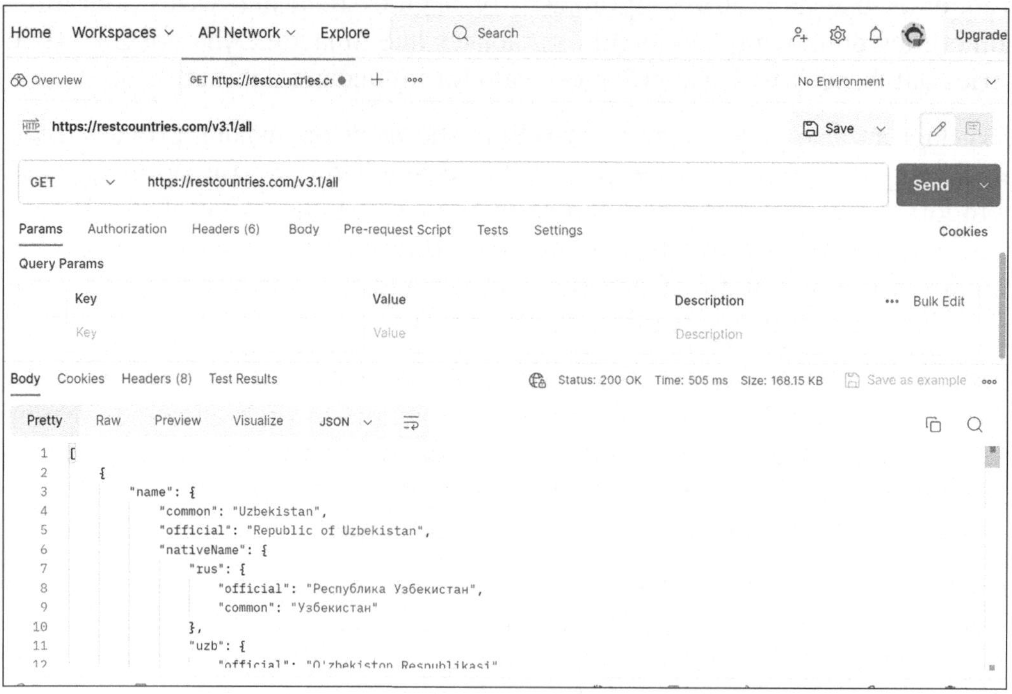

Figure 3.6: *API Request to restcountries.com Using Postman*

When it comes to data collection via APIs, Postman offers numerous features that streamline the process. First, it allows you to easily set up and send requests to pull data from various endpoints, making it a great tool for the '`pull`' method of data collection. Its built-in environment variables and parameterization capabilities allow you to customize requests, enabling dynamic data collection across different API endpoints. Additionally, Postman includes features for automating API interactions, such as running collections of requests in a specified sequence. This is particularly useful for large-scale data extraction tasks.

Another advantage of Postman is its collaborative features. The platform supports sharing of collections, environments, and variables, which is essential when working in team settings. It also offers robust documentation features, so you can generate and maintain API documentation effortlessly. This ensures that as you collect data, you also keep an organized record of your data sources, methods, and configurations. The combination of these features makes Postman an invaluable tool for data collection when working with APIs, enhancing both the efficiency and effectiveness of the process.

Processing Data Requests with Python

While this chapter focuses on leveraging AWS services to do most of the legwork, there are times when we will need to rely on some code to ensure our custom use case gets implemented properly. Python is the ideal programming language for this purpose, and we will focus on learning the essentials aspects to empower you to build effectively on AWS.

Python is one of the most versatile languages for data collection tasks, owing largely to its rich ecosystem of libraries and frameworks. Libraries like **requests** [2] simplify the process of fetching data from web APIs, while BeautifulSoup and Scrapy assist in web scraping tasks. If you are dealing with structured data formats like CSV, JSON, or XML, Python's standard library and third-party packages like Pandas offer robust parsing capabilities. This breadth of options means that Python can handle virtually any data source you are likely to encounter, from websites and APIs to spreadsheets and databases.

One of Python's biggest selling points is its readability and ease of use. Even those with limited programming experience find Python's syntax intuitive, which is a significant advantage for data collection tasks that may require custom coding. You can easily automate repetitive tasks such as fetching daily metrics from an API or scraping periodic updates from a web page. Libraries like Schedule or native Python modules like time and datetime can help you set up automated data collection routines with minimal hassle.

Python's capability to integrate with other tools and services sets it apart as a data collection tool. Whether you need to store collected data in an SQL database, send it to a cloud storage service like AWS S3, or even forward it to a data visualization tool, Python has libraries and SDKs to make that process straightforward. Moreover, Python's active community continually contributes to its ever-growing selection of data-centric libraries, ensuring that the language remains up-to-date with the latest data collection techniques and best practices. Therefore, choosing Python for your data collection tasks offers both flexibility and future-proofing.

Querying Data with SQL - DBeaver

DBeaver [3] is an open-source database management tool that provides a unified interface for interacting with a wide variety of databases. Whether you are working with SQL-based databases like MySQL, PostgreSQL, and SQLite, or NoSQL databases like MongoDB, DBeaver has you covered. Its user-friendly graphical interface makes it easier to navigate through database structures, run SQL queries, and manage data. The tool offers a plethora of functionalities, including data export and import, SQL script generation, and schema diagramming, among others:

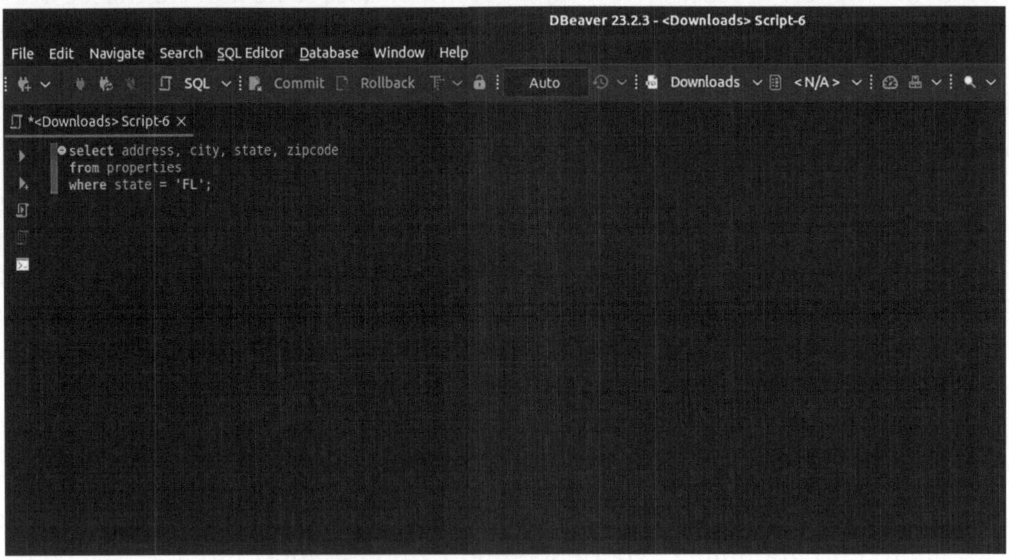

Figure 3.7: *Simple SQL Query Running in DBeaver*

When it comes to querying data, DBeaver stands out for several reasons. First, its SQL editor is rich in features like syntax highlighting, auto-completion, and SQL formatting, which make writing and debugging queries more efficient. The tool also allows you to run queries in multiple tabs, making it easier to compare results and perform complex analyses. With DBeaver, you can execute stored procedures, manipulate data directly within the interface, and even visualize query results through charts and graphs. This makes it a versatile tool for both data analysis and database management tasks.

Another advantage of DBeaver is its extensibility. Since it's open-source, a strong community of developers continually contributes to its capabilities. This means that you can often find plugins or extensions that add specific functionalities tailored to your needs. Moreover, DBeaver supports various data export formats, including CSV, JSON, and HTML, allowing you to easily share your query results with others or import them into other tools for further analysis. All these features make DBeaver an invaluable tool for anyone who frequently interacts with databases, enabling streamlined querying and data management.

Strategies for Data Storage

Now that we have reviewed different ways to inspect and collect data, let's review some tried-and-tested strategies for how to store this data.

Using S3 for All the Things

Amazon S3 stands out as the premier choice for storing data after the collection stage of a data engineering pipeline for several reasons. First, it offers unparalleled scalability. Unlike traditional file systems or databases that might have size or performance constraints, S3 can scale infinitely to store any amount of data. As your data grows, you don't have to worry about re-architecting your storage solution. You can continue to add data to your S3 buckets without experiencing performance degradation, making it an ideal choice for projects that will evolve over time.

Second, S3 excels in data durability and availability. It offers 99.999999999% (11 9's) durability over a given year, which means your data is extremely safe. Data gets automatically distributed across a minimum of three physical facilities within an AWS region. This level of redundancy ensures that your data remains available and accessible, even if one or more facilities experience an issue. Such robustness is particularly beneficial in the post-collection stage when you can't afford to lose any data.

Third, Amazon S3 provides a wide range of storage classes designed for various use cases and cost optimization. For example, S3 Standard offers high durability and low latency for frequently accessed data, whereas S3 Glacier is more cost-effective for long-term archival. By selecting the appropriate storage class, you can effectively balance between accessibility and cost, without compromising on data integrity.

Fourth, S3 integrates seamlessly with other AWS services, such as AWS Glue for data cataloging, Amazon Athena for SQL queries, and AWS Lambda for event-driven computing. This makes it easier to build end-to-end data engineering pipelines that are both robust and flexible. For instance, you can set up a Lambda function to trigger whenever new data gets uploaded to an S3 bucket, allowing for real-time processing and analytics.

Lastly, S3 comes with a robust set of security and compliance features. You can use AWS **Identity and Access Management** (**IAM**) to set granular permissions on your S3 buckets or even on individual objects. Encryption options are available both for data at rest and in transit. Additionally, S3 supports auditing and logging features that enable you to track access and modifications to your data, which is critical for compliance with regulations like GDPR or HIPAA.

In summary, Amazon S3's scalability, durability, flexibility, and security features make it the go-to storage solution after the data collection stage in a data engineering pipeline. Its variety of storage classes and seamless integration with other AWS services provide the additional layers of customization and automation that modern data projects require.

Building a Catalog

A data catalog serves as a centralized repository for metadata and schema information in the AWS Glue ecosystem. It plays a critical role in organizing, accessing, and managing raw data that resides in various data stores such as Amazon S3, Amazon RDS, and Amazon Redshift. AWS Glue automatically scans your data sources and populates the data catalog with tables, schema definitions, and other metadata. This auto-discovery feature eliminates the need for manual cataloging, which can be both time-consuming and error-prone.

The data catalog assists in data preparation and transformation tasks. When using AWS Glue ETL jobs, you can refer to the catalog to quickly identify the datasets you need. The ETL jobs can then use this metadata to apply the necessary transformations to the raw data. For example, if you have raw CSV files in an S3 bucket and the data catalog contains the schema information, an ETL job can automatically map the CSV columns to the corresponding data types, ensuring that the data is correctly transformed and loaded into the destination data store.

Beyond ETL jobs, the data catalog also integrates with other AWS services such as Amazon Athena and Amazon QuickSight for seamless querying and data visualization. You can directly run SQL queries on the cataloged datasets without the need to move or transform the data. This feature accelerates the time-to-insight, enabling you to quickly glean actionable intelligence from your raw data.

Access control and security also benefit from using a data catalog. AWS Glue integrates with AWS IAM, allowing you to specify granular permissions on who can access or modify the cataloged datasets. This feature helps you maintain a robust security posture while making data easily discoverable and accessible for authorized users.

In essence, a data catalog in AWS Glue acts as the backbone for data discovery, transformation, and governance. It streamlines the data preparation process, enhances collaboration among data teams, and ensures that you can securely and efficiently turn raw data into actionable insights.

Storing Raw and Transformed Data

Storing raw and transformed data separately offers several advantages, starting with data integrity. Keeping raw data in its original state ensures you have an untouched, historical record of the data, often referred to as the "**source of truth**." If any issues arise during the transformation process, such as data corruption or loss, you can always revert to the raw data. This approach provides a safety net that allows for auditing, troubleshooting, and reprocessing if necessary.

Another benefit focuses on flexibility and adaptability. As your business evolves, so do your data transformation needs. Storing raw data independently allows you to apply new transformations or update existing ones without affecting the original datasets. For example, if you initially transform raw logs into summarized daily metrics but later decide you need hourly metrics, you can easily perform the new transformation on the raw data. This adaptability becomes increasingly important as you fine-tune analytics, apply machine learning models, or meet new regulatory requirements.

Data accessibility and compliance also come into play. In some industries, regulations mandate the retention of raw data for a specific period, often requiring that it remain unaltered. Storing raw and transformed data separately simplifies compliance with such regulations, as you can set different retention policies for each. Moreover, having raw data available ensures that you can meet any ad-hoc, exploratory, or forensic data analysis needs that arise, without having to reverse-engineer transformed or summarized data.

Cost optimization is another reason for keeping raw and transformed data separate. AWS, for example, offers different storage solutions optimized for varying needs, such as Amazon S3 Standard for frequently accessed data and Amazon S3 Glacier for long-term archival. Raw data, which you might not need to be accessed frequently once transformed, can be moved to cheaper storage solutions, while keeping the transformed data in more readily accessible storage. This strategy allows for better cost management, enabling you to allocate resources more efficiently based on usage patterns.

In summary, storing raw and transformed data separately enhances data integrity, provides flexibility for future transformations, simplifies regulatory compliance, and allows for cost optimization. Each type of data serves different purposes and has distinct storage requirements, making it ideal to keep them separate for more effective data management.

Putting It All Together: Collecting Real Estate Data

Now that we have reviewed the basics of data formats, collection, and storage, let's dive in and put these concepts to use. Suppose you have just won the lottery. Instead of splurging on fancy cars or volatile cryptocurrency, you choose to invest in a more stable, predictable industry: real estate. Your goal is to ride the recent wave of build-for-rent and institutional interest and buy up properties that can then be rented out to consumers. However, the age-old saying that "*real estate is local*" still holds true today. In other words, markets can differ significantly in terms of their demographics and population trends, which can have a material impact on your expected ROI investments.

Let's review some public datasets that can help inform our analysis. The beauty of this exercise, as with most data analytics projects, is that this is not a one-time, static analysis of a snapshot in time. We can and should automate projects like this to keep an eye on how our investment thesis plays out and get proactively alerted of any significant shifts to our original assumptions.

Review Sources

Here are a few data sources that can help us get a clearer picture of how to make our real estate investment decisions:

- **The Zillow Research Team** [4] regularly publishes economic data on residential home sales, rental prices, and inventory. While CSV data is available, Zillow recommends using the Housing Market Metrics API [5] to do recurring data collection. You can follow the instructions on the "Introduction" page to request an account and get API access.

- The **U.S. Census** datasets [6] offer a wealth of demographic and socio-economic information about the population of the United States. They cover various topics, such as age, gender, race, income levels, educational attainment, and housing data, and are usually updated every 10 years for the decennial census and more frequently for other surveys like the **American Community Survey** (**ACS**). These datasets serve as valuable resources for understanding community characteristics, which can inform a variety of decisions, including real estate investment.
- The **FBI Crime Data API** [7] provides access to various crime statistics across the United States, compiled by the Federal Bureau of Investigation. The data includes information on violent crimes, property crimes, and arrests, broken down by location and time period. This resource is valuable for assessing the safety of potential real estate investment areas.

Collecting Data on S3 Using AWS Lambda

Now that you have followed the above instructions and have access to the datasets, let's configure our initial pipeline on AWS.

Creating a Bucket on S3 to Store Data

1. Navigate to the AWS Console and the S3 service.
2. Click `Create bucket`.
3. Name the bucket (for example, "real-estate-ROI-data"), accept the default configuration, and click `Create bucket` once more to finish setup:

    NOTE: Bucket naming is governed by several rules [8] such as uniqueness and restrictions on using uppercase letters, so you might need to try a few different names to get the bucket to save properly:

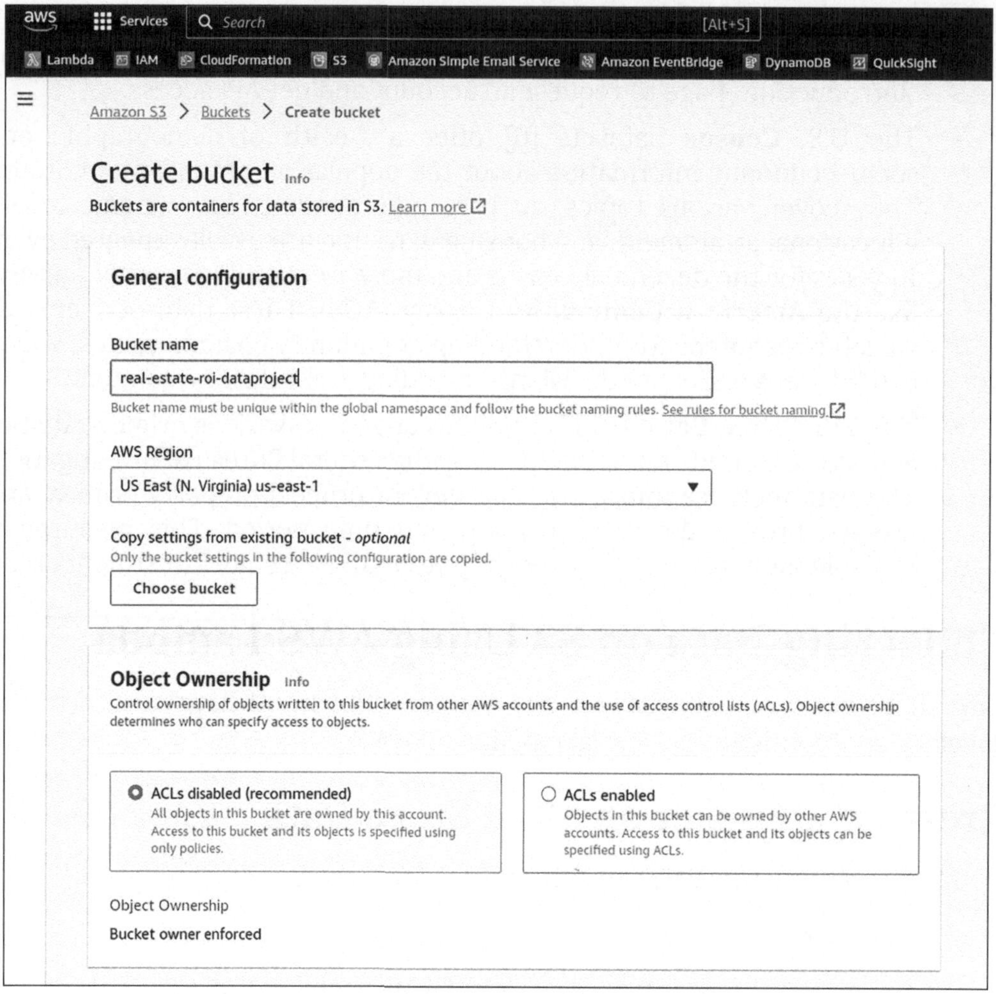

***Figure 3.8**: Creating a Bucket on S3*

Creating an IAM Role for Permissions

As we have mentioned, AWS does a great job of keeping security front and center. This means that before our Lambda can talk to our new S3 bucket, we need to define an IAM role that grants Lambda write permissions:

1. Navigate to the IAM Console.
2. Click **`Roles`**, and then **`Create role`**.
3. From the **`Select trusted entity`** page, select AWS Service as the Trusted entity type, and then select Lambda as the use case.

4. From the Permissions policies page, search for AmazonS3FullAccess and add that permission to this role:
    a. This gives full read and write access to all buckets on the given account. For more fine-grained control, you can add/update policies that focus on specific operations (read-only vs. read-write) and specific buckets.
5. Give your role a name (for example, `real-estate-roi-data-s3`) and save it.

Creating an AWS Lambda Function to Download Data

1. Navigate to the AWS Console and the AWS Lambda service.
2. Click `Create function`.
3. Keep the default `Author from scratch` option selected.
4. Enter a function name (for example, `download-real-estate-data`) and select the latest version of Python for the runtime.
5. Configure the timeout to be 10 minutes to ensure we have sufficient time to download the full dataset:
    a. If the Lambda doesn't complete within the timeout duration, the Lambda will stop processing and throw an error.
    b. The maximum timeout to use is 15 minutes, underscoring how Lambdas are designed for short, focused tasks (however, they can be highly parallelized too!).
6. Under the Execution role section, select Use an existing role and select the role we created in our previous IAM process (`real-estate-roi-data-s3`):

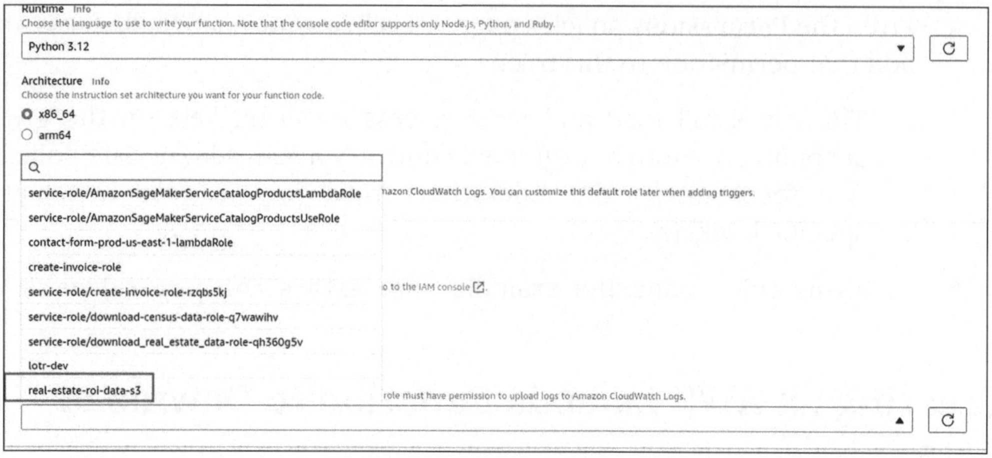

***Figure 3.9**: Creating a Lambda Function*

7. Once created, edit the function, as illustrated in *Figure* 3.10, by replacing the default source code with the code, as follows:

***Figure 3.10**: Editing a Newly Created Lambda*

Lambda source in Python:

```
import json
import boto3
import urllib.request
```

```
s3 = boto3.client('s3')

def lambda_handler(event, context):
    #url for the Zillow Home Value Index (ZHVI), latest url can be found 
at https://www.zillow.com/research/data/
    url = 'https://files.zillowstatic.com/research/public_csvs/zhvi/
Metro_zhvi_uc_sfrcondo_tier_0.33_0.67_sm_sa_month.csv?t=1707444908'

    response = urllib.request.urlopen(url)
    csv_data = response.read()

    bucket_name = 'real-estate-roi-data'
    key_name = 'zhvi.csv'

    s3.put_object(Bucket=bucket_name, Key=key_name, Body=csv_data)

    #it is customary to return a success/failure message to conclude 
your lambda. The statusCode: 200 is a common HTTP response code 
indicating a successful response.
    return {
        'statusCode': 200,
        'body': 'File downloaded and uploaded to S3 successfully!'
    }
```

8. Save this script and create a test event from the **Test** dropdown.
    a. While some Lambda request events might need to follow a specific JSON format, our Lambda will not be reading any incoming event fields, so you can use any JSON body for your test.
9. To test the Lambda, you must first click **Deploy** to save your latest code changes. Then, click the main **Test** button to execute the Lambda.
10. If successful, you should see our Lambda response being returned with metadata about the final request statistics. You should also see the **zhvi.csv** file in your S3 bucket:

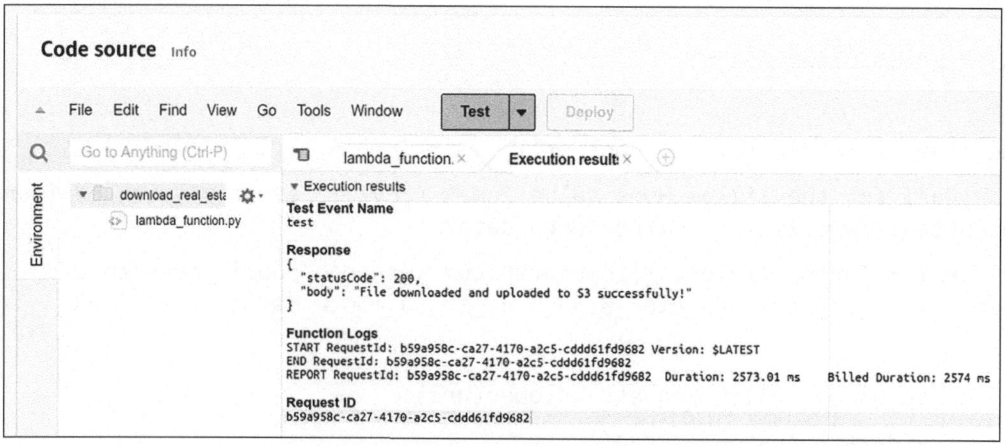

Figure 3.11: *Executing Your Lambda and Seeing the Results*

Repeat this process for the other two datasets. You should now have three Lambdas that can pull data directly from each data source and persist it to S3.

Note that to schedule this for automatic execution (say you want to pull weekly price data from Zillow), you can use Amazon EventBridge [9] to schedule Lambda executions and view the results from the Lambda console.

Return to the S3 console and confirm that you can see the persisted files in your S3 bucket. You should notice that the S3 bucket is structured just like any file system, with folders and files. As you download more sources, you can customize your folder structure to separate by data source or by date/time, depending on your use case.

Conclusion

The efficient collection and storage of data lay the foundation for impactful analytics. As we saw in this chapter, AWS provides a versatile toolkit, enabling you to build automated, scalable data pipelines. Whether you need to pull from APIs, receive pushed data, or run large batch jobs, AWS can simplify it. Choosing the right data formats and separating raw and processed data ensures flexibility. By leveraging AWS to remove drudgery from data collection, you can focus on deriving meaning from the data through insightful analysis and visualization. In the next chapter, we will tackle the construction of robust data processing pipelines on AWS, employing AWS Glue for seamless data orchestration and cleaning.

Points to Remember

- There are common data types such as text, numerical, time-series, and geospatial data, each with optimal formats like JSON, CSV, and Parquet, depending on the use cases.
- Tools like Postman, Python requests, and SQL clients help collect, parse, and query data from APIs, websites, and databases.
- AWS supports both "push" and "pull" data collection strategies. Pull involves actively fetching data, while push allows sources to directly send data.
- For large datasets, batch processing is more efficient than real-time streaming. However, streaming enables instant analysis.
- AWS services like S3 and Lambda allow automating recurring large-scale data collection tasks and building robust pipelines.

References

1. "Benchmarking Apache Parquet", https://blog.cloudera.com/benchmarking-apache-parquet-the-allstate-experience/
2. "Python requests library", https://pypi.org/project/requests/
3. "DBeaver Community", https://dbeaver.io/
4. "Real Estate Metrics", https://www.zillowgroup.com/developers/api/public-data/real-estate-metrics/
5. "Housing Market Metrics API", https://documenter.getpostman.com/view/9197254/UVsFz93V#intro
6. "ACS Demographic and Housing", https://data.census.gov/table/ACSDP1Y2022.DP05
7. "FBI Crime Data API", https://cde.ucr.cjis.gov/LATEST/webapp/#/pages/docApi
8. "Bucket naming rules", https://docs.aws.amazon.com/AmazonS3/latest/userguide/bucketnamingrules.html?icmpid=docs_amazons3_console
9. "Schedule AWS Lambda functions using Eventbridge", https://docs.aws.amazon.com/eventbridge/latest/userguide/eb-run-lambda-schedule.html

CHAPTER 4

Processing Data on AWS

Introduction

Businesses rely on analyzing massive amounts of data to find insights that can give them a competitive edge. However, before we can even begin to find these insights, we need to clean and shape the data we have collected to make sense of it.

The art of proposing a question must be held of higher value than solving it

- Gregor Cantor, Mathematician

This is where AWS Glue comes in. Glue is a fully-managed **Extract, Transform, and Load (ETL)** service that provides a visual, easy-to-use interface for preparing and cleaning data to make it ready for analysis. In this chapter, we will explore the key concepts and components of an AWS Glue data pipeline. You will learn how to leverage features like automatic schema inference, pre-built transforms, and intuitive graphical workflows to tackle your data transformation challenges. We will walk through hands-on examples of using crawlers to catalog data, building ETL jobs, and best practices around pipeline testing, monitoring, and security. By the end, you will have practical knowledge to start harnessing the power of your data using AWS Glue. Let's get started!

Structure

In this chapter, we will cover the following topics:

- Data Processing Using AWS Glue
- Anatomy of a Data Pipeline
- Crawling Your Data

- Using the Data Catalog
- Transforming Your Data with Glue Jobs
- AWS Glue Best Practices

Data Processing Using AWS Glue

Let's continue our data analytics journey by building an end-to-end data processing pipeline for our data. AWS Glue is a fully managed ETL service that makes it simple and cost-effective to categorize your data, clean it, enrich it, and move it reliably between various data stores. As with most AWS services, you can manage and visualize this entire workflow from the AWS Console, checking each step along the way.

As with other AWS services, Glue is serverless, which means that you don't need to provision a specific amount of capacity upfront. Glue will scale up and down to meet your data traffic needs. And while the out-of-the-box features of Glue should help you build a working real-time pipeline with minimal configuration, Glue also provides ways to customize your pipelines via custom scripting to further improve performance. ShopFully, a marketing technology company, turned to Glue to process over 100 million events in 20 minutes, a 6x performance improvement [1].

One of the keys to Glue's processing power is a data processing framework called **Apache Spark** [2]. Spark is a powerful tool designed to handle big data - think of it as a supercharged engine for processing vast amounts of information quickly and efficiently. Imagine you have a huge library of books, and you need to find every instance of the word "adventure" across all books. Doing this manually would take forever, but Spark uses advanced computing techniques to divide this huge task into smaller, manageable parts, and then works on them simultaneously, drastically speeding up the process. As Spark does this parallel processing in-memory, this results in significant performance gains, providing Glue the power it needs to transform data at large scale.

Anatomy of a Data Pipeline

Let's walk through the basic concepts in building a data processing pipeline on AWS Glue, as depicted in *Figure 4.1:*

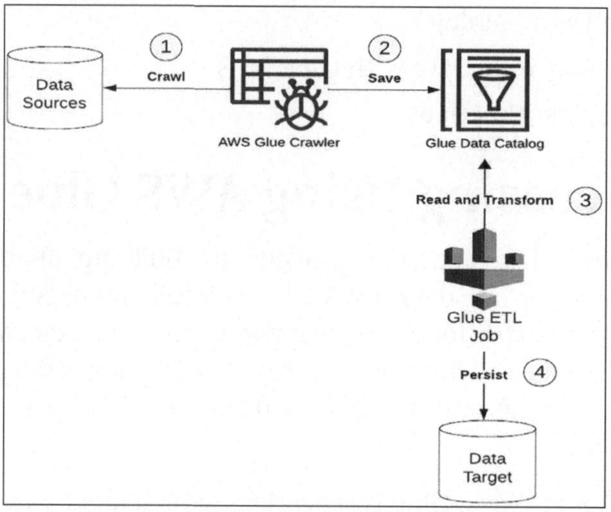

Figure 4.1: *High-Level Overview of an AWS Glue ETL Job*

Data pipelines start with one or more **Data Sources.** This could be one of any of the data stores offered by AWS, including RDS, DynamoDB, and S3. To keep our example simple, we will work with the data we consumed from the previous chapter. However, note that the interface we are building here could apply to other data sources as well.

To start building our pipeline, we need to first define **Crawlers**. Crawlers scan our data in S3 and automatically create metadata tables in the Glue Data Catalog. These tables are crucial because they define the structure of your data, which guides the transformation process. It's akin to reading a map before starting a journey; understanding your data's layout helps in planning how to process and transform it.

The **Data Catalog** serves as the central metadata repository for all of the data assets in the pipeline. It will help generate code and serve as the central source of truth for your data assets.

With the metadata in place, you move on to creating an **ETL Job** in AWS Glue. This job is a piece of logic, which you can author in an AWS Glue-generated script or write yourself in Python or Scala. It will transform your data to the required shape. The 'transform' phase can include data cleaning, joining different datasets, or even discarding irrelevant information. It's this stage where your raw data is honed into something of value.

Once your ETL job is ready, you set up triggers. **Triggers** in AWS Glue are mechanisms that start your data processing workflow. They can be set to activate on a schedule, like once every hour, or in response to an event, like the arrival of new data in your S3 bucket. Triggers ensure that your data pipeline runs smoothly, and your data is processed as needed.

The end result of a data pipeline is clean transformed data being stored at a **Data Target**. Similar to how we configured data sources to start our pipeline, we also define where to load our final transformed data. We simply choose from the list of sources supported by AWS and provide the necessary credentials and access permissions to ensure that AWS Glue has write access to the destination.

Finally, you might find that you want multiple Glue jobs to run in a specified order (that is, these jobs are dependent on one another). To orchestrate this process, Glue provides **Workflows** to manage the dependency graph of your jobs to ensure they are executed in the proper sequence.

All throughout the pipeline build and execution process, the Glue console provides highly visual tools to help you manage these complex data transformation pipelines. Now, let's dive into each component to understand what each is and how to use it in Glue.

Crawling Your Data

Cataloging data effectively in AWS Glue is a foundational step to organize and manage your data assets, which allows for smoother data processing and analysis in the cloud. Let's start building out our **Data Catalog** by creating a **Crawler** to parse our data on S3.

Creating a Crawler

1. From the AWS Glue console, click `Crawlers` in the left-hand pane under the `Data catalog` section.
2. Click the `Create crawler` button to start the crawler configuration process.
3. Specify a name and a description (optional).
4. Add a data source; in this case, we will choose `S3`, but we can pick from any standard storage format used on AWS:
    a. Select the path in `S3` where your data resides. You can browse your `S3` buckets or input the `S3` path directly:

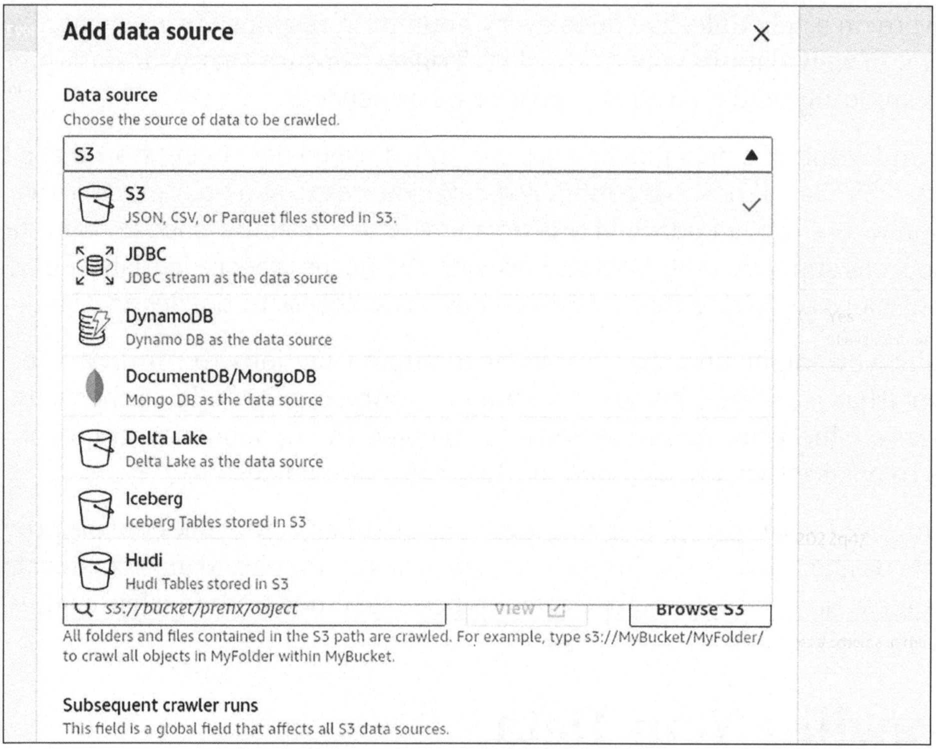

***Figure 4.2**: Glue Data Sources*

5. Optionally, create a **`Classifier`** for the incoming data, which will tell Glue how to parse the data and define custom data types for each field.
6. Confirm we have an IAM role to confirm security settings.
7. Finalize the output target table and its properties, and schedule the crawler:
   a. On-demand works fine for now, but for regular data updates, you can schedule this to run on a regular basis.
   b. Select or create a database in the AWS Glue Data Catalog where the crawler will store the metadata. You can also configure the crawler to add prefixes to the tables (or use the folder names as table names) and to update the table definitions in the Data Catalog.
8. Review all the configuration settings. If everything looks correct, click **`Finish`**.

After the crawler is configured, select it from the list and click the **`Run crawler`** button to start the crawling process. Once the crawler has completed, go to the **`Tables`** section of the Data Catalog in AWS Glue to confirm your tables have been created correctly.

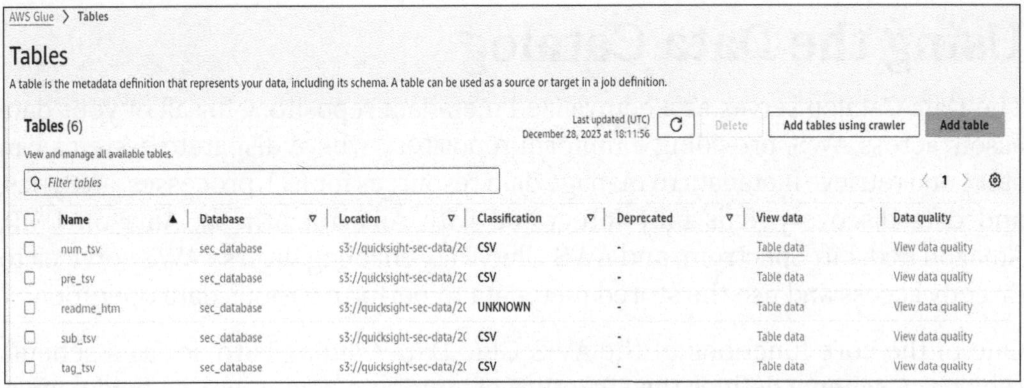

***Figure 4.3**: Glue Tables*

Additionally, you can click **`Table data`** to confirm that the schema matches the structure you expect. This will take you to Athena, which allows you to both inspect the table structure and run ad-hoc queries once the tables are populated with data:

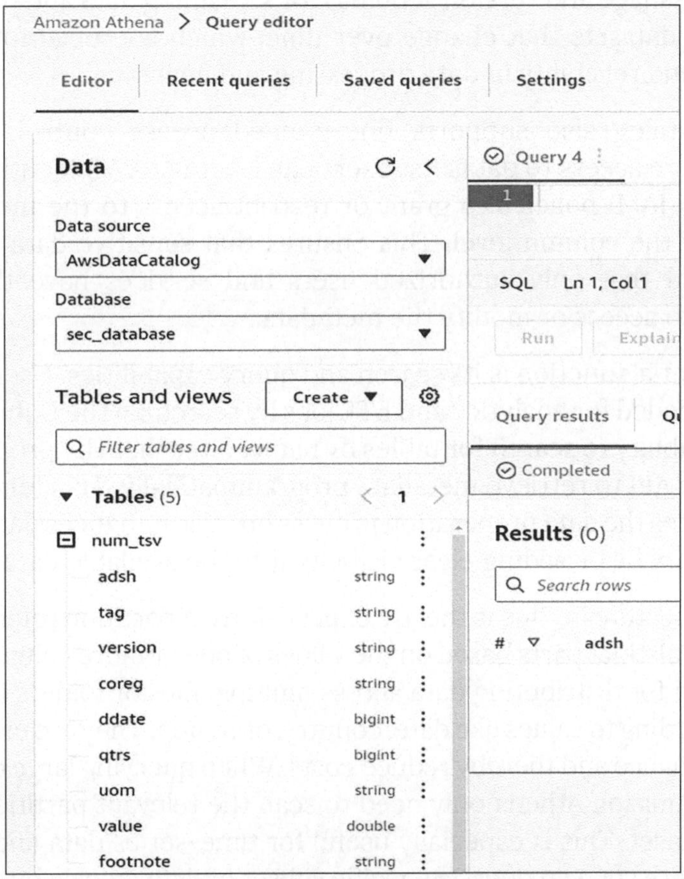

***Figure 4.4**: Glue Table Structure in Athena*

Using the Data Catalog

The Data Catalog serves as a centralized metadata repository for all of your data assets across AWS, providing a uniform repository where disparate systems can store and retrieve metadata to manage data resources for ETL processes, analytics, and data discovery. It is fully integrated with Amazon Athena, Amazon EMR, Amazon Redshift Spectrum, and AWS Glue ETL, enabling diverse AWS services to directly access and use the stored metadata to perform various data operations.

One of the core functions of the AWS Glue Data Catalog is to act as a schema registry. A **schema** defines the structure of your data, documenting field names, field types, and other metadata. When AWS Glue crawlers scan your data sources, they automatically infer schemas and create table definitions in the Data Catalog. This not only allows for schema versioning and schema change policies but also enables seamless schema discovery for ETL jobs and data analysis. The Data Catalog can manage and version schemas for streaming data and handle schema evolution for datasets that change over time, which is crucial for maintaining consistency and reliability in data processing and analytics.

The Data Catalog also supports fine-grained access control to metadata, ensuring secure access to datasets. Users can leverage AWS Identity and Access Management (IAM) policies to grant or restrict access to the metadata at the table level or the column level. This ensures that sensitive data is adequately protected and that only authorized users and services have the necessary permissions to access or modify the metadata.

Another essential function is its search and query capabilities. Users can quickly locate data needed for analytics and ETL jobs by searching the Data Catalog. This includes the ability to search for tables by name, filter them by properties, or use the AWS Glue API to retrieve metadata programmatically. This functionality not only accelerates the data preparation process but also enhances data governance and data quality by providing clear visibility into the available data assets.

An important feature in Glue is the use of **partitions**. A partition refers to a division of a table into distinct parts based on the values of one or more columns. Partitions are often used for distributing data across multiple files or folders in Amazon S3, typically according to values like date, country, or region. They are used to improve query performance and thereby reduce costs. When querying large datasets, AWS services like Amazon Athena only need to scan the relevant partitions instead of the entire dataset. This is especially useful for time-series data and other large-scale data where you can query a specific subset of data quickly by only scanning the relevant partitions (for example, a specific time range).

Generating Column Statistics

Another important feature of Glue's data catalog is column statistics. The data catalog can compute descriptive statistics for any data stored in cataloged tables (for example, minimum/maximum values) and other important information like the presence of null values and the maximum lengths of values in a specific column.

To generate column statistics for a given table in the Data Catalog, follow these steps:

1. Navigate to the AWS Glue console and select **`Data Catalog`** > **`Tables`**.
2. Click on a table name.
3. From the table overview screen, click the "**`Column statistics`**" tab.
4. Follow the on-screen prompt to generate statistics for all of the fields:

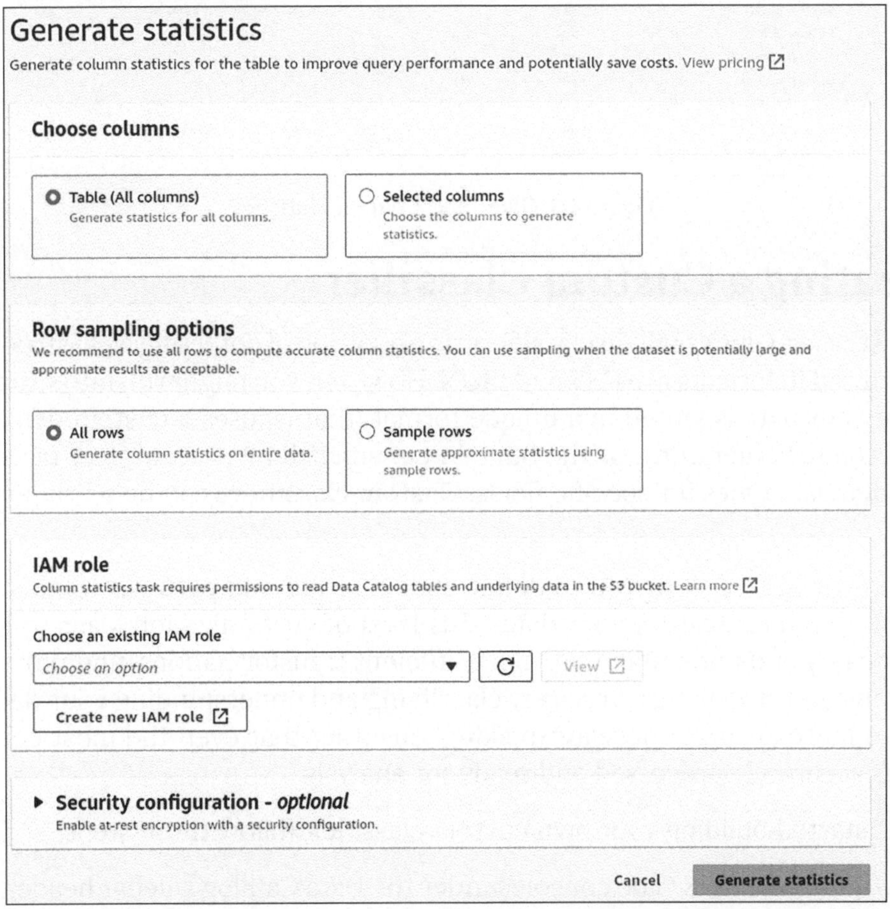

***Figure 4.5**: Glue Table Column Statistics Generation*

   a. Create a new IAM role to execute this action if one does not already exist.

5. Click **`Generate statistics`** to allow Glue to start performing its calculations. This may take several minutes depending on the size of your data and the fields selected for calculation.

Once complete, you should now see column statistics for your data. This is useful to help you understand the shape and boundaries of your data, specifically to understand date ranges, numeric value ranges, and to understand the presence of null values in your data:

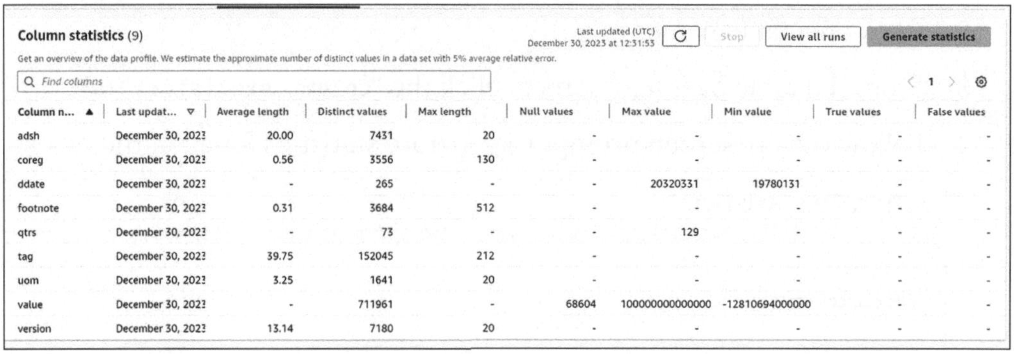

Column n...	Last updat...	Average length	Distinct values	Max length	Null values	Max value	Min value	True values	False values
adsh	December 30, 2023	20.00	7431	20	-	-	-	-	-
coreg	December 30, 2023	0.56	3556	130	-	-	-	-	-
ddate	December 30, 2023	-	265	-	-	20320331	19780131	-	-
footnote	December 30, 2023	0.31	3684	512	-	-	-	-	-
qtrs	December 30, 2023	-	73	-	-	129	-	-	-
tag	December 30, 2023	39.75	152045	212	-	-	-	-	-
uom	December 30, 2023	3.25	1641	20	-	-	-	-	-
value	December 30, 2023	-	711961	-	68604	100000000000000	-12810694000000	-	-
version	December 30, 2023	13.14	7180	20	-	-	-	-	-

***Figure 4.6**: Glue Table Column Statistics*

Creating a Custom Classifier

In most cases, Glue's built-in classifiers do a good job of detecting well-structured data stored in formats like CSV and JSON. However, you might run into situations where your data is stored in a unique format (that is, uses a custom delimiter), has a complex hierarchy, or the built-in classifier did not accurately target the intended data types for specific fields. **Custom classifiers** can help bridge these gaps.

Custom classifiers allow you to define specific rules and patterns to match the unique characteristics of your data. This level of customization leads to better data quality and understanding, more efficient transformations, and ultimately, more insightful analytics. Precisely classifying and understanding your data can lead to more accurate decision-making, ensuring that even the most complex data is accurately processed and ready for analysis.

To get started building your own custom classifier, follow these steps:

1. From the AWS Glue console, under the Data Catalog sidebar header, click **`Classifiers`**.

2. Click **`Add classifier`**.
3. Name your classifier and choose a starting data format for the data. For this example, we will choose **`CSV`**.
4. Customize the parsing options (delimiter, quote symbol, column heading) and optionally choose to customize the data types of each column:

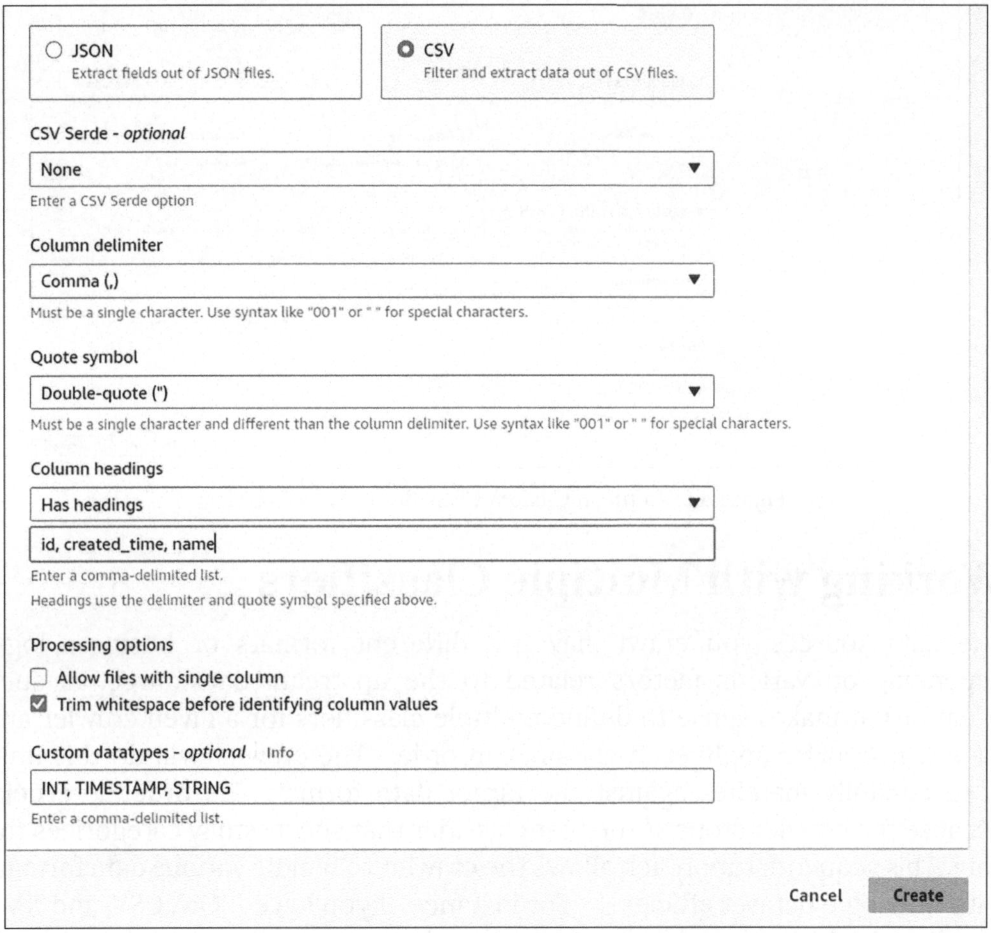

Figure 4.7: *Custom Classifier Configuration*

   a. For this example, we chose to manually enter the three column names and added custom datatypes to ensure the target fields get typed correctly.
   b. Custom datatypes include "`BINARY`", "`BOOLEAN`", "`DATE`", "`DECIMAL`", "`DOUBLE`", "`FLOAT`", "`INT`", "`LONG`", "`SHORT`", "`STRING`", "**`TIMESTAMP`**". Unsupported datatypes will display an error [3].

5. Click **`Create`** to finalize creation of your classifier.

To use your custom classifier, edit one of your existing crawlers and edit the "`data sources and classifiers`" section to add your custom classifier to the crawler.

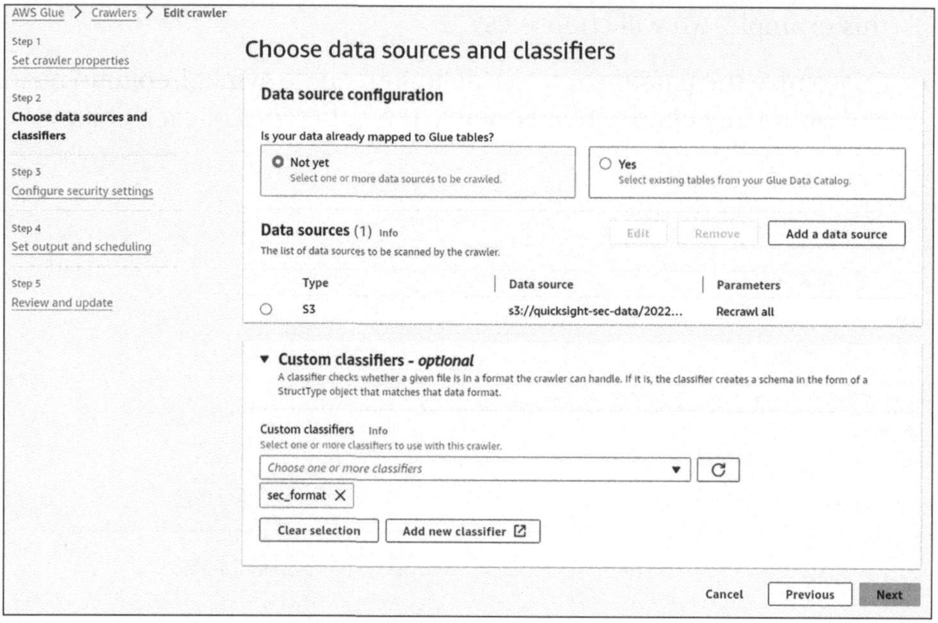

Figure 4.8: *Adding a Custom Classifier to Your Crawler*

Working with Multiple Classifiers

The data sources you crawl may use different formats or business logic depending on various factors related to the upstream datasource. In such situations, it makes sense to define multiple classifiers for a given crawler and have that crawler apply each classifier in order. The crawler will do this until it successfully matches against the target data format. The order is crucial because the crawler stops at the first classifier that successfully categorizes the data. This sequential approach allows the crawler to handle various data formats within a single dataset efficiently. For instance, if you have JSON, CSV, and XML files in your data store, the crawler can apply the respective classifier to each file type. However, if the first classifier is too broad or improperly configured, it might incorrectly classify data, leading to inaccurate schema inference.

For best practices, it's essential to prioritize your classifiers effectively. Start with the most specific classifiers for unique or custom data formats and follow with more generic built-in classifiers. This prioritization ensures that specialized data is correctly identified before the crawler defaults to broader classifications. Regular monitoring and adjusting of the classifier list are also crucial. Analyze the crawler logs to understand which classifiers are being used and which are not and adjust the order accordingly. Remove or reconfigure any that consistently misclassify data or are never used. Additionally, consider the performance impact. A long list of classifiers might slow down your crawls, especially if the correct classifier is usually at the end of the list. By regularly reviewing and optimizing the order and configuration of your classifiers, you can maintain an efficient, accurate, and speedy classification process in Glue.

Transforming Your Data with Glue Jobs

Data transformation is the heart of any data analytics process. Its where raw data is refined into a format that's ripe for analysis. Now that we have our data stored in well-defined tables, we can use Glue Studio, specifically Visual ETL, to build a graphical definition of the steps of our ETL job. Let's first review the concepts and then build our ETL job step-by-step:

- **ETL** stands for **Extract, Transform,** and **Load**. Our crawlers and classifiers extract raw data from data sources. Our core ETL job, defined in Glue Studio, will define the business logic to transform that raw data to suit our needs. The logic resides in a script generated by AWS Glue; optionally, you can write your own custom transformations in programming languages like Python. Common transformation operations include filtering, reshaping, and joining data. The final stage is loading transformed data to a target end source, making it available to data consumers like QuickSight for visualization purposes.
- **Glue Studio** is an intuitive graphical interface that simplifies the creation, running, and monitoring of ETL jobs in AWS Glue. It's especially useful for those who prefer a visual approach to defining data flows and transformations without writing code:

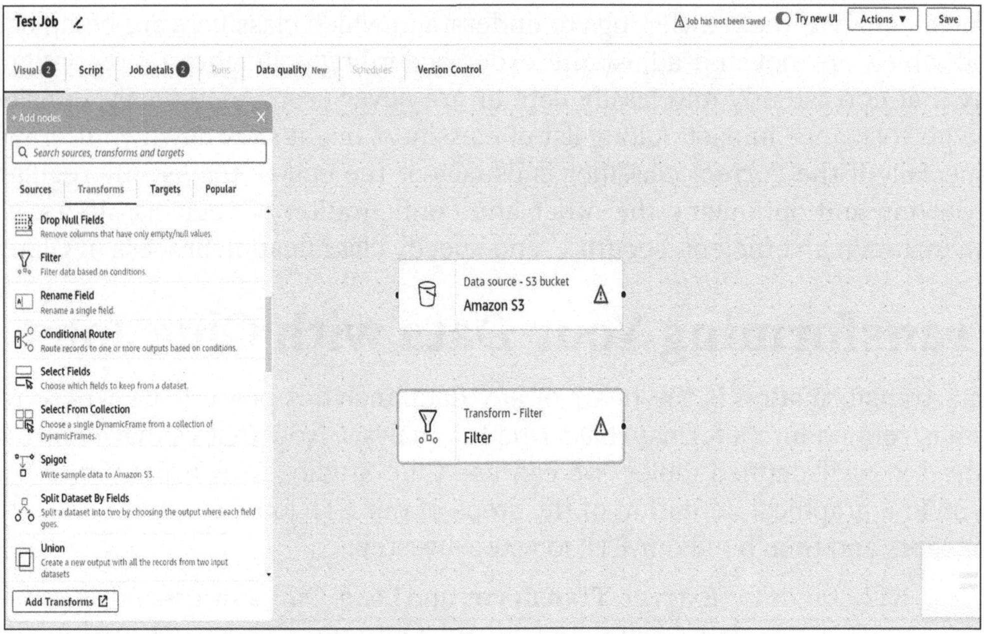

***Figure 4.9**: Visual ETL View of an AWS Glue Job*

- **Transforms** are the specific operations applied to your data within an ETL job. AWS Glue supports many built-in transforms, such as:
  - `Map`: Applies a function to each record in your dataset.
  - `DropNullFields`: Removes fields that have null values.
  - `Join`: Combines two datasets based on a common key.
  - `SelectFields`: Picks specific fields from your dataset.

As the user builds the job graphically, Glue generates a **`Script`** that implements the logic described in the visual ETL. This script is an **`Apache Spark`** script, which Glue executes to perform your transformations:

***Figure 4.10**: Raw Script of a Glue ETL Job*

Building the Pipeline with Visual ETL

Here are the steps for building the pipeline with Visual ETL:

1. In the AWS Glue console, click **`ETL jobs`** in the left navigation pane, and then click the **`Visual ETL`** button to create a new ETL job.

2. Enter a name for your job in the upper left-hand corner.

3. Define a data source by selecting the **`AWS Glue Data Catalog`** node and choosing the source data you wish to transform.

4. Add one or more Transforms to the graph, making sure to add your Transforms in the proper sequence.

5. Finally, add a Target data source to store the transformed data:

   a. You can select from a range of AWS data stores such as Amazon S3, Amazon RDS, Amazon Redshift, and more.

   b. Configure the target by specifying object format (for example, CSV, Parquet) and other relevant settings.

6. Click the **Job Details** tab, confirming that all required fields are populated.
7. Review the final visual diagram of your data sources, transformations, and data targets to ensure that it matches your desired ETL workflow. If all required fields are populated, click **Save** to save your job.
8. You should now see your new job in the **ETL Jobs** section. From the Actions dropdown, you can choose to run your job now or schedule a run for later.

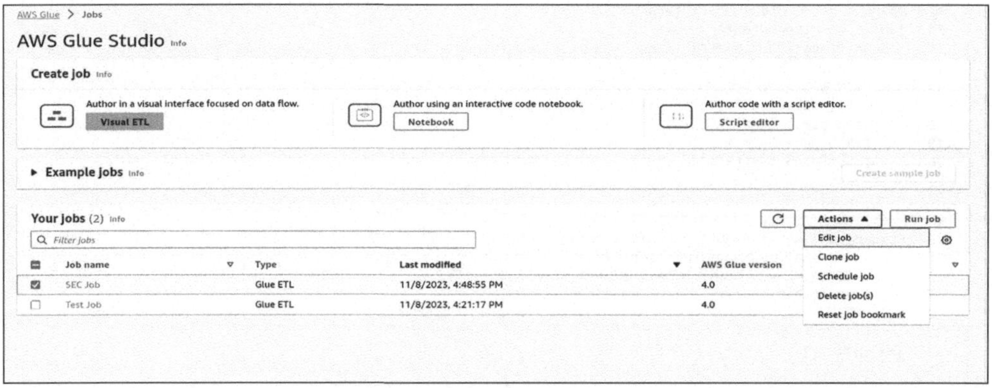

Figure 4.11: *Glue Job Completed*

Congratulations! You should now have a basic AWS Glue job transforming your data.

Creating Jobs Using Jupyter Notebooks

Jupyter notebooks [4] offer an interactive computing environment that is ideal for exploring and experimenting with data, making them an excellent choice for authoring ETL jobs in AWS Glue, especially in situations with more complex transformations that require rapid iterative development and testing. Notebooks also help you explore new data sources and give you real-time feedback on your data during different stages of transformation. Additionally, notebooks help facilitate better documentation and collaboration, as you can include detailed explanations (using Markdown) and visualizations alongside your code. Finally, notebooks provide seamless integration with other Python libraries and tools, enhancing the capabilities of your ETL jobs beyond what's inherently available in Glue. This approach fosters a more intuitive and exploratory development experience, leading to more accurate and efficient data processing workflows.

To create an ETL job using Jupyter notebooks, follow these steps:

1. From the AWS Glue console, click **`ETL jobs`**.
2. From the ETL jobs dashboard, click **`Notebook`**
3. Choose **`Spark(Python)`** as the type of notebook and click **`Create notebook`**:

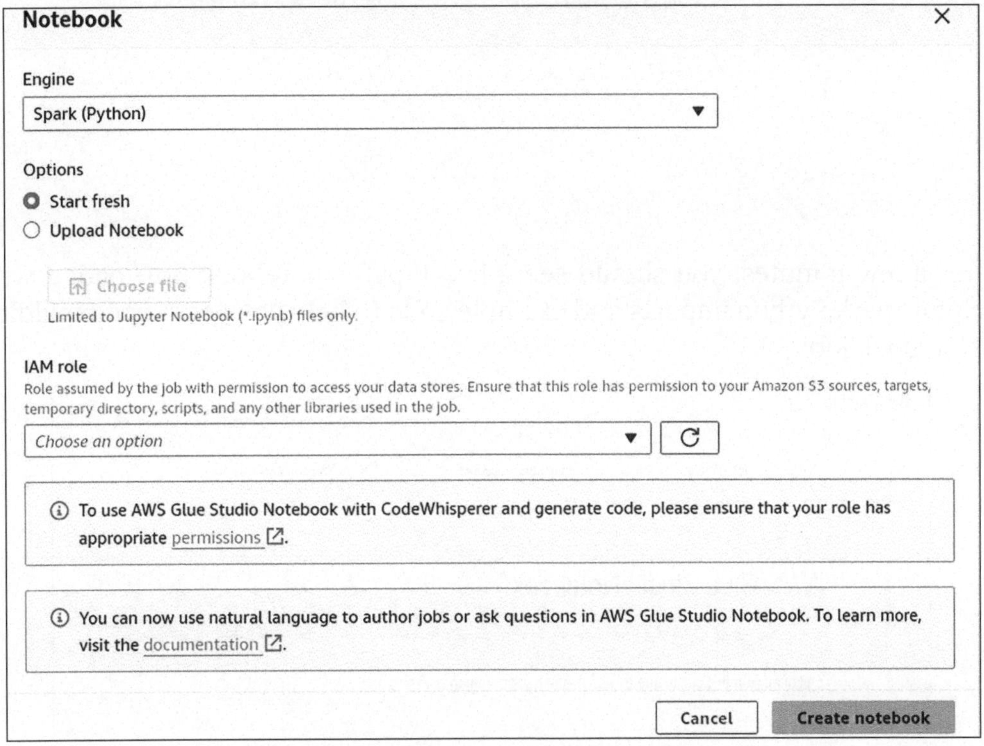

***Figure 4.12**: Creating a Notebook-based Glue Job*

   a. You can also upload an existing notebook.

   b. Ensure that the IAM role you choose has access to your data sources (ideally in S3), as otherwise, the notebook will not be able to access the data. The role should also have a policy similar to the one below to ensure you can start a Glue session from within the notebook.

```
{
    “Version”: “2012-10-17”,
    “Statement”: [
        {
            “Sid”: “Statement1”,
            “Effect”: “Allow”,
```

```
            "Action": "iam:PassRole",
            "Resource": "arn:aws:iam::598578551199:role/AWSGlueNotebooks",
            "Condition": {
                "StringEquals": {
                    "iam:PassedToService": "glue.amazonaws.com"
                }
            }
        }
    ]
}
```

After a few minutes, you should see a live Jupyter notebook pre-loaded with helpful Spark Python imports and example code to help you get started building a Notebook job:

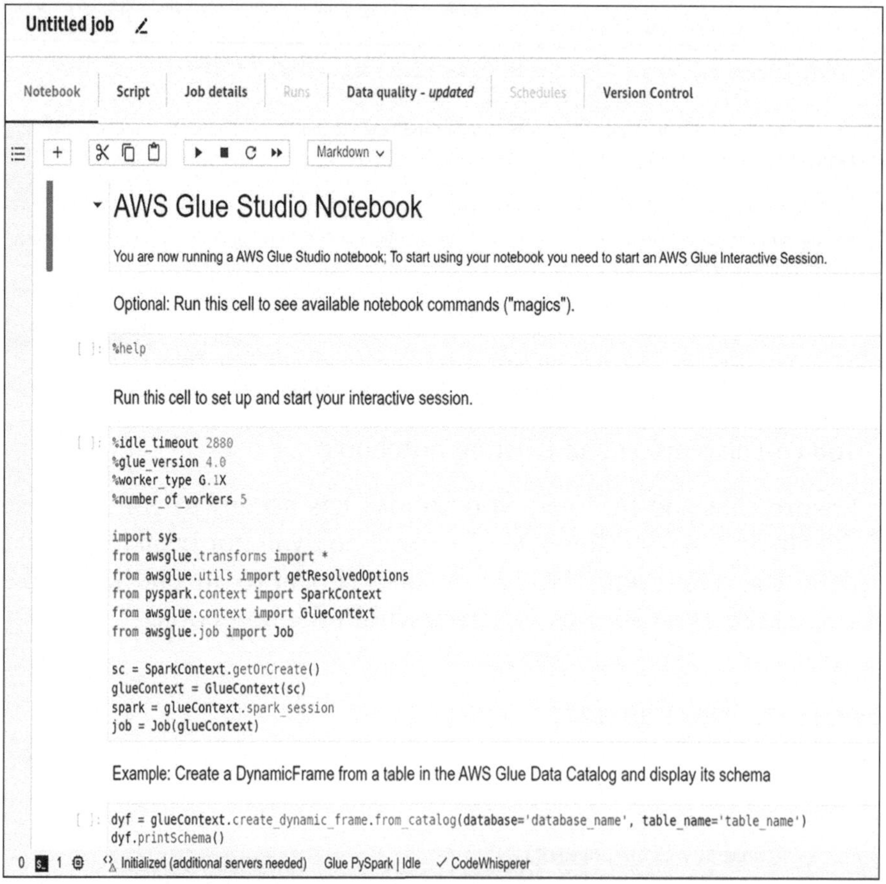

Figure 4.13: *Viewing Notebook Cells in a Glue Notebook Job*

From here, you can work with the example code to create a session and write job code that might look like the following:

```
job.init(args['JOB_NAME'], args)

# Extract: Load data from the AWS Glue Data Catalog
datasource0 = glueContext.create_dynamic_frame.from_catalog(
    database = "your_database_name", # Replace with your database name
    table_name = "your_table_name",  # Replace with your table name
    transformation_ctx = "datasource0")

# Transform: Apply a mapping
applymapping1 = ApplyMapping.apply(frame = datasource0, mappings = [
    ("column1", "string", "column1_new", "string"), # Replace with your
column mappings
    ("column2", "long", "column2_new", "long")      # Replace with your
column mappings
    ], transformation_ctx = "applymapping1")

# Load: Write the data to S3
datasink2 = glueContext.write_dynamic_frame.from_options(
    frame = applymapping1, connection_type = "s3",
    connection_options = {"path": "s3://your-bucket/target-path/"}, #
Replace with your S3 path
    format = "parquet", transformation_ctx = "datasink2")

job.commit()
```

While this is a simple example script, it shows the basic flow that you can then extend using Python functionality and modules to allow for custom business logic [5].

AWS Glue Best Practices

Now that you understand the basics of creating Glue jobs, let's review some common best practices to help ensure you can execute data pipelines safely and effectively.

Testing Your Glue Jobs

Testing and validating the data quality of an AWS Glue job is an essential step to ensure that your ETL process is correct and efficient. When you are dealing with data analytics, the integrity and quality of your data are not just important; they are everything. Here is how you can systematically approach this validation process.

First, it's vital to understand the purpose of data validation. The process is not just about checking if your job runs without errors, but also about ensuring that the data transformation aligns with your business rules and analytics needs. To start the validation, run your Glue job with a subset of data that is representative of your entire dataset. This allows for quick iteration and debugging without incurring high costs or long processing times. Once you are confident that the job works as expected on this sample, you can scale up to larger data volumes.

Additionally, AWS Glue provides transforms that help validate data as it flows through your pipeline. **Detect Sensitive Data** scans your data for sensitive personal identifiable information (PII), such as personal email or social security numbers, and lets you either replace it or add a column with information on what was found and where. Another transform, **Evaluate Data Quality**, performs basic data hygiene checks, such as column counts, uniqueness, and descriptive statistics, on the data:

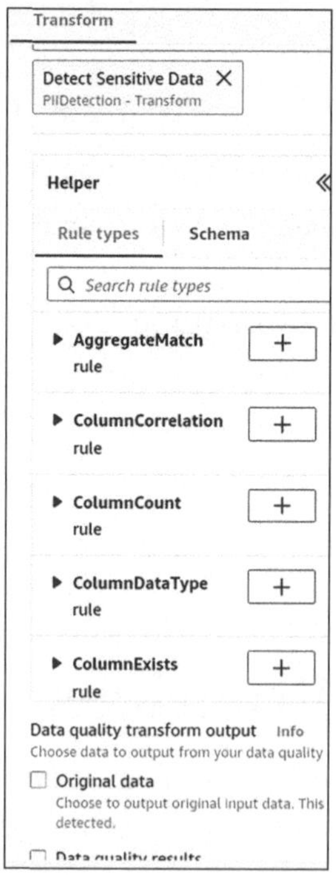

Figure 4.14: *Detect Sensitive Data Transform*

Another way to confirm data quality is to use the AWS Glue Data Catalog to define the metadata about your data sources and to verify schema consistency before and after the ETL process. Schema changes can often lead to unexpected results in data analytics, so maintaining consistency is key. If your data schema changes, the Data Catalog will catch this error upstream and throw an error to review in the `Runs` tab.

In addition, AWS Glue logs every step of your ETL job execution in CloudWatch Logs. These logs are your first stop for testing your pipeline's results, providing details on what happened during the job. They can help identify errors, such as failed transformations or write operations, and offer insights into performance issues, such as slow-running jobs.

Securing Your Glue Jobs

Here are some common ways you can secure your Glue jobs to prevent unauthorized access to your data:

- **Job Encryption**: Secure your job's data by enabling encryption. In the job configuration, set up encryption for data at rest and in transit. Choose the encryption method for data stored in S3, Job Bookmarks, and Logs.
- **Network Security**: Configure your job to run in a **Virtual Private Cloud (VPC)** for network isolation. Set up security groups and Network ACLs to control inbound and outbound traffic for your Glue jobs.
- **Data Access Control**: Apply fine-grained access controls to your data resources using AWS Lake Formation or S3 bucket policies.
- **IAM Role Permissions**: Ensure that your Glue IAM role only has permissions for the required data in S3.
- **Audit Logs**: Regularly review CloudTrail and CloudWatch Logs to monitor for any unauthorized access or unexpected job activities. Enable continuous monitoring with tools like AWS Config to keep a check on resource configurations and changes.
- **Security Configurations**: Make use of security configurations in AWS Glue to manage S3 encryption, CloudWatch Logs encryption, and job bookmarks encryption. You can create a security configuration and assign it when you create or edit a Glue job.

Monitoring Your Glue Jobs

Finally, here are ways you can monitor your Glue jobs on an ongoing basis:

1. View Metrics via AWS Glue Console:
    a. Log in to the AWS Management Console.
    b. Navigate to the AWS Glue service.
    c. In the AWS Glue console, click **`Jobs`** in the left navigation pane under the **`ETL`** section to view a list of your Glue jobs.
    d. Select a job from the list to view its details.
    e. On the job details page, you can see the **`Run history`**, which provides the status of each job run (**`Succeeded`**, **`Stopped`**, **`Failed`**, or **`Running`**).
    f. For detailed logs, click the **`Logs`** link next to a specific job run. This will redirect you to Amazon CloudWatch Logs where you can view the execution logs.
2. Monitor metrics over time:
    a. Navigate to the Amazon CloudWatch console and select **`Metrics`**.
    b. Choose the **`Glue`** namespace to explore the available Glue metrics such as **`DataBytesRead`**, **`DataBytesWritten`**, **`JobRunTime`**, and more.
    c. In CloudWatch, you can create alarms based on specific metrics thresholds. Go to **`Alarms`** in the CloudWatch console and select **`Create alarm`**. Choose the Glue metric you want to monitor, specify the threshold, and set the notification action (like an email alert).
3. Job Audit via CloudTrail:
    a. Use AWS CloudTrail to track actions taken by a user, role, or AWS service in Glue. CloudTrail logs can be used for auditing job activity.

Conclusion

You should now have a solid grasp of the end-to-end process for building data transformation pipelines. The visual interface, automatic crawling capabilities, and pre-built transforms make it simple to ingest, prepare, and load datasets for analysis. AWS Glue provides all the tools you need to get your data ready for analytics and decision-making.

In the next chapter, we will unlock additional value from your clean, analysis-ready data using Amazon QuickSight. This visual analytics service allows you to create interactive dashboards to surface key insights and trends from your datasets. We will explore features like auto-generated visualizations and natural language query to quickly build reports tailored to your analysis needs.

Points to Remember

- AWS Glue provides a visual, no-code interface to build and manage data transformation pipelines. The graphical workflow and pre-built transforms simplify ETL without needing to write scripted jobs.
- Crawlers automatically scan and catalog your data sources, making schemas readily available for downstream ETL jobs. This kickstarts the pipeline process.
- The AWS Glue Data Catalog serves as a central metadata store and schema registry for your data assets across services. It enables discovery, governance and data quality.
- Serverless Spark execution engines provide flexibility to scale data processing on demand. You only pay for the resources consumed running each job.
- In-built monitoring, logging, encryption, and access control features enable you to build secure and auditable data pipelines. Validate output quality using schema checks and data validation transforms.

References

1. "ShopFully Improves Marketing Campaign Efficiency by 6x Using AWS Glue", https://aws.amazon.com/solutions/case-studies/shopfully-case-study/
2. "Apache Spark", https://spark.apache.org/
3. "Writing custom classifiers", https://docs.aws.amazon.com/glue/latest/dg/custom-classifier.html?icmpid=docs_console_unmapped#custom-classifier-csv
4. "Project Jupyter", https://jupyter.org/try
5. "Overview of using notebooks", https://docs.aws.amazon.com/glue/latest/dg/using-notebooks-overview.html

CHAPTER 5

Descriptive Analytics on AWS

Introduction

Descriptive analytics forms the foundation of data analysis by summarizing data to uncover patterns and trends. As data volumes grow exponentially in the digital age, the ability to effectively describe and make sense of data is crucial. This chapter explores descriptive analytics techniques on the AWS Cloud, focusing on tools like Amazon Athena, to handle and understand large datasets stored in any format.

Structure

In this chapter, we will cover the following topics:

- Introduction to Descriptive Statistics
- Introduction to Amazon Athena
- Creating a Database and Table in Athena
- Querying Your Data Using Athena
- How to Optimize Athena for Performance and Security

Introduction to Descriptive Statistics

Descriptive statistics form the cornerstone of data analysis, serving as a fundamental tool for summarizing and understanding data. At its core, it involves summarizing large datasets to make them understandable at a glance. Unlike more complex statistical analyses, which infer complex patterns or try to test hypotheses, descriptive statistics describe the shape and size of the data in a straightforward and intuitive manner:

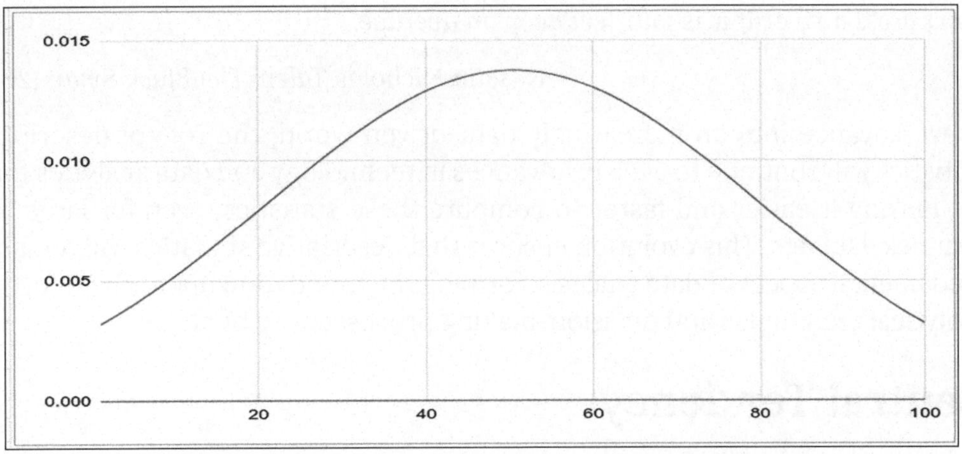

***Figure 5.1**: Normally Distributed Data (that is, "bell curve")*

The key elements of descriptive statistics include measures of **central tendency** and measures of **variability**. Measures of central tendency, such as the mean, median, and mode, provide a single value representing the center point of a dataset. On the other hand, measures of variability, such as the range, variance, and standard deviation, offer insights into the spread or dispersion of the data. These elements collectively give a quick and simple overview of the data's characteristics.

Descriptive statistics have practical applications across a vast range of fields. In business, they help in understanding market trends, customer preferences, and sales patterns. In healthcare, they assist in summarizing patient data and medical research findings. Similarly, in education, they are used to analyze student performance and educational outcomes. This universal applicability makes descriptive statistics an invaluable tool in any data-driven decision-making process.

In today's era of big data, the importance of descriptive statistics has grown exponentially. With the surge in data generation, the ability to quickly summarize and understand large volumes of data is crucial. Descriptive statistics offer a starting point for deeper analysis, allowing data analysts to sift through vast amounts of information and extract meaningful patterns and insights.

While descriptive statistics are powerful, they come with their own set of limitations. They provide a summary view of the data but don't delve into the underlying reasons driving patterns. Misinterpretation of descriptive statistics can lead to erroneous conclusions. Therefore, it is essential to approach them with a critical mind and understand their context within broader data analysis efforts.

Don't cross a river if it is four feet deep on average.

-*Nassim Nicholas Taleb, The Black Swan* (2010)

As we advance into an increasingly data-driven world, the role of descriptive statistics will continue to evolve. Advances in technology and data analytics tools are making it easier and faster to compute these statistics, even for large and complex datasets. This evolution ensures that descriptive statistics will remain a fundamental aspect of data analysis, forming the foundation upon which further analytical techniques and decision-making processes are built.

Central Tendency

Central tendency is a cornerstone concept in the realm of descriptive statistics, often used in data analysis to summarize a set of data by identifying the central point within that dataset. When applied in the context of AWS and Data Analytics, understanding central tendency provides invaluable insights for both recent graduates and business professionals with limited technical backgrounds:

- The **mean**, commonly known as the average, is perhaps the most familiar measure of central tendency. It is calculated by adding up all the values in a dataset and then dividing by the number of values. In the field of data analytics on AWS, the mean is especially useful for analyzing data like sales figures, customer ratings, or performance metrics. For instance, calculating the average daily sales from a cloud-based database can provide a quick overview of a company's performance.
- The **median**, on the other hand, represents the middle value in a dataset when it is arranged in ascending or descending order. If there is an even number of values, the median is the average of the two middle numbers. This measure is less affected by outliers and skewed data, making it more reliable in certain scenarios than the mean. For example, in analyzing income data stored in AWS, where a few high incomes can skew the average, the median provides a more accurate representation of a typical income.
- The **mode** refers to the most frequently occurring value in a dataset. There can be one mode, more than one mode, or no mode at all if no number repeats. The mode is particularly useful in analyzing categorical data, such as customer preferences or most-used services in an AWS environment. For instance, determining the most common error messages in a log file can help in pinpointing recurring issues.

As an example, let's assume we have cleaned and transformed customer service data for our company and now have a resulting dataset of weekly customer service calls for the last seven weeks stored in the following list:

```
[15, 13, 15, 18, 15, 20, 12]
```

To calculate the **mean** (average), add all the numbers together and divide by the number of data points. Here, (15 + 13 + 15 + 18 + 15 + 20 + 12) ÷ 7 equals 15.43. Thus, this company receives around 15 calls daily.

For the **median**, which is the middle value in an ordered list, arrange the data in ascending order: 12, 13, 15, 15, 15, 18, 20. Since there are seven data points, the median is the fourth value, which is 15. The median indicates that half of the days have calls below or equal to 15 and the other half have calls above or equal to 15.

Finally, the **mode** represents the most frequently occurring value. In this dataset, the number 15 occurs three times, more often than any other number, making it the mode. The mode reflects the most common daily call volume.

It's crucial to understand the differences between these measures and choose the right one according to the nature of the data and the specific question being addressed. Accuracy in calculating and interpreting mean, median, and mode ensures that the insights drawn from the data are valid and applicable to real-world scenarios.

Variability

Variability, also known as dispersion, is a key concept in statistics that measures how much data points in a set differ from each other and the mean. Understanding variability is essential in data analysis as it provides insight into the consistency and predictability of data. Three primary measures of variability are the range, variance, and standard deviation, each offering a unique perspective on the spread of data:

- **Range** is the simplest measure of variability. It is calculated by subtracting the smallest value in a dataset from the largest value. The range gives a quick sense of the spread of the data, but it's sensitive to outliers and doesn't provide information about how data is distributed around the mean.
- **Variance** is a more comprehensive measure of variability. It quantifies how much the data points in a set deviate from the mean. To calculate variance, subtract the mean from each data point, square these differences, sum them up, and then divide by the number of data points (for a population) or by the number of data points minus one (for a sample). The result is the

average of the squared differences from the mean, providing a detailed picture of the data's spread.

- **Standard deviation**, often considered the most useful measure of variability, is the square root of the variance. It is expressed in the same units as the data, making it more interpretable than variance. A small standard deviation indicates that the data points tend to be close to the mean, while a larger standard deviation suggests that the data points are spread out over a wider range.

Variance and standard deviation are particularly useful in determining the reliability of the mean. If the standard deviation is small, it means that the mean is a reliable measure of central tendency for the data. Conversely, a large standard deviation indicates that the mean might not be as representative of the data set.

In practical data analysis, these measures of variability are used to assess the predictability and consistency of data. For example, in financial data analysis, a high standard deviation in stock prices might indicate a more volatile and risky investment.

Let's consider a simple dataset that represents the weekly sales (in units) of a product over a five-week period:

```
[50, 55, 60, 45, 50]
```

Range is the simplest measure of variability. In this context, it shows the difference between the highest and lowest sales weeks. To calculate the range, subtract the lowest sales figure (45 units) from the highest (60 units), resulting in a range of 15 units. This range indicates the extent of fluctuation in weekly sales.

Variance provides a deeper understanding of sales fluctuations around the average weekly sales. First, calculate the mean (average) sales: $(50 + 55 + 60 + 45 + 50) \div 5 = 52$ units. Next, calculate each week's deviation from the mean, square these deviations, and average them. The squared deviations are: $(2^2 + 3^2 + 8^2 + 7^2 + 2^2) = 138$. The variance is calculated as $138 \div (5 - 1) = 34.5$ units^2. This variance quantifies the average squared deviation of weekly sales from the mean, offering a detailed view of sales variability.

Standard deviation, which is the square root of variance, translates this variability into more understandable terms. The square root of 34.5 is approximately 5.87 units. This standard deviation means that, on average, weekly sales deviate from the average sales figure by about 6 units. A smaller standard deviation would suggest more consistent sales, while a larger one indicates greater fluctuation.

In a business context, understanding these variability measures helps managers plan their inventory and forecast sales. The range provides a quick overview of sales volatility, while the standard deviation offers more precise insight into typical sales variations from week to week. For instance, if the company is planning production or inventory levels, knowing that sales can vary by approximately 6 units from the average can help in making more informed decisions.

Describing Your Data Using Amazon Athena

Descriptive statistics are a fundamental aspect of data analysis, providing a simple and powerful way to understand the shape and size of data. **Amazon Athena**, a serverless query service, makes it straightforward to analyze your data that lives in Amazon S3 using simple SQL notation. This will be one of our primary tools to perform descriptive statistics against large datasets stored on AWS:

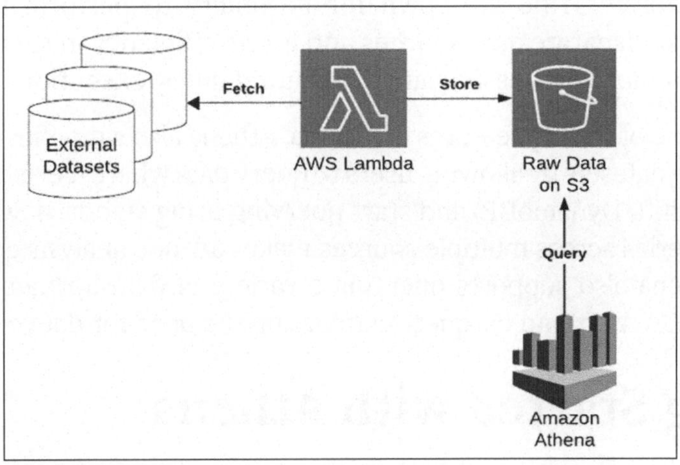

Figure 5.2: *Overview of Querying Data Using Amazon Athena*

Athena is an ideal tool for handling descriptive statistics because it allows us to quickly inspect unstructured and structured data for ad-hoc analysis without requiring excessive data transformation or preparation. Additionally, since it's serverless, there's no need to create and manage a database to talk to our data.

Enerbrain, an Italian proptech company, designed its data analytics platform with Athena [1] to make sense of massive volumes of sensor data as part of their IoT energy optimization solution. Athena allowed them to make real-time decisions about HVAC system performance and spot early warning signs of system failure:

***Figure* 5.3**: *Depiction of Analyzing Energy Sensor Data, Generated by ChatGPT*

Athena is based on Trino SQL (formerly known as **PrestoSQL**), an open-source, distributed SQL query engine designed for running interactive analytic queries against data sources of all sizes, ranging from gigabytes to petabytes. It allows users to query data where it lives, including in various databases, data lakes, and even different file formats, without needing to move the data into a separate analytics database. Trino is known for its ability to perform fast analytical queries against disparate data sources and for its efficiency in executing queries by using in-memory processing and distributed query execution.

Trino is just one of the key features of Athena. Athena also simplifies the process of querying large datasets by allowing users to query data where it exists (for example, S3, RDS, Redshift, DynamoDB) and start querying using standard SQL. This use of federating queries across multiple sources makes ad-hoc analysis quick and cost-effective. Athena also supports querying a variety of data formats (for example, CSV, JSON, ORC, Avro, and Parquet), eliminating the need for data conversion.

Getting Started with Athena

To begin using descriptive statistics with Athena, the first step is setting up your data in Amazon S3 in a format that Athena can query. This often involves structuring your data in common formats like CSV, JSON, or Parquet. Once your data is in place, you create a table in Athena that references the data location and schema. This table configures the data types and partitions that allow Athena to efficiently query your data.

However, if you use AWS Glue (as we did in our working example), you should already have tables defined and ready to use out-of-the-box by Athena. This is one of the most significant benefits of building solutions using a platform like AWS. Most of the services on AWS integrate seamlessly with one another, and as a result, you typically realize benefits and "get things for free" just by virtue of being on the platform!

Creating a Database and Table in Athena

Let's review the process of creating a table from scratch, using a simple CSV dataset stored on S3. We will use the online retail dataset on Kaggle [2] as an example as it has relatively few fields, and we can apply our descriptive statistics methods to it in a straightforward way.

First, let's upload our dataset to S3:

1. **Download the file from Kaggle:** This should download as a zip file. Unzip the contents to your local computer and rename the `online_retail_II.xslx` file to `online_retail_II.csv`.
2. **Upload this file to S3:** Pick a bucket (in this example, we will use a bucket called `online-retail-data-analytics`) and upload this file to a folder called **`data`**.

Now, let's query this data using Athena:

1. **Open Amazon Athena**: From your AWS Management Console, navigate to the Amazon Athena service. Choose the option **`Query your data with Trino SQL`**.
2. **Set Up a Query Result Location in S3**: Before executing any queries in Athena, you must specify an S3 bucket for storing query results. Go to **`Settings`** in the Athena console and enter an S3 bucket location (for this example, we will create a bucket called `athena-retail-query-execution-results`).
3. **Navigate to the Query Editor**: In Athena, go to the Query Editor. Here, you will write and execute SQL queries to interact with your data.
4. **Create a Database**: Before creating a table, you need to work from a database in Athena. Execute a simple SQL command to create one:

   ```
   CREATE DATABASE IF NOT EXISTS retail;
   ```

5. **Create a Table**: Now, create a table that corresponds to the structure of your CSV file. Use a `CREATE TABLE` statement, specifying column names and types that match your CSV file's format. When creating the table, ensure that no other CSV file of the same format is present in the path, as all files will be detected during this process. For our online retail dataset:

```
CREATE EXTERNAL TABLE IF NOT EXISTS retail.transactions(
Invoice string,
StockCode string,
Description string,
Quantity integer,
InvoiceDate date,
Price decimal(10,2),
`Customer ID` string,
Country string
)
ROW FORMAT DELIMITED
FIELDS TERMINATED BY ','
LOCATION 's3://online-retail-data-analytics/data/'
TBLPROPERTIES("skip.header.line.count"="1");
```

a. While there are several data types to choose from when defining columns, in general, you will work with character-based fields (`string`), numeric fields (`integer`, `decimal`), `true/false` fields (`boolean`), and date fields (`date`, `timestamp`) [3].

6. **Run the Query**: Execute the `CREATE TABLE` query. Athena will process this command and create a table structure in the specified database.

   a. Whenever possible, try to define column names without using spaces. The ideal naming strategy is using lowercase names and separating words with underscores [4].

7. **Verify the Table Creation**: To ensure your table has been created successfully, you can run a `SELECT` query to view the top rows of your table. Running the following query should return 541,911 (the total number of records):

```
select count(*) as total_transactions
from retail.transactions;
```

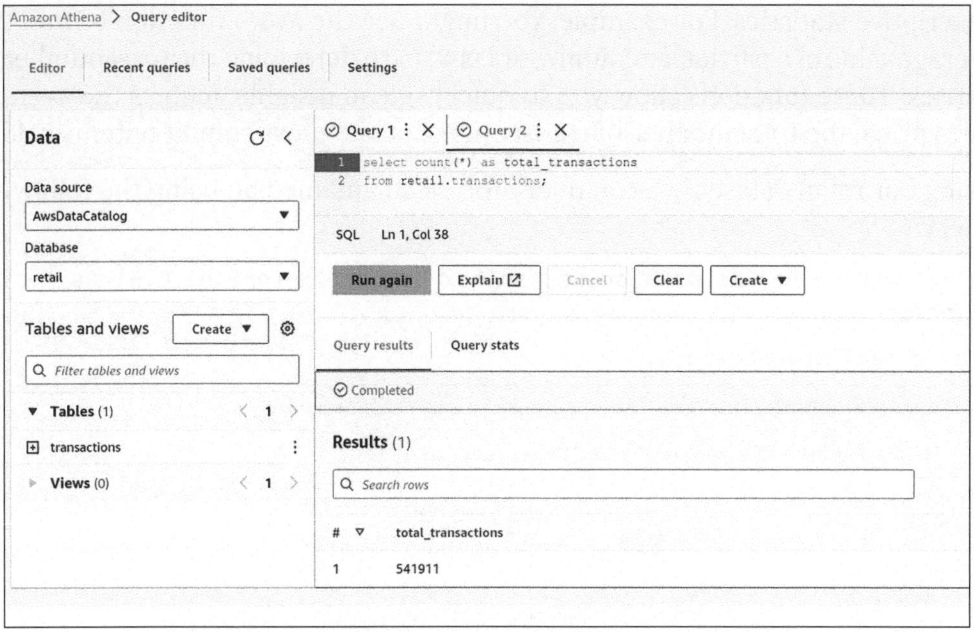

Figure 5.4: *Amazon Athena Console and Query Execution*

Querying Your Data

Structured Query Language (SQL) is the standard language used for querying and manipulating data in databases, and Amazon Athena employs SQL for data querying, allowing users to interact with their data stored in Amazon S3. Athena uses a variant of standard SQL with some differences and additional features tailored for its serverless architecture and integration with other AWS services.

Athena's SQL capabilities enable users to perform a wide range of data operations. This includes selecting and filtering data, aggregating results, joining tables, and even complex analytical functions. For example, users can execute `SELECT` statements to retrieve specific data from tables, use `WHERE` clauses to filter data based on certain conditions, and utilize JOIN operations to combine data from multiple tables based on a related column. Athena also supports aggregate functions like `COUNT`, `SUM`, `AVG`, `MIN`, and `MAX`, which are crucial for summarizing large datasets.

Central Tendency Queries

With your data set up, you can start running SQL queries to calculate various descriptive statistics. For example, you might use the `AVG()` function to find the average value of a particular column, or `COUNT()` to determine the total number of entries. These functions allow you to quickly glean insights such as the average sales price, the total number of transactions, or the most common items sold.

Using our retail dataset, we can query for mean and median using the following query:

```
select AVG(price) as mean_price, approx_percentile(price, 0.5) as medi-
an_price
from retail.transactions;
```

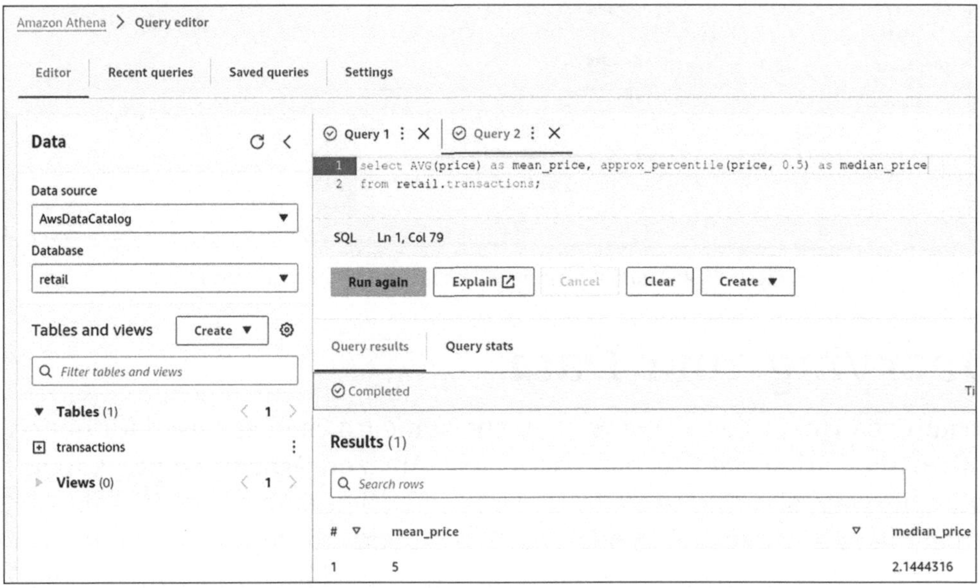

***Figure 5.5**: Athena Queries for Mean and Median*

Variability Queries

More complex statistics like standard deviation or variance can also be computed using built-in SQL functions in Athena. For instance, the `STDDEV()` function calculates the standard deviation of a dataset. This can be particularly useful for understanding the variability in your data, such as fluctuations in daily website traffic or sales figures.

Adding standard deviation and variance to our query shows that we get a standard deviation of approximately 97 with a variance of 9428:

```
select min(price) as min, max(price) as max, avg(price) as mean, std-
dev(price) as std_dev, variance(price) as var
from retail.transactions;
```

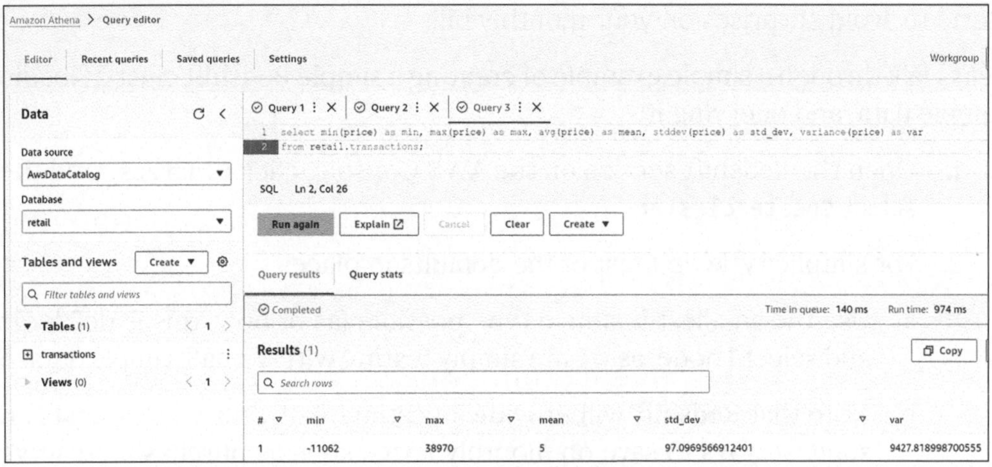

Figure 5.6: *Athena Queries for Standard Deviation and Variance*

Athena also supports more advanced statistical analyses with window functions and aggregations. You can use these to perform calculations across different segments of your data. For instance, calculating a running total, a moving average, or comparing the average sales figures across different regions. This flexibility allows businesses to perform detailed analyses tailored to their specific needs.

Using Redshift for Larger Datasets

While Athena is excellent for basic aggregations and summaries, for more advanced statistical analysis, you might need to integrate with other AWS services, such as Amazon Redshift for data warehousing. Redshift's cloud-based data warehouse service is designed to analyze terabytes and petabytes of data efficiently as it supports massive parallelization when running queries. It is important to note that as Redshift is a data warehouse, it is designed for Online Analytical Processing (OLAP) use cases for aggregating insights across large datasets, and should not be used to store your application's day-to-day transactions, which are more suitable for a relational database like Amazon RDS (OLTP - Online Transaction Processing).

There are two main ways to use Redshift: either provision your own cluster or use Redshift Serverless. Creating your own cluster involves choosing a specific node type and number of nodes to suit your data size and performance requirements, whereas Serverless only requires a few clicks to get started. Managing your own cluster can help optimize performance and save on costs, whereas Serverless requires no work on your part but will typically cost more. As with all AWS services, make sure to keep a close eye on cost and usage, and create billing alerts to avoid surprises on your monthly bill.

Let's walk through a simple example of creating a simple Redshift cluster, loading sample data, and querying it:

1. Open the Redshift service on the AWS Console, click **`Clusters`**, and then select **`Create cluster`**.
2. For simplicity, keep most of the defaults in place:
    a. Use the smallest instance type possible (as of now, this is dc2.large), and select 1 node, as we are simply testing with a small sample dataset.
    b. Note that Redshift will provide an estimate of your cluster costs and suggest ways to save on monthly costs, such as purchasing reserved nodes in advance.

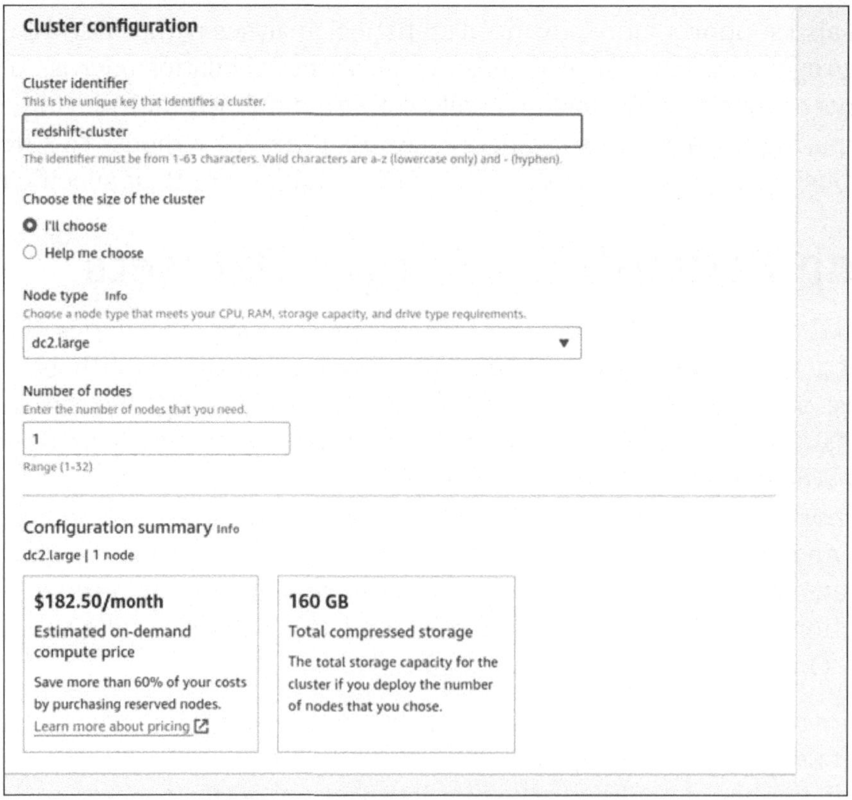

Figure 5.7: *Creating a Cluster on Redshift*

   c. Click **`Load sample data`** to load the Tickit sample dataset during cluster creation.

   d. In the **`Database configurations`** tab, define admin credentials for your database. While AWS Secrets Manager is a great choice for storing this (providing managed access to secret key/values), for testing our sample dataset, we will use the default admin username (**`awsuser`**) and a custom password.

   e. In the Cluster permissions section, click Manage IAM roles, then Create IAM role to create the proper permissions for operating this cluster (if we were copying data from S3, we would specify the bucket here).

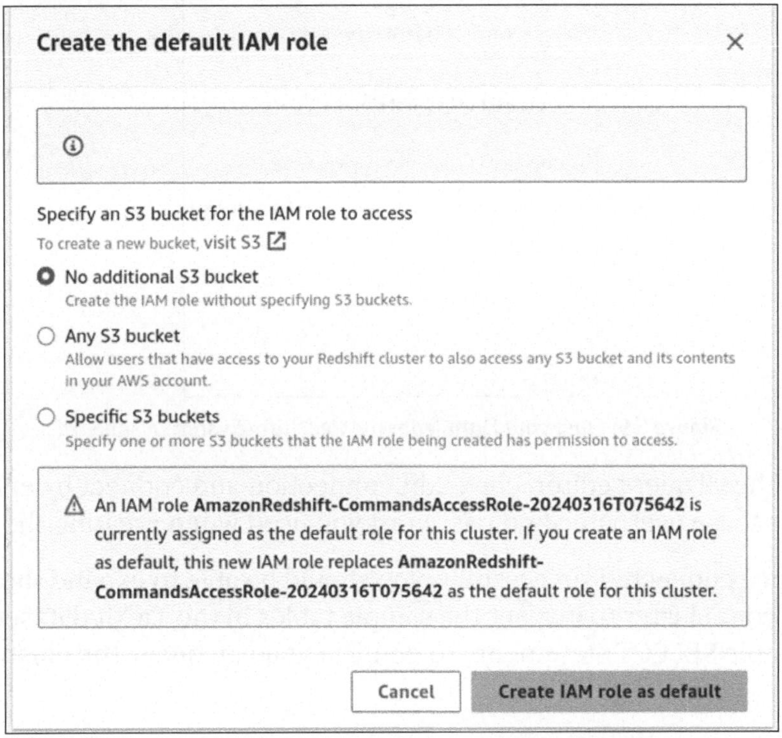

Figure 5.8: *Creating an IAM Role for Redshift Operations*

   f. In the Networking section, create or use a VPC to host your cluster. The VPC must have at least three subnets available for use.

3. Click Create cluster, and your cluster will begin provisioning and loading sample data. This process typically takes about 10 minutes on average. However, as we are provisioning a smaller cluster, it should take closer to 1-2 minutes.

Once your cluster is up and running, you can upload and query your data to Redshift. Data is usually uploaded to Amazon S3 and then copied into Redshift, though direct uploads are also possible using tools like AWS Data Pipeline or Amazon Kinesis.

For this example, we will work with the sample dataset to begin querying data right away:

1. From your newly created cluster's dashboard, click **`Query data`** to begin querying our sample data using the v2 editor (this provides a more advanced web interface to connect to your cluster, building and sharing notebooks, and visualizing your data).

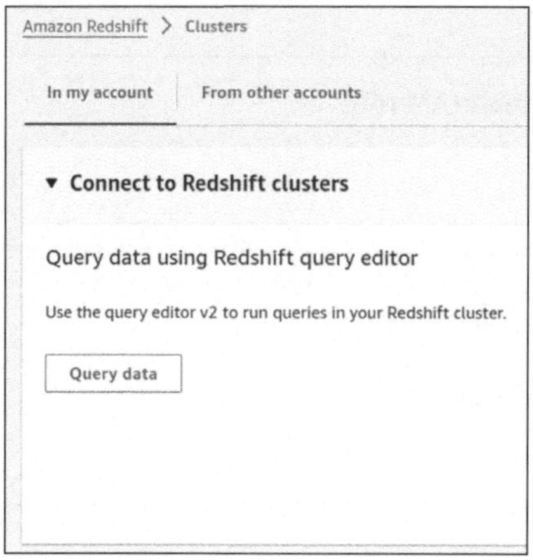

***Figure 5.9**: Querying Data from the Redshift Cluster Dashboard*

2. In the v2 query editor, click Edit connection and connect by entering the Database username and password you used when creating the cluster.
3. Once connected successfully, you should be able to expand the tree view of your cluster to inspect the sample tables in the Tickit dataset. Execute simple SELECT statements to confirm you can query the cluster.

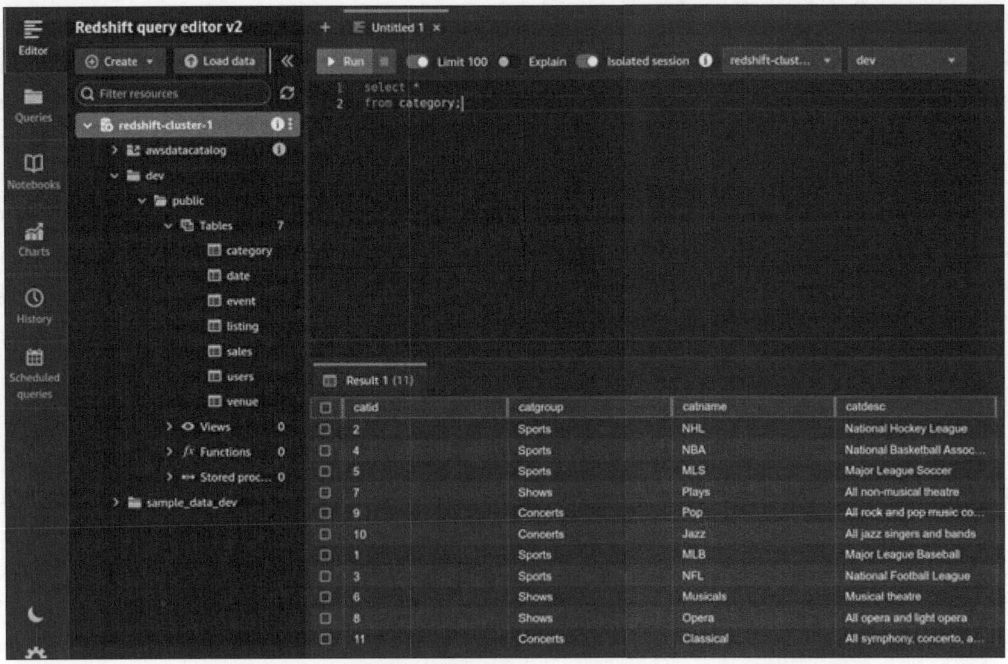

Figure 5.10: *Selecting All Categories from the Tickit Dataset*

With your data in place, you can start using SQL queries to compute descriptive statistics. Redshift's SQL capabilities allow you to calculate common statistics such as average (`AVG`), minimum (`MIN`), maximum (`MAX`), sum (`SUM`), and count (`COUNT`). These functions can be used to quickly get a sense of your data, such as understanding the average sales per product or the total number of transactions in a dataset. Note that the v2 editor allows for autocompletion while you type out your query.

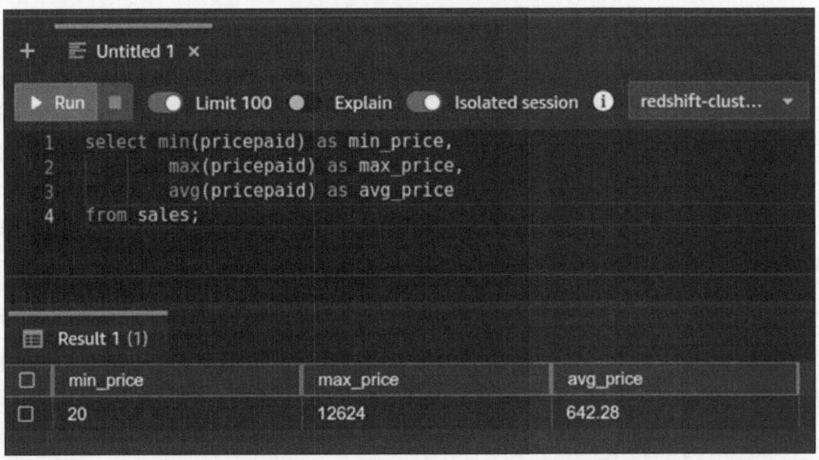

Figure 5.11: *Describing the Shape of Tickit Sales*

For more advanced statistical measures like standard deviation or variance, Redshift provides functions like `STDDEV` and `VARIANCE`. These can help you understand the dispersion or spread of your data. For example, you could use these functions to analyze the consistency of sales over a period or to understand the variability in customer spending habits. Redshift also allows for the use of window functions, which can be particularly useful for more complex descriptive statistical tasks. Window functions enable calculations across sets of rows that are related to the current row, allowing for sophisticated analyses such as running totals, moving averages, or comparing current results with historical data.

In sum, Redshift offers a robust platform for performing descriptive statistical analysis on large datasets. Its SQL-based interface makes it accessible to those familiar with relational databases, and its integration with other AWS services allows for a comprehensive analytical workflow, from data storage and processing to visualization and reporting. As with any data analysis tool, the key to effective use is a thorough understanding of your data and the specific statistical techniques that will yield the most meaningful insights for your particular use case.

Optimizing Athena Performance

The best place to start looking at optimizing performance is with data storage. Data in Amazon S3 should be stored in a **columnar** format, such as Apache Parquet or ORC. These formats allow Athena to read only the required columns for a query, significantly reducing the amount of data scanned and improving query performance. Additionally, compressing your data files and partitioning them based on frequently queried columns or date ranges can lead to both performance gains and cost savings.

Another key practice is efficient data querying. It's important to structure your SQL queries to take advantage of Athena's strengths. For instance, making use of partition columns in your `WHERE` clause can limit the amount of data scanned, saving both time and money. Also, using `SELECT` statements to retrieve only the columns needed, rather than using `SELECT *`, can greatly reduce the amount of data Athena needs to process.

Indexing is an often-overlooked aspect that can dramatically improve query performance. While Athena itself does not support traditional indexing, using AWS Glue to create and maintain a data catalog can optimize how Athena accesses and reads the data. The AWS Glue Data Catalog provides column statistics and table partitions, which Athena can utilize to optimize query execution.

When dealing with large datasets, query performance can be enhanced by splitting larger queries into smaller, more manageable ones. This approach not only speeds up individual query execution but also helps in better resource allocation and management. Additionally, consider using Athena's workgroup feature to separate query execution environments, allowing for more efficient resource allocation and cost tracking.

Cost management is also a crucial aspect of using Athena effectively. Since Athena charges based on the amount of data scanned, reducing the amount of data scanned by queries can lead to significant cost savings. Tools like AWS Cost Explorer and Athena's query execution plan can be used to monitor and optimize costs. Additionally, implementing data partitioning and columnar formats, as mentioned earlier, also contributes to cost efficiency.

By adhering to these best practices, users can maximize Athena's capabilities for efficient and cost-effective data analytics. Whether you are analyzing log files, conducting business intelligence, or performing data science tasks, these strategies will empower you to leverage Athena's full potential in your data analytics endeavors on AWS.

Securing Athena

Managing and maintaining security when querying data with Athena is crucial, especially considering the sensitive nature of data and compliance requirements. Here are some best practices and strategies to ensure security while using Amazon Athena:

Encrypting data is a fundamental aspect of securing your information. With Amazon Athena, data stored in S3 can be encrypted at rest using AWS **Key Management Service** (**KMS**). This ensures that your data is secure and accessible only to authorized personnel. Additionally, Athena supports encryption of query results stored in S3, as well as encrypting data in transit using SSL. It's important to ensure that all data layers, both at rest and in transit, are encrypted to safeguard against unauthorized access.

Controlling access to your data is essential for maintaining its security. Amazon Athena integrates with AWS **Identity and Access Management** (**IAM**) to manage access permissions. Create IAM policies that define who can execute queries and access data. It is recommended to follow the principle of least privilege, granting users only the permissions necessary to perform their job functions. For instance, a data analyst may only need read access to specific S3 buckets, whereas a database administrator might require broader permissions.

AWS Lake Formation can be used in tandem with Athena for more granular control over data access. Lake Formation allows you to set column-level and row-level security policies, ensuring that users can access only the specific data they are authorized to view. This is particularly useful in scenarios where you have sensitive data intermingled with less-sensitive data in the same dataset.

Regularly monitoring and auditing your environment can help detect and respond to security incidents swiftly. AWS CloudTrail can be used to log and monitor actions taken by a user, role, or an AWS service in Athena. This provides visibility into query execution and data access patterns. Amazon CloudWatch can also be used to set alarms and notifications for unusual or unauthorized query activities, enhancing the overall security posture.

Lastly, ensure the security of the environment where queries are being executed. This includes securing the client systems and networks used to access Athena. Maintain up-to-date antivirus software, enforce strong authentication mechanisms, and regularly patch and update systems to protect against vulnerabilities.

Incorporating these security practices into your usage of Amazon Athena will help ensure that your data querying processes are not only efficient but also secure, aligning with best practices and compliance standards. This holistic approach to security is vital in today's data-driven environment, where the integrity and confidentiality of data are paramount.

Reviewing Practical Applications

In the business world, descriptive statistics play a vital role in transforming raw data into meaningful insights. Businesses of all sizes generate vast amounts of data, from sales figures to customer feedback. Descriptive statistics help in summarizing this data, providing a clear, concise view of what the data says about the business's performance, customer behaviors, and market trends.

One of the primary applications of descriptive statistics in business is in understanding market trends. For instance, a retail company might analyze sales data over time to identify which products are selling the most. By calculating the mean and median sales figures for different product categories, the company can determine which items are the most popular and at what times of the year.

Descriptive statistics are also invaluable in customer analysis. For example, a business might collect data on customer age, income, and purchase history. By analyzing the mode and range of this data, the business can identify the most common customer profile and tailor its marketing strategies, accordingly, ensuring they target the most relevant audience.

Businesses often use descriptive statistics to track performance. **Key performance indicators (KPIs)** like monthly sales, customer acquisition costs, and churn rates are essentially descriptive statistics. By regularly calculating these, businesses can get a quick snapshot of their current performance and track changes over time.

In financial analysis, descriptive statistics provide a summary of a company's financial health. Measures such as the average quarterly revenue, the range of yearly profits, or the standard deviation of monthly expenses offer valuable insights into the company's financial stability and can help in forecasting and budgeting.

Descriptive statistics also find use in evaluating employee performance and operational efficiency. For example, the average time taken to complete certain tasks, or the number of sales closed per salesperson per month, can highlight areas of strength and opportunities for improvement within the workforce.

It's important to note the limitations of descriptive statistics in business. They provide a snapshot of the data but do not explain why certain trends or patterns exist. Additionally, ethical considerations, such as data privacy and the potential for data misrepresentation, must always be at the forefront when using statistics in business contexts.

Conclusion

In this chapter, we explored the fundamentals of descriptive statistics and conducted hands-on analysis using Amazon Athena. The ability to efficiently summarize and describe data is crucial for extracting actionable insights. As data continues to grow in scale and complexity, leveraging serverless services like Athena equips us with the capability to keep pace. While descriptive techniques uncover surface-level trends, applying advanced analytics unearths deeper patterns.

In the next chapter, we will utilize the full breadth of AWS's machine learning services on Amazon SageMaker to take our data analysis to the next level. We will train powerful predictive models to optimize business decisions, identify growth opportunities, and deliver cutting-edge intelligence. By complementing descriptive capabilities with prescriptive solutions, AWS empowers us to create incredible value from data.

Points to Remember

The key points to take away from this chapter are as follows:

- Descriptive statistics such as measures of central tendency and variability provide simple yet powerful ways to summarize and make sense of data. Building fluency in these fundamental concepts equips us with the right analytical mindset.
- Amazon Athena allows running SQL queries against data in S3 to easily calculate descriptive statistics at scale. Its serverless architecture enables ad-hoc analysis without infrastructure overhead.
- Following best practices around data formats, query structuring, cataloging, and workgroups is key to optimizing Athena performance and cost efficiency.
- Encryption, access controls, monitoring, and auditing are crucial when working with sensitive data to ensure Athena queries are executed securely.
- Descriptive techniques form the foundation of data analysis workflows. However, to drive impactful business insights, we need to complement them with more advanced analytics like machine learning to uncover hidden patterns and optimize decisions. The next chapter explores these advanced capabilities.

References

1. "Scaleup Enerbrain Builds on AWS to Develop Smart Building Energy Management System", https://aws.amazon.com/solutions/case-studies/enerbrain-case-study/
2. Online retail dataset, Kaggle. https://www.kaggle.com/datasets/lakshmi25npathi/online-retail-dataset
3. "Data types in Amazon Athena", Amazon Athena documentation. https://docs.aws.amazon.com/athena/latest/ug/data-types.html
4. "Names for tables, databases, and columns", Amazon Athena documentation. https://docs.aws.amazon.com/athena/latest/ug/tables-databases-columns-names.html

Chapter 6
Advanced Data Analysis on AWS

Introduction

Data is everywhere. Every website visited, product purchased, or photo shared generates yet another data point, contributing to the vast oceans of information companies accumulate. While data holds tremendous potential value, realizing actionable insights requires sophisticated tools to store, process, and analyze these massive datasets. In this chapter, we explore how AWS provides a robust, flexible platform, enabling organizations to tap into the power of their data through advanced analytics. We discuss key machine learning concepts, examine tools like Amazon SageMaker that simplify building ML models, and review common use cases across industries transformed by data-driven decision making. Whether you are new to data science or a seasoned expert, this chapter serves as your guide to unlocking impactful analytics in the cloud. Buckle up as we dive into the essential concepts, services, and step-by-step examples that demonstrate how AWS empowers anyone to make the most of their data.

Structure

In this chapter, we will cover the following topics:

- Introduction to Machine Learning and Its Concepts
- Approaches and Use Cases to Machine Learning
- Introducing Amazon SageMaker
- Machine Learning Using SageMaker Notebooks and Python
- No-Code Model Development Using SageMaker Canvas
- Getting Started with SageMaker
- Making Predictions Using SageMaker Canvas
- Additional SageMaker Features and Use Cases

Introduction to Machine Learning

Machine learning (**ML**), a branch of **artificial intelligence**, has become a pivotal element in the realm of data analytics. The world is awash in data, and machine learning helps to find unique patterns in data to find actionable insights. It's hard to understate the importance of these techniques, especially in comparison to traditional programming.

"Machine learning is the last invention that humanity will ever need to make."

– Nick Bostrom, AI philosopher and professor

Most software applications (even today) require manually encoding rules and business logic. This involves maintaining and updating this logic over time to meet user needs. Machine learning, in contrast, dynamically recognizes patterns over time and makes decisions with minimal human intervention.

Concepts of Machine Learning

At its core, machine learning involves teaching computers to learn from data and translate that learning into an actionable model. This process is akin to how humans learn from experience. However, instead of using human experience, machines use data to discern patterns and make predictions:

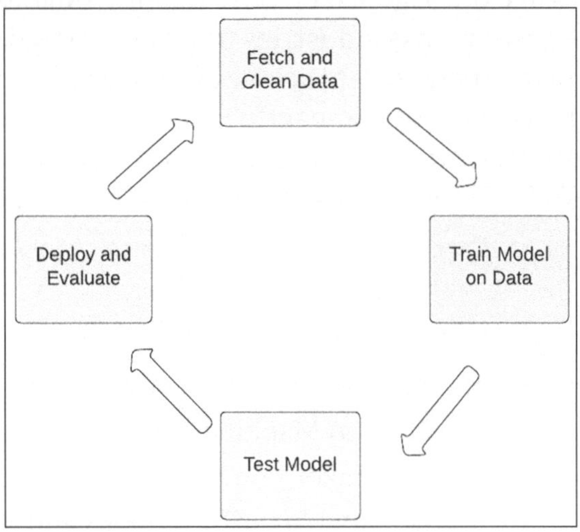

Figure 6.1: *Overview of the Machine Learning Process*

The first step in machine learning is **training**. Training involves feeding a basic machine learning model (designed for a specific objective like classification) with data to help it learn. This data, known as the training dataset, usually includes both the input data and the correct output. The model's job is to learn the relationship between the two using basic statistical methods to predict outcomes and measure performance. For instance, in a weather prediction model, the input might be temperature, humidity, and wind speed, while the output would be the weather forecast.

Feature selection is a critical part of the training process. Features are individual measurable properties of the phenomena being observed. The goal is to select the most relevant features that contribute to the accuracy of predictions. Think of it as choosing the right ingredients for a recipe. The quality of the ingredients (features) significantly impacts the quality of the final dish (predictions).

A common challenge to navigate during the training process is **overfitting** and **underfitting**. Overfitting occurs when the model learns the training data too well, becoming too narrowly focused on all data nuances, resulting in poor performance on new, unseen data. It's like memorizing the answers to a test without understanding the underlying concepts. On the other hand, underfitting happens when the model is too simple and fails to capture the complexity of the data, leading to poor performance both on the training data and on new data.

To this end, we should strive to include **validation** as part of our machine learning pipeline. Validation assesses how well your machine learning model performs. This is typically done using a separate set of data (held back from the training process) known as the **validation dataset**. The validation set is used to tune the model's parameters to improve its performance. This process is akin to a practice test (with new questions) to evaluate your knowledge before the final exam.

Testing is the final step in the machine learning process. Once the model has been trained and validated, it is tested using another separate set of data called the test dataset. This step is critical as it gives an unbiased evaluation of the final model's performance and is indicative of how it will perform in the real world.

A metric often used during both validation and testing is the **Root Mean Square Error (RMSE)**. The RMSE measures the square root of the differences (squared) between the actual observations and the model predictions. A lower RMSE indicates that the model is performing well, whereas a higher value indicates poor model performance. The fact that differences are squared helps to ensure that models are penalized for making larger errors.

In summary, machine learning involves several key steps: training the model with data, selecting the right features, avoiding overfitting and underfitting, and carefully evaluating, validating, and testing the model. Each step is crucial in developing a robust machine learning model that can make accurate predictions or decisions based on data. By understanding and applying these concepts, you can harness the potential of machine learning in data analytics.

Approaches to Machine Learning

There are various approaches to machine learning, each suited to different problems and data types. Understanding these approaches offers insight into how machines can learn and make decisions:

- The first major approach is **supervised learning**. This involves training a model on a labeled dataset, where the desired output is known. The model learns to map input data to the corresponding output. Common applications include regression, where the model predicts a continuous output, and classification, where it predicts discrete labels. For example, in a spam detection system (common in most popular email clients), the model is trained on emails labeled as 'spam' or 'not spam,' and it learns to classify new emails accordingly.
- **Unsupervised learning**, in contrast, deals with unlabeled data. Here, the model explores the data to find patterns or structures without any explicit guidance on the outcome. A common unsupervised learning task is clustering, where the model groups similar data points together. For instance, a company might use unsupervised learning to segment its customers into different groups based on purchasing behavior, without any predefined categories.
- **Semi-supervised** learning falls between supervised and unsupervised learning. It uses a small amount of labeled data along with a larger set of unlabeled data. This approach is particularly useful when labeling data is expensive or time-consuming. The model leverages the labeled data to learn the structure of the dataset and makes predictions for the unlabeled data. Semi-supervised learning is often used in scenarios where acquiring labeled data is challenging, such as in image or speech recognition tasks.
- **Reinforcement** learning is another type, distinguished by its focus on making sequences of decisions. In this approach, an agent learns to achieve a goal in an uncertain, complex environment. The agent receives feedback from the environment in the form of rewards or penalties and learns to take actions that will maximize its long-term reward. This type of learning is often used in robotics, gaming, and navigation systems.
- **Deep learning**, a subset of machine learning, has gained prominence for its ability to process and learn from large amounts of data. It uses neural networks with many layers (hence 'deep') to model complex patterns

in data. Deep learning is particularly effective for tasks like image and speech recognition, where it can learn from a large set of labeled data.

- Finally, **transfer learning** is a method where a model developed for one task is reused as the starting point for a model on a second task. It's particularly useful when the first task has a large amount of data, and the second task has less. For example, a model trained to recognize cars could be adapted to recognize trucks with minimal additional training.

Each type of machine learning has its strengths and applications, making the field incredibly versatile. From processing vast datasets to making intelligent decisions, these methods enable machines to perform tasks that, until recently, were thought to be the exclusive domain of human intelligence.

Use Cases for Machine Learning

Machine learning has become an integral part of various business processes, offering innovative solutions across a range of industries. Its diverse set of applications have revolutionized how businesses approach problem-solving and decision-making:

- One of the most common uses of machine learning is in **making predictions**. This involves using historical data to forecast future events, such as stock market trends in the financial industry or customer purchasing behavior in retail. These predictive models help businesses manage inventory, invest in companies, and operate more efficiently in response to dynamic markets. For example, Amazon uses machine learning to pre-emptively stock its fulfillment centers, predicting what products consumers will buy before they buy them [1]. As we will see, Amazon Sagemaker plays an important role in orchestrating the creation, execution, and orchestration of models to make these predictions:

Figure 6.2: *Rendering the Optimization of a Fictional Factory, Generated by ChatGPT*

- **Classification** is another significant application of machine learning (typically found in **natural language processing** (**NLP**) tasks) where data is automatically categorized into predefined classes. This technique has profound implications in various sectors. For instance, email services use machine learning to classify emails as 'spam' or 'not spam,' enhancing user experience. In healthcare, machine learning models classify individuals based on their risk of developing certain conditions, aiding in early diagnosis and personalized treatment plans. Similarly, **sentiment analysis** analyzes text data from social media and customer feedback and gauges public sentiment towards a brand or product (typically in categories of "positive", "negative", or "neutral"). This insight is invaluable for shaping marketing strategies and understanding customer satisfaction.
- **Amazon Comprehend** is an NLP service that utilizes machine learning to uncover insights and relationships in text. The service is designed to analyze and interpret the content of documents or collections of text, enabling users to extract information such as key phrases, entities (like people, places, and dates), language, sentiments, and more. This capability is significant for a wide range of applications, from sentiment analysis in customer feedback to content organization and trend analysis in large volumes of unstructured data. We will explore Comprehend in greater detail in *Chapter 7: Additional Use Cases for Data Analysis*.
- **Anomaly Detection**, a critical aspect of machine learning, plays a vital role in security and fraud detection. Banks and financial institutions leverage machine learning algorithms to monitor transaction patterns, flagging anomalies that could indicate fraudulent activities. This not only secures financial transactions but also builds customer trust. Features like anomaly detection are crucial for large financial institutions that manage billions of transactions and cannot reasonably inspect each transaction manually or with a traditional programming language.
- **Amazon Lookout for Metrics** is an anomaly detection service designed to help businesses and organizations identify unusual patterns or outliers in their data that deviate from the norm. By leveraging machine learning, Lookout for Metrics automatically detects and diagnoses anomalies in business and operational data, such as sudden dips in sales revenue, spikes in website traffic, or unusual changes in system performance metrics. This capability is crucial because it enables companies to respond quickly to potential issues, optimize operations, and make data-driven decisions without requiring deep expertise in machine learning or data science. By providing timely insights into data anomalies, Amazon Lookout for Metrics helps businesses maintain operational efficiency, enhance customer experiences, and ultimately drive better outcomes.

- **Recommendation Systems**, widely used in entertainment and e-commerce, exemplify machine learning's role in personalizing user experience. These systems use both explicit data (users liking or disliking movies) and implicit data (users watching movies for a long time) and compare them to similar users to find titles the user might like. These techniques help users find movies and buy products, driving engagement and sales and giving companies that can wield this power a competitive edge.
- **Amazon Personalize** is a machine learning service that enables developers to create personalized user experiences for their applications, based on the same technology used at Amazon.com. It allows for the easy integration of personalized recommendations into apps, websites, and content management systems without requiring extensive machine learning expertise. This service is important because personalized experiences can significantly enhance user engagement, satisfaction, and loyalty by delivering content, products, and recommendations that are tailored to individual user preferences and behaviors. By leveraging Amazon Personalize, businesses can improve conversion rates, increase average order value, and enhance customer retention. The service automatically processes and analyzes data, adjusts recommendations in real-time, and scales with the size and complexity of the dataset, making it a powerful tool for businesses aiming to offer a more customized and responsive user experience.
- In the realm of image and video analysis, machine learning (particularly deep learning) models excel at **interpreting visual data**. This capability is harnessed in the automotive industry for developing autonomous vehicles and in retail for features like virtual try-ons in clothing apps, enhancing customer experience and safety:

Figure 6.3: *An Autonomous Vehicle Using Visual Data to "See", Generated by ChatGPT*

- Lastly, **resource optimization** through machine learning algorithms is transforming logistics, supply chain management, and manufacturing. By optimizing delivery routes and production schedules, businesses achieve increased efficiency and reduced operational costs.

Together, these applications demonstrate the versatility and transformative potential of machine learning in providing practical and efficient solutions across various business sectors. As machine learning technology continues to evolve, its ability to innovate and improve business processes grows exponentially.

Introducing Amazon SageMaker

Amazon SageMaker is a fully managed service that provides developers and data scientists with the ability to build, train, and deploy machine learning models quickly. SageMaker removes the heavy lifting from each step of the machine learning process to make it easier to develop high-quality models:

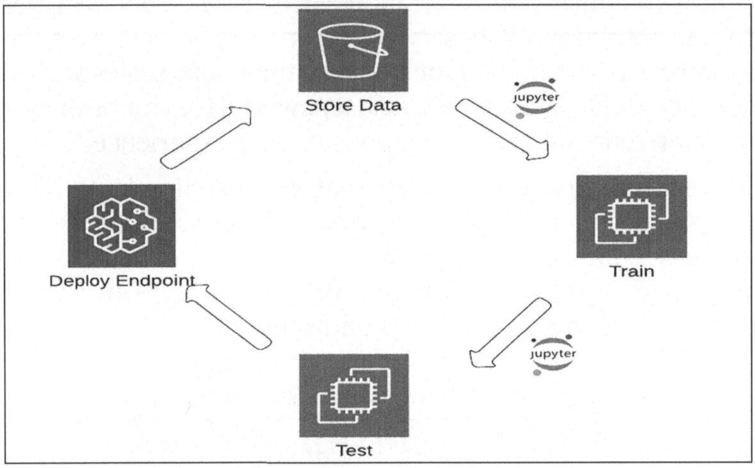

***Figure 6.4**: The Machine Learning Flow on Amazon SageMaker*

SageMaker offers a powerful and flexible environment for handling various aspects of the machine learning workflow. It simplifies the process of building models by providing everything you need to quickly connect to your data source, select and optimize the best algorithms and frameworks, and set up and manage the automatic data processing pipelines necessary for model training.

One of the key features of SageMaker is its ability to streamline the training of machine learning models. It automates complex aspects of the training process, such as managing the underlying infrastructure (for example, EC2 instances running Jupyter notebooks), adjusting model parameters, and optimizing algorithms. This automation significantly reduces the time and effort required to train models, from days to minutes, allowing data scientists to focus more on the strategic aspects of their models rather than the operational details.

Model deployment is another area where SageMaker excels. It simplifies the process of deploying your machine learning models into a production-ready hosted environment with just a few clicks. This feature enables businesses to quickly move from model development to deployment, reducing the time to market for new machine learning-driven capabilities.

SageMaker also stands out due to its scalability and flexibility. It can easily scale to accommodate large datasets and complex models, a necessity for handling the vast amounts of data generated by businesses today. Moreover, SageMaker supports a broad array of machine learning algorithms and frameworks, allowing data scientists and developers to choose the best tools for their specific needs.

Another unique feature of Amazon SageMaker is its built-in integration with other AWS services. This integration allows for seamless data flow between various AWS services, such as Amazon S3 for storage, Amazon RDS, and AWS Lambda for application services. This connectivity streamlines the machine learning workflow, making it more efficient and less prone to errors.

SageMaker's approach to security and compliance is also noteworthy. It provides robust security measures at all levels, from the data processing and model training phases to model deployment and monitoring. This comprehensive security ensures that the entire machine learning workflow meets the strict compliance and data privacy standards required by many businesses.

In conclusion, Amazon SageMaker is a versatile and comprehensive solution that addresses various challenges in the machine learning workflow. Its ease of use, combined with powerful and flexible features, makes it an ideal platform for businesses looking to leverage machine learning to solve complex problems, like the ones mentioned in the previous use cases. Whether it's predictive analytics, personalization, fraud detection, or any other machine learning application, SageMaker provides the tools and environment necessary to develop, train, and deploy models efficiently and effectively.

Machine Learning Using SageMaker Notebooks and Python

SageMaker relies on **Jupyter Notebooks** to enable data scientists and machine learning engineers to write code for processing data, training models, and deploying these models to production [2]. These notebooks are live, interactive environments that allow users to write and execute code from their browser. This removes the need for collaborators to write code locally and deploy the code remotely to use it:

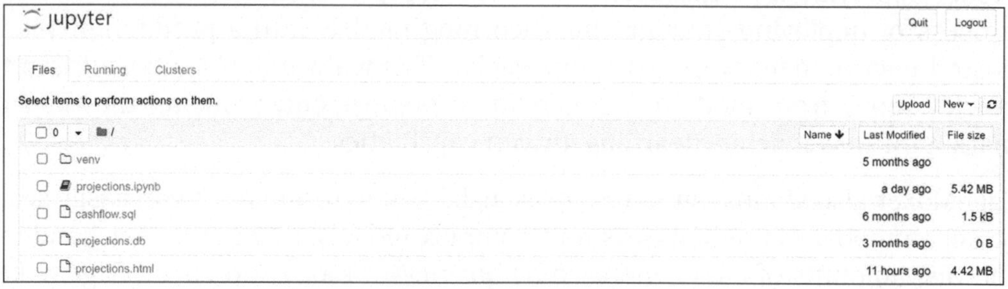

Figure 6.5: *Jupyter Notebook Directory*

Notebooks include a mix of both documentation (in Markdown format) and executable code blocks (generally in Python). These latter blocks will be used in SageMaker to write training and model configuration code:

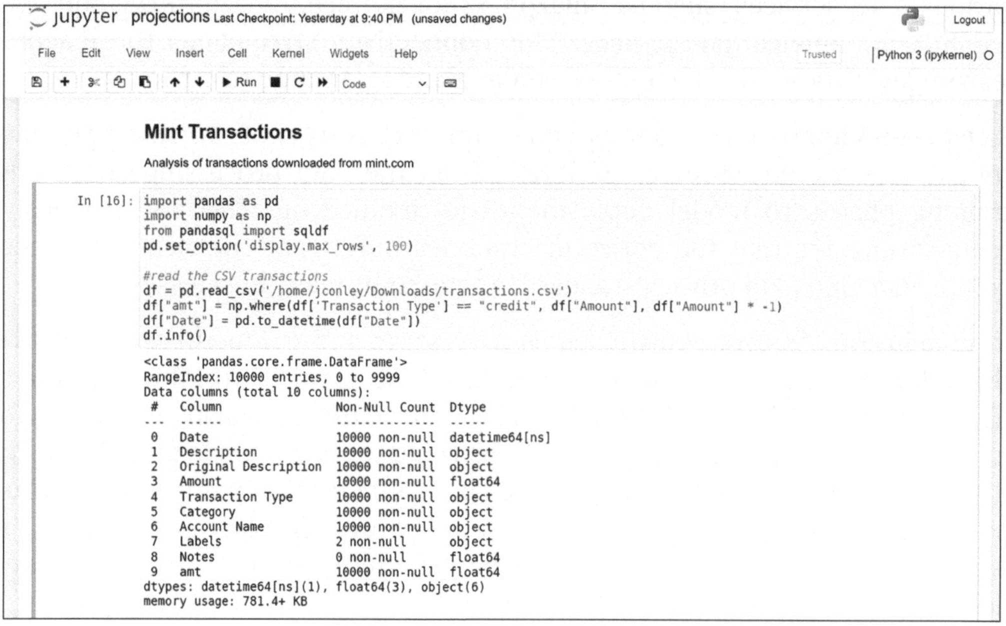

Figure 6.6: *Jupyter Notebook with Markdown and Python Code*

The first step in using SageMaker notebooks is to create and launch a notebook instance. Once the instance is up and running, users can select the desired Jupyter notebook kernel, such as Python, and begin the process of building their model. The notebooks offer direct integration with various AWS services, allowing for easy data import from sources like Amazon S3. SageMaker also provides built-in algorithms and supports popular machine learning frameworks like TensorFlow and PyTorch, enabling users to select the best tools for their specific needs.

Data preprocessing is a vital step in model building, and SageMaker notebooks facilitate this with various tools and libraries. Users can clean, transform, and prepare their data within the notebook environment. After preprocessing, the model training process begins. SageMaker streamlines this by offering options for parameter tuning and optimization. The platform's ability to scale and manage compute resources effectively ensures efficient model training, even with large datasets.

Once a model is trained and evaluated, deploying it is the next crucial step. SageMaker simplifies deployment with a few lines of code. Users can deploy their models to a SageMaker endpoint, which automatically provisions and manages the underlying infrastructure. This endpoint acts as a scalable and secure model hosting service, allowing for real-time inferences.

SageMaker also supports A/B testing and automatic scaling of these endpoints. Users can specify the initial number of instances and the scaling policies based on the expected traffic. This ensures cost-effectiveness and high availability of the model for inference.

After deployment, the model is ready to make predictions. Applications can simply send data to the SageMaker endpoint, and the model returns the predictions. This process can be integrated into various applications and services, allowing for real-time analytics and decision-making.

SageMaker's notebook environment provides tools for monitoring the performance of the model in production. This includes logging and metrics that help in understanding the model's usage and behavior. Additionally, SageMaker offers features for updating and maintaining models, such as easy retraining and redeployment, ensuring that the models remain accurate and relevant over time.

In essence, Amazon SageMaker notebooks offer a comprehensive and user-friendly platform for the entire machine learning lifecycle - from building and training models to deploying and using them for predictions. The integration with other AWS services, combined with the scalability and flexibility of SageMaker, makes it an excellent tool for data scientists and developers looking to leverage machine learning in their projects.

No-Code Model Development Using SageMaker Canvas

While Jupyter notebooks are a vital tool for collaborating on machine learning models, we will focus instead on a simpler, no-code approach for building machine learning pipelines, called **SageMaker Canvas**:

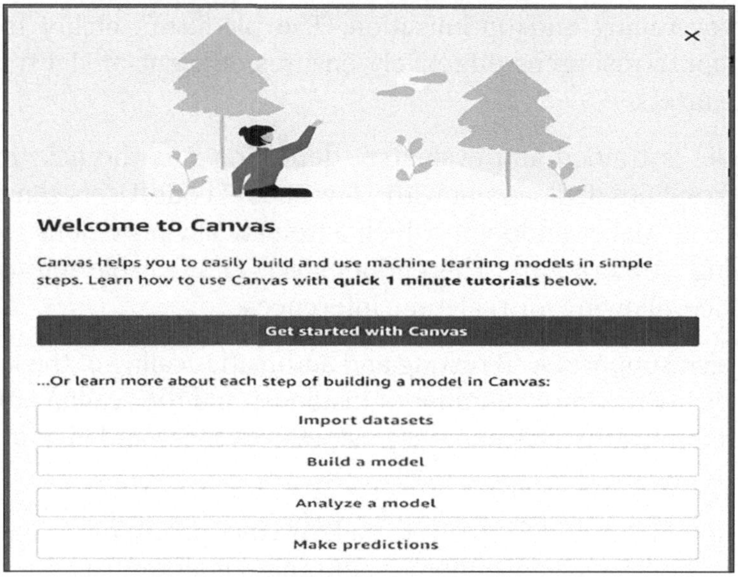

***Figure 6.7**: Welcome Screen for SageMaker Canvas*

Canvas empowers users to analyze data using a simple interface that abstracts away the complexities of building pipelines in Jupyter notebooks. This innovative tool is designed to make data analytics more accessible, enabling users to create and deploy machine learning models with ease. The intuitive interface of SageMaker Canvas simplifies the process of data exploration, allowing users to import data from various sources such as Amazon S3, Redshift, and even Excel files. Once the data is in place, Canvas offers an array of pre-processing capabilities to clean and prepare the data for analysis.

One of the standout features of SageMaker Canvas is its ability to build machine learning models without requiring users to write a single line of code. This feature is particularly beneficial for individuals who are new to the field of data analytics or those who prefer a more visual approach. Users can simply select their target variable, and Canvas automatically recommends the best model for their data. This not only saves time but also allows users to focus on understanding the results and making data-driven decisions.

Moreover, SageMaker Canvas is not just about model creation; it excels in model interpretation as well. The platform offers insightful visualizations and explanations of the model's predictions, making it easier for users to comprehend and trust the outcomes. This aspect is particularly important in business settings, where explaining the rationale behind predictions is as crucial as the predictions themselves. Additionally, once a model is ready, deploying it is just a matter of a few clicks. SageMaker Canvas handles the complexities of deployment, allowing users to share their models with others easily or integrate them into business applications.

Getting Started with SageMaker

Starting a project with Amazon SageMaker involves several key steps. First, let's review a popular use case for SageMaker and apply it to our project.

Predicting Housing Prices

The California Housing dataset [3] is a well-known dataset in the field of machine learning. This dataset, derived from the 1990 California census, provides a comprehensive set of data points covering house values and other housing-related features across various California districts. It includes metrics like median house value, median income, housing median age, as well as additional details such as the number of rooms, bedrooms, population, and households in each district. This dataset is commonly used for regression analysis and to demonstrate machine learning algorithms, particularly because of its real-world relevance and the diversity of features it uses. It serves as a benchmark dataset for experimenting with and evaluating various prediction models.

Making Predictions Using SageMaker Canvas

Here's a simplified checklist to guide you through the process of using the California Housing dataset in SageMaker Canvas [4]:

1. **Download the Dataset**
   a. From the dataset home page, click `Input` and download `housing.csv`.
2. **Upload Your Data to Amazon S3**
   a. Store your dataset in an Amazon S3 bucket. SageMaker uses data stored in S3 for training and deploying models.

3. **Initialize SageMaker Canvas**:
    a. From the SageMaker console, go to Domains and then **`Create a Domain`**. Follow the prompts to create a simple single-user domain.
        i. For more advanced enterprise configurations, create a domain that supports and allows for multiple users.
    b. From your new domain, click **`Launch`** and then **`Canvas`**.

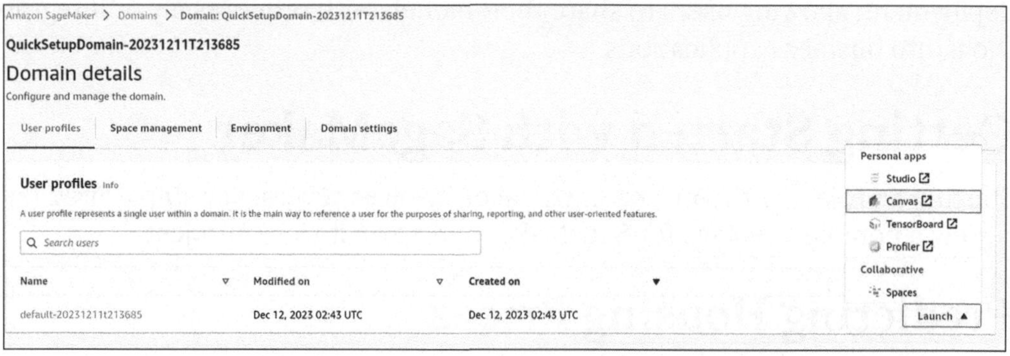

Figure 6.8: *SageMaker Domain Setup*

    c. The initial launch will likely take a few minutes as Canvas provisions all of the underlying resources necessary to manage data and train models.

4. **Upload Your Data to Canvas**
    a. Once your Canvas environment is ready, click **`Data Wrangler`** to see the available sample datasets. Then, click **`Create`** to import your data from S3. Click **`Create`** to create a tabular dataset, and select Amazon S3 as the data source to complete the upload:

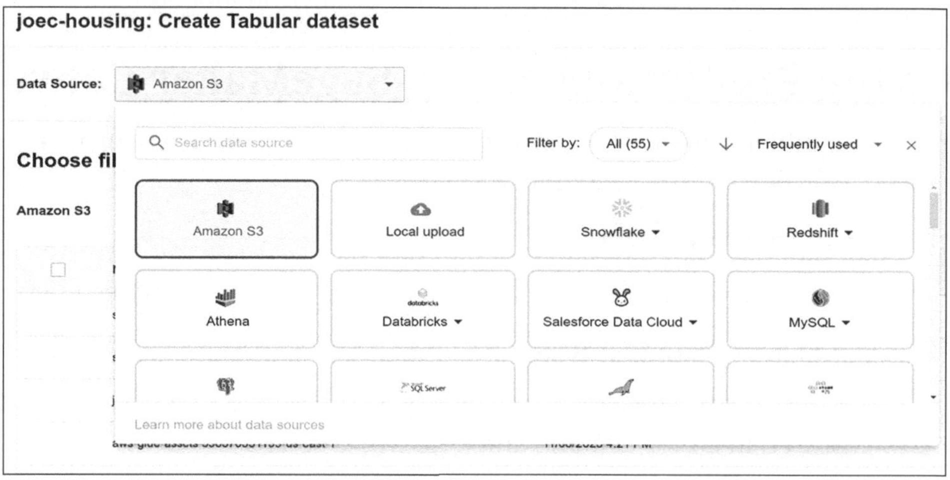

Figure 6.9: *SageMaker Canvas Data Source Upload*

   b. You can use the **Preview** functionality to review the first set of records and also indicate if there is a header row present in the data.

5. **Create a Model**

   a. Go back to the main Canvas screen and click **My Models -> Create new model:**

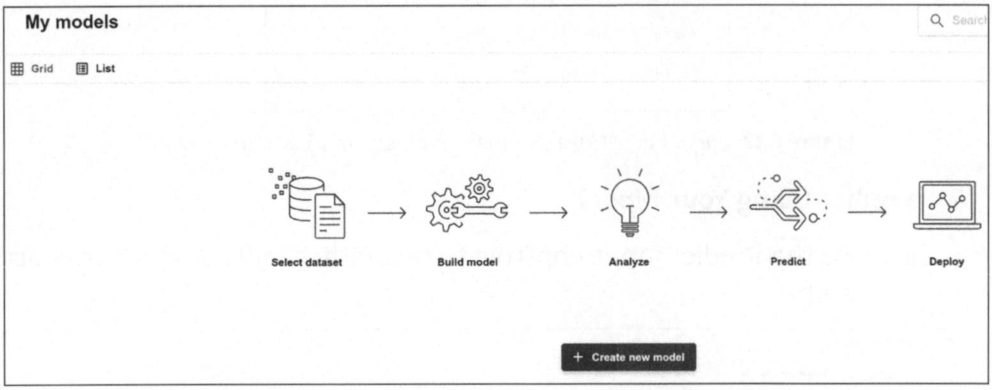

***Figure 6.10**: SageMaker Canvas Model Creation Screen*

   b. Choose **Predictive Analysis** and give the model a name (for example, "`California Housing Analysis`").

6. **Build Your Model**

   a. Follow the prompts to select your dataset, build, analyze, predict, and then deploy your model.

   b. Select the California housing dataset you uploaded previously.

   c. Under the **Build** tab, select the **median_house_value** feature as the field on which we will run predictions. Canvas will suggest a model to use based on this selection. Additionally, click **Preview model** to see the Estimated RMSE for the model:

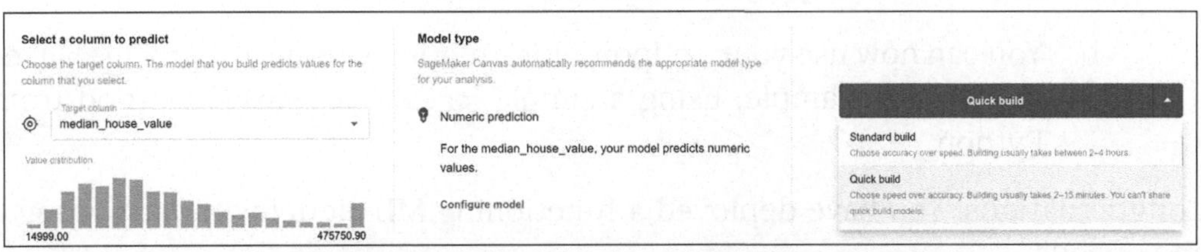

***Figure 6.11**: SageMaker Canvas Model Build Screen*

   d. For our California Housing dataset, our RMSE should be 46150, which means our housing price predictions could be off by as much as $46k.

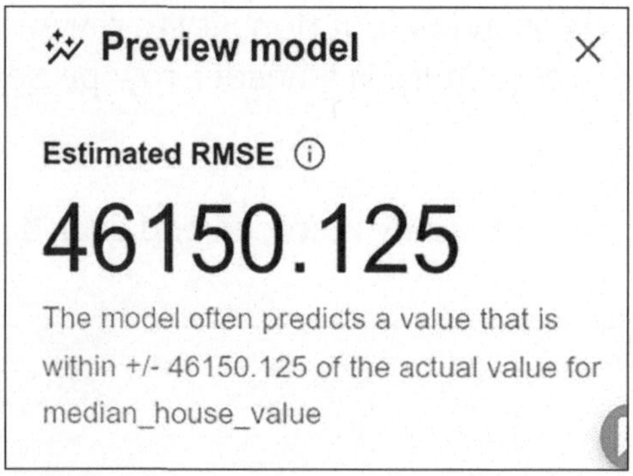

***Figure 6.12**: SageMaker Canvas Model Preview and Estimated RMSE*

7. **Predict Using Your Model**

    a. Use the Predict input controls to test either individual records or in batch:

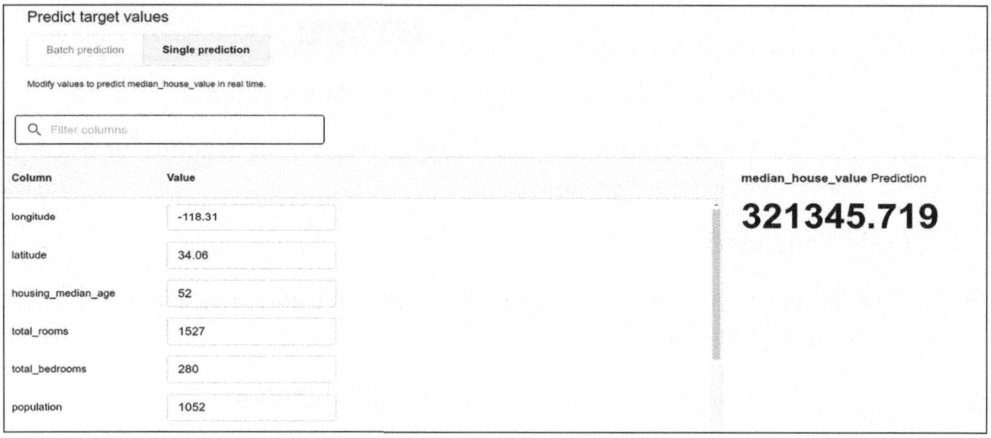

***Figure 6.13**: SageMaker Canvas Model Prediction*

8. **Deploy the Model**

    a. Click `Create Deployment` to deploy the model.

    b. You can now use your endpoint information like any other SageMaker model, for example, using a simple `create_endpoint` method from Python.

Congratulations! You have deployed a functioning ML model without writing a line of code.

Additional SageMaker Features

While Canvas is the easiest solution to use due to its no-code configuration, there are additional SageMaker features you should be aware of.

Studio

Amazon SageMaker Studio is a fully **integrated development environment (IDE)** for machine learning, designed to provide a more streamlined and user-friendly experience in building, training, and deploying machine learning models. As a part of the AWS suite, SageMaker Studio centralizes all aspects of the machine learning workflow into one interface, enhancing both efficiency and ease of use.

One of the key features of SageMaker Studio is its single, web-based visual interface that consolidates all the tools needed for machine learning development. This includes everything from preparing and building datasets to experimenting with and tuning models. SageMaker Studio supports a variety of machine learning frameworks and languages, such as TensorFlow and PyTorch, allowing users to work in familiar environments. It also integrates with Jupyter notebooks, providing a familiar interface for data scientists to write and test their code. The IDE enables easy tracking and comparison of different model versions and training runs, making it simpler to evaluate and select the best models.

Furthermore, SageMaker Studio enhances model building and deployment with its powerful automation and optimization tools. Features like AutoML allow users to automate the process of model selection and tuning, making machine learning accessible even to those with limited domain expertise. The ability to deploy models with just a few clicks directly from the Studio is another significant advantage, simplifying the transition from model development to production. In addition, SageMaker Studio offers robust monitoring and debugging tools, ensuring that deployed models are performing as expected and simplifying the troubleshooting process. Overall, SageMaker Studio represents a significant step forward in making machine learning more accessible and manageable, particularly for teams looking to streamline their machine learning workflows.

JumpStart

Amazon SageMaker JumpStart is a pivotal component of the Amazon SageMaker ecosystem, designed to simplify and accelerate the **machine learning (ML)** journey for users at all skill levels. As a part of AWS, SageMaker JumpStart democratizes ML by offering pre-built solutions and models, making it easier for users to deploy and experiment with ML technologies without requiring deep expertise in the field.

A standout feature of SageMaker JumpStart is its extensive library of pre-built and pre-trained machine learning models. These models cover a wide range of applications, from image and text classification to time-series forecasting, enabling users to easily find and deploy models that suit their specific use cases. These models are optimized for SageMaker, ensuring high performance and scalability. This is particularly beneficial for users new to ML or those looking to quickly prototype solutions, as it significantly reduces the time and effort required to start from scratch.

In addition to models, SageMaker JumpStart provides a variety of end-to-end solutions that address common business problems. These solutions are complete with necessary data processing steps, model training, and deployment processes. Users can easily customize these solutions to fit their unique requirements, making them highly versatile for a range of industries and applications. This feature of SageMaker JumpStart not only accelerates the deployment of ML solutions but also serves as an educational tool for users looking to understand how ML can be applied in real-world scenarios.

Moreover, SageMaker JumpStart integrates seamlessly with the rest of the AWS ecosystem. Users can easily access and manipulate data stored in AWS services like Amazon S3, and deploy models on SageMaker with optimal resource management. The integration also extends to other AWS services, allowing for the creation of comprehensive, scalable, and efficient ML workflows.

Overall, Amazon SageMaker JumpStart is a powerful tool that lowers the barrier to entry for machine learning. By providing pre-built models, solutions, and seamless integration with AWS services, it empowers users to harness the power of ML quickly and effectively, regardless of their expertise level. Whether for businesses seeking to implement ML solutions or individuals keen on exploring ML, SageMaker JumpStart offers a practical and accessible starting point.

Other Popular Use Cases for SageMaker

We have reviewed a complete example of how to create prediction models using SageMaker. Let's now review other popular machine learning use cases that we can achieve using SageMaker.

Recommendation

The process of building a recommendation model in SageMaker typically begins with data preparation, which is crucial for the success of any machine learning model. SageMaker facilitates this step by providing seamless integration with AWS data storage services like Amazon S3. Users can easily import their datasets, which might include user behavior data, item metadata, or historical transaction records. SageMaker's data preprocessing capabilities enable users to clean, normalize, and transform this data into a suitable format for training recommendation models.

For the model development phase, SageMaker supports various machine learning algorithms that are well-suited for recommendation systems, such as factorization machines, neural topic models, and deep learning-based approaches. Users have the flexibility to either use these built-in algorithms or bring their own custom models developed in frameworks like TensorFlow or PyTorch. Additionally, SageMaker provides hyperparameter optimization tools to fine-tune the model for better accuracy.

Once the model is trained, deploying it is straightforward with SageMaker. The platform allows for the easy creation of scalable, managed endpoints that can handle real-time recommendation requests. These endpoints can be integrated with websites, mobile apps, or other customer-facing platforms to provide personalized recommendations to users. Moreover, SageMaker's A/B testing capabilities enable users to experiment with different models or model versions, ensuring the best possible recommendation system is in place.

In summary, Amazon SageMaker streamlines the process of building and deploying recommendation models, offering a comprehensive set of tools and services for each step of the machine learning lifecycle. From data preparation to model training and deployment, SageMaker provides a conducive environment for developing sophisticated and personalized recommendation systems.

Classification

Amazon SageMaker provides a powerful and user-friendly platform for building classification models, a fundamental task in machine learning used for various applications like spam detection, image recognition, and sentiment analysis. SageMaker streamlines the entire process of developing these models, from data preparation to deployment, making it accessible for both experienced data scientists and newcomers to the field.

The journey of building a classification model in SageMaker begins with data preparation. SageMaker integrates seamlessly with AWS storage services like Amazon S3, allowing users to easily import their datasets. These datasets can be in various forms, such as text, images, or tabular data. SageMaker's data processing capabilities enable efficient handling of this data, including tasks like cleaning, labeling, feature extraction, and splitting the data into training and testing sets. This pre-processing step is crucial to ensure the quality and reliability of the machine learning model.

For the model training phase, SageMaker supports a wide range of built-in algorithms suitable for classification tasks, including linear learners for simple binary classification, and more complex algorithms like XGBoost and neural networks for multi-class classification. Users can also utilize popular machine learning frameworks such as TensorFlow or PyTorch to develop custom models. SageMaker's environment is designed to facilitate easy experimentation with different algorithms and parameters, aided by tools for automatic model tuning and optimization. Once the model is trained and evaluated, deploying it is straightforward with SageMaker. The service allows for the easy creation of scalable, fully-managed endpoints for making real-time predictions. These endpoints can be integrated into various applications, enabling them to perform classification tasks such as identifying whether an email is spam or not, categorizing customer feedback, or recognizing objects in images.

In summary, Amazon SageMaker provides a comprehensive and efficient pathway for building classification models. Its integration with AWS services, support for various machine learning algorithms and frameworks, and capabilities for easy deployment make it a versatile and powerful tool for tackling a wide range of classification problems in machine learning.

Decision-Making

Amazon SageMaker offers a conducive environment for building decision tree models, widely used for their simplicity and interpretability in various machine learning tasks such as classification and regression. SageMaker simplifies the process of developing, training, and deploying decision tree models, making it accessible for both seasoned data scientists and those new to machine learning.

The process of building a decision tree model in SageMaker starts with data preparation. SageMaker facilitates seamless integration with AWS data storage services such as Amazon S3, allowing users to easily import their datasets, which could include a wide range of features relevant to the problem at hand.

The platform provides robust data preprocessing capabilities that are crucial for decision tree models, like handling missing values, encoding categorical variables, and feature selection. Once the data is prepared and split into training and testing sets, users can proceed to model training.

SageMaker supports various algorithms suitable for decision tree models, including popular ones like XGBoost and Random Forest, which are essentially ensembles of decision trees. Users can leverage these algorithms directly or customize them according to their specific requirements. The platform also provides tools for hyperparameter tuning, helping to optimize the model for accuracy and efficiency. This is particularly important for decision tree models, where parameters like tree depth and the number of trees (in the case of ensemble methods) significantly impact performance.

After training the model and evaluating its performance, deploying the decision tree model is streamlined in SageMaker. The platform allows for the creation of scalable and secure endpoints for real-time inference with just a few lines of code. These endpoints can be integrated into various applications, enabling them to make data-driven decisions based on the model's predictions.

In conclusion, Amazon SageMaker provides a comprehensive suite of tools for building decision tree models, covering all aspects from data preparation to deployment. Its ease of use, coupled with the flexibility to customize and optimize models, makes SageMaker a valuable tool for a wide range of applications that require the interpretability and effectiveness of decision tree models.

Conclusion

Through the concepts, tools, and examples covered in this chapter, it is evident how Amazon SageMaker provides a robust, fully-managed environment to build, train, and deploy machine learning models with ease. By abstracting away the heavy lifting of infrastructure management and automation, SageMaker empowers novices and experts alike to focus on the strategic aspects of developing high-quality models. Whether using the no-code convenience of Canvas or the flexible notebooks, organizations can leverage SageMaker to turn their data into actionable insights.

In the next chapter, we will build on these fundamental machine learning techniques to explore more advanced use cases such as time series forecasting for demand planning and graph analysis for fraud detection. We will discuss specialized algorithms, data needs, and model evaluation metrics tailored to these complex tasks. The chapter will demonstrate how customization, performance optimization, and tight integration with other AWS services unlock the full potential of SageMaker for tackling advanced analytics challenges.

Points to Remember

The key points to take away from this chapter are as follows:

- Machine learning models uncover valuable insights from data that would not be visible to humans, transforming decision-making across industries.
- Amazon SageMaker provides a fully managed platform to quickly build, train, and deploy machine learning models, with no infrastructure management needed.
- Core concepts like training datasets, feature engineering, overfitting vs. underfitting, and model evaluation are key to developing accurate models.
- SageMaker Canvas enables users to create machine learning models without any coding required, using a simple point-and-click interface.
- SageMaker integrates seamlessly with other AWS services like S3 and Lambda to enable complete ML workflows, from data processing to model deployment.

References

1. "How artificial intelligence helps Amazon deliver", https://www.aboutamazon.com/news/innovation-at-amazon/how-artificial-intelligence-helps-amazon-deliver
2. "Introduction to the JupyterLab and Jupyter Notebooks", https://jupyter.org/try-jupyter/notebooks/?path=notebooks/Intro.ipynb
3. "California Housing Prices", https://www.kaggle.com/datasets/camnugent/california-housing-prices
4. "Lab 2 - Housing Prices (Real Estate)", https://catalog.us-east-1.prod.workshops.aws/workshops/80ba0ea5-7cf9-4b8c-9d3f-1cd988b6c071/en-US/1-use-cases/2-real-estate

CHAPTER 7

Additional Use Cases for Data Analysis

Introduction

This chapter explores additional use cases for leveraging data analytics on AWS across key areas such as time series forecasting, text analytics, graph database analytics, and IoT data. Time series forecasting with Amazon Forecast enables predicting future values based on historical data, offering insights that inform planning and decision-making. Text analytics using Amazon Comprehend facilitates deriving meaning from unstructured text data through natural language processing. Graph databases and Amazon Neptune allow modeling and querying complex data relationships as networks of interconnected nodes and edges. Finally, IoT Analytics helps analyze IoT sensor data in real time. Together, these services demonstrate the versatility of AWS's analytics capabilities in transforming diverse data types into actionable business intelligence. The chapter provides a hands-on look at building models using these services through step-by-step examples, elucidating their value in real-world business contexts.

Structure

In this chapter, we will cover the following topics:

- Time Series Forecasting with Amazon Forecast
- Text Analytics with Amazon Comprehend
- Graph Database Analytics with Amazon Neptune
- IoT Data with IoT Analytics

Time Series Forecasting

Time series analytics is a fascinating field, especially in today's data-driven world where we can use devices to capture high volumes of data over time. Techniques specific to time series data help us extract patterns from this data and make accurate predictions about the future.

Time series datasets are unique in their sequential nature and temporal element. Unlike conventional datasets, where each data point stands alone, time series data is characterized by a continuous sequence of values recorded over specific intervals of time. This aspect is crucial because the value at a given time point often depends on previous values, making the data inherently chronological. Understanding time series data is essential as it underpins many real-world applications such as financial market analysis, weather forecasting, and even predicting consumer behavior trends:

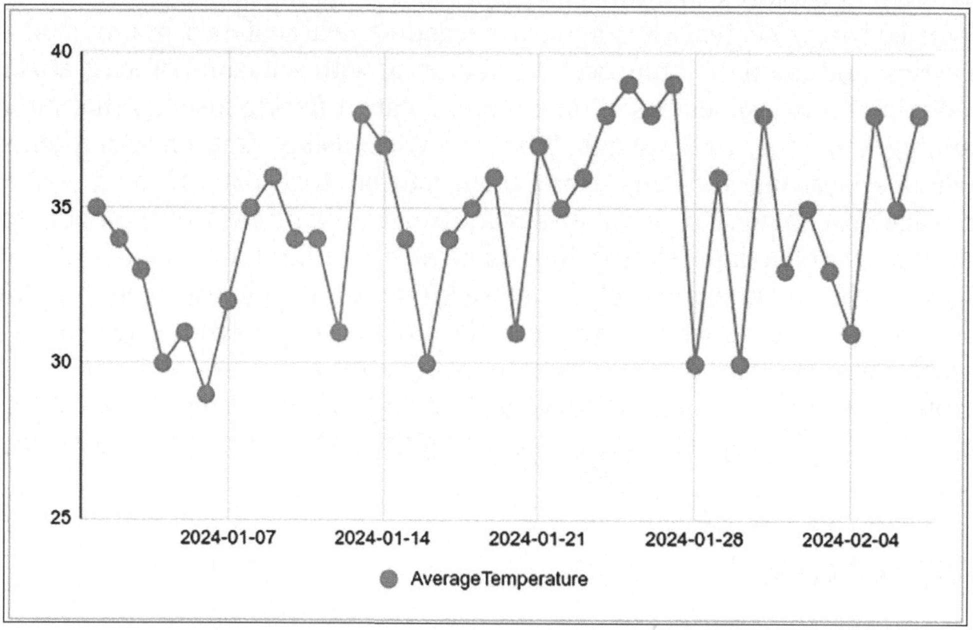

***Figure 7.1**: Graph of a Time Series Temperature Dataset*

One of the fundamental attributes of time series data is its seasonality and trend components. **Seasonality** refers to patterns that repeat over known, fixed periods of time, such as the uptick in retail sales during holiday seasons or temperature fluctuations across seasons. **Trends**, on the other hand, indicate a long-term direction in the data, such as a gradual increase in average global temperatures over the years. Identifying and understanding these components is crucial because they help in making accurate predictions and understanding underlying patterns in the data.

Autocorrelation refers to the correlation of a time series with its own past and future values. It's a measure of how much the current value in a series is influenced by its previous values. For instance, in financial markets, the stock price today might be correlated with its price yesterday or last week. Autocorrelation helps in identifying repeating patterns or trends over intervals within the data, which is crucial for forecasting and modeling. High autocorrelation implies that past values have a strong influence on current values, a feature that many time series forecasting models, such as **AutoRegressive Integrated Moving Average (ARIMA)**, heavily rely upon. However, it's also a double-edged sword; excessive autocorrelation can lead to models that are too dependent on their immediate past, potentially overlooking longer-term trends.

Frequency and **granularity** in time series data are closely related concepts that dictate the level of detail and the intervals at which data is recorded or observed. Frequency refers to how often data points are recorded - it could be hourly, daily, weekly, and so on. Granularity, on the other hand, is about the level of detail or aggregation of the data. For example, temperature data could be recorded every minute (high granularity) or averaged out over a day (lower granularity). The choice of frequency and granularity has a significant impact on data analysis. High-frequency granular data can capture minute changes and offer a detailed view, but may also introduce noise and require more computational resources. Lower frequency data might miss short-term fluctuations but can provide a clearer view of long-term trends. The key is to strike a balance that aligns with the objectives of the analysis and the nature of the phenomena being studied.

Stationarity is a property of a time series whereby its statistical characteristics such as mean, variance, and autocorrelation are constant over time. In practical terms, a stationary time series has a consistent structure over time, making it easier to model and predict. Most classical time series models assume stationarity because it simplifies the modeling process and makes the models more reliable. However, many real-world time series data are non-stationary, exhibiting trends, seasonality, or varying variances over time. To deal with non-stationarity, analysts often use techniques like differencing, where the difference between consecutive data points is taken, or transformation methods like logarithms, to stabilize the variance. Ensuring stationarity is a critical step in time series analysis, as it directly impacts the accuracy and reliability of forecasting models. AWS's sophisticated analytics tools often incorporate features to test and ensure stationarity, thereby enhancing the quality of insights derived from the data.

Another significant aspect of time series data is its susceptibility to external factors leading to **anomalies** (or outliers). These are data points that deviate significantly from the overall pattern and can be caused by unexpected events or errors in data collection. Detecting these anomalies is a critical step in time series analysis as they can provide valuable insights or indicate potential issues in the data collection process. AWS tools offer sophisticated methods for anomaly detection, helping users identify and address these irregularities effectively.

When dealing with time series data, the focus often shifts to handling large volumes of data efficiently. AWS provides scalable solutions that can store and process vast amounts of time series data, enabling users to perform complex analyses without the need for extensive technical infrastructure. This capability is especially valuable in scenarios where data accumulates rapidly, such as in sensor data analysis or real-time financial transaction tracking.

In summary, time series datasets are distinguished by their sequential nature, with each data point connected to its predecessors through time. This connection adds complexity but also richness to the data, offering insights into trends, seasonal patterns, and potential anomalies. Understanding these characteristics is crucial for anyone venturing into data analytics on AWS, as it lays the groundwork for more advanced analyses and applications.

Business Applications

Time series forecasting offers valuable insights aiding strategic decision-making across various business sectors. One prominent use case is in the financial sector, where time series forecasting helps inform stock market analysis, economic forecasting, and risk management. Financial institutions use historical data to predict stock prices, currency exchange rates, and market trends, allowing investors and analysts to make informed decisions. This predictive capability is not just limited to stocks; it's also crucial in forecasting economic indicators like GDP growth rates, inflation, and unemployment rates. These forecasts help governments and policymakers in planning and implementing economic policies.

In the retail industry, time series forecasting plays a crucial role in inventory management and demand forecasting. Retailers analyze past sales data to predict future demand for products, enabling them to optimize inventory levels, reduce holding costs, and minimize stockouts. This forecasting is particularly vital in managing seasonal products, where demand can fluctuate significantly throughout the year. Additionally, it aids in planning marketing strategies and promotions, ensuring that they align with anticipated customer demand.

The energy sector also greatly benefits from time series forecasting, particularly in electricity demand and price forecasting. Energy companies use historical consumption data to predict future demand, which is essential for grid management and reducing the risk of power outages. Accurate demand forecasts enable energy providers to optimize their production, allocate resources efficiently, and plan maintenance schedules effectively. Similarly, predicting energy prices helps in strategic planning and financial risk management, especially in volatile markets.

Supply chain management is another area where time series forecasting is indispensable. By analyzing historical data on supply chain variables such as delivery times, order volumes, and supplier performance, businesses can predict future supply chain disruptions and bottlenecks. This foresight enables them to take proactive measures, such as diversifying suppliers or adjusting inventory levels, to ensure smooth operations and maintain customer satisfaction.

Lastly, in the realm of digital marketing and online business, time series forecasting is used to analyze website traffic, user engagement, and online sales. This analysis helps businesses understand consumer behavior patterns, predict future trends in website visits, and optimize their digital marketing campaigns. It also assists in budget allocation for advertising, ensuring that resources are invested in channels and times that yield the highest returns.

In conclusion, time series forecasting has become an integral part of business strategy across various industries. Its ability to provide forward-looking insights makes it a valuable asset for financial analysis, inventory management, energy demand planning, supply chain optimization, and digital marketing strategies. As data analytics tools and technologies evolve, the precision and scope of these forecasts are continually improving, enabling businesses to make more informed data-driven decisions.

Introducing Amazon Forecast

Amazon Forecast is a fully managed service provided by AWS that leverages machine learning to deliver highly accurate time series forecasting. This powerful tool is designed to handle the complexities of time series data and make predictive technology accessible to both developers and data scientists alike. It builds on the same technology used at Amazon.com for forecasting product demand, making it a robust and well-tested solution for a variety of business applications.

One of the key features of Amazon Forecast is its ability to automatically process and analyze complex time series data without requiring users to have expertise in machine learning. The service takes care of the heavy lifting involved in building, training, and deploying sophisticated forecasting models. Users simply provide the historical time series data, and Amazon Forecast automatically selects the best algorithm and model based on the data characteristics. This automation greatly simplifies the forecasting process, making it more efficient and accessible, especially for users with limited machine learning experience.

Amazon Forecast is highly versatile and can handle multiple time series data inputs simultaneously, a feature particularly useful for large-scale forecasting tasks. This capability allows businesses to incorporate related time series datasets and additional variables, such as product features or store locations, to enhance the accuracy of their forecasts. The service can predict key business metrics such as product demand, sales, web traffic, and resource requirements, with the forecasts being tailored to specific items, locations, or time intervals as needed.

Another significant advantage of using Amazon Forecast is its scalability and integration with other AWS services. It can easily scale to handle large volumes of data and complex forecasting tasks, making it suitable for businesses of all sizes. Additionally, it integrates seamlessly with other AWS data storage and processing services like Amazon S3 and AWS Lambda, facilitating a smooth data pipeline and efficient workflow. The service also offers robust security features, ensuring that the data used for forecasting is securely stored and processed.

In summary, Amazon Forecast stands out as a powerful, user-friendly solution for time series forecasting. Its machine learning capabilities, coupled with automation and scalability, make it an invaluable tool for businesses looking to harness the power of their data for predictive insights. By simplifying the forecasting process and providing accurate predictions, Amazon Forecast helps organizations optimize operations, plan resources, and make informed decisions for the future.

Analyzing Time Series Data Using Amazon Forecast

Let's start with a simple example of analyzing stock prices from a recent five-year period [1].

Creating Your Datasets

1. From the AWS Console, navigate to **`Amazon Forecast`** and create a dataset group:

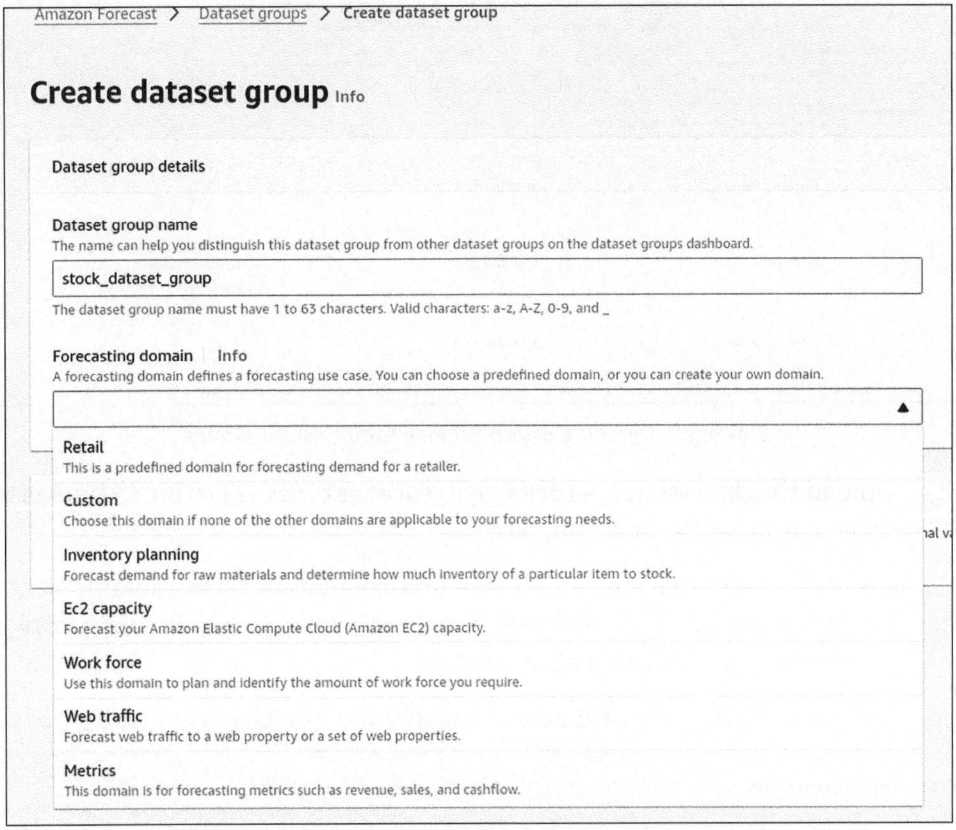

***Figure 7.2**: Creating a Dataset Group in Amazon Forecast*

  a. Enter a valid **`Dataset group name`**, adhering to the name requirements noted below.

  b. Choose **`Custom`** for the **`Forecasting domain`**. We will use a predefined dataset of stock quotes that adheres to this format. Other domains require different formatting and values.

2. The next screen should allow you to import the actual dataset:

  a. Give your dataset a valid name.

  b. Use the default schema.

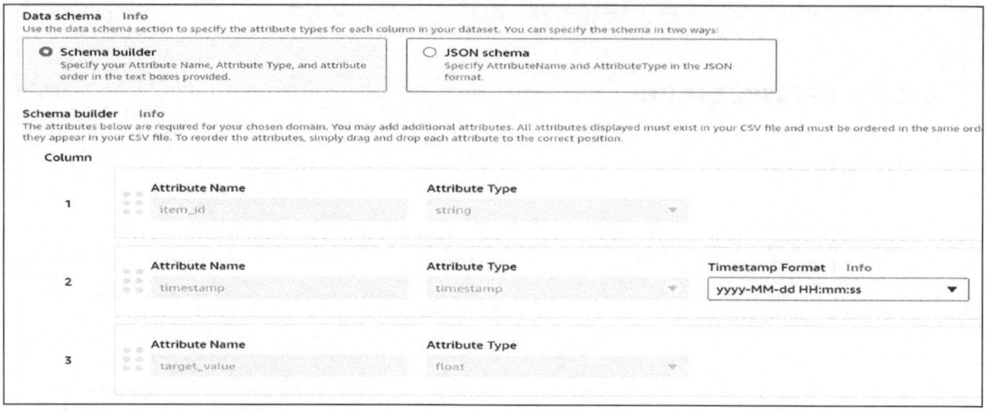

Figure 7.3: *Default Custom Schema for a Dataset Group*

3. Upload the dataset **`all_stocks_5yr_forecast.csv`** [2] to an S3 bucket and make a note of the resulting key:
    a. Make sure that the CSV you upload matches the default schema noted above. This file will already be structured in the **<item_id, timestamp, target_value>** format.
4. Enter the **`Import file type`** as **`CSV`**, and enter the key you just uploaded:

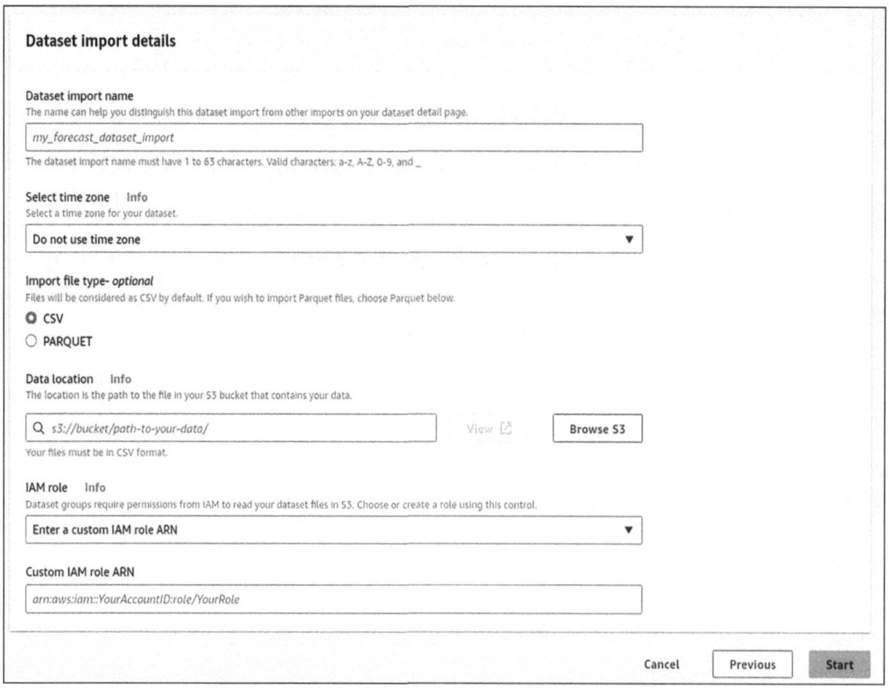

Figure 7.4: *Importing a Dataset in Forecast*

5. Create a custom IAM role to handle the upload.
6. Click **Start** and Forecast will begin the import process.

Training a Predictor and Making a Forecast

1. Now that our data has been imported, the next step is to build a **predictor** that will take in additional configuration. From the dataset group dashboard, click **Train predictor**.
2. Give a name to your predictor, and optionally set configuration items for granularity, horizon, and quantiles:

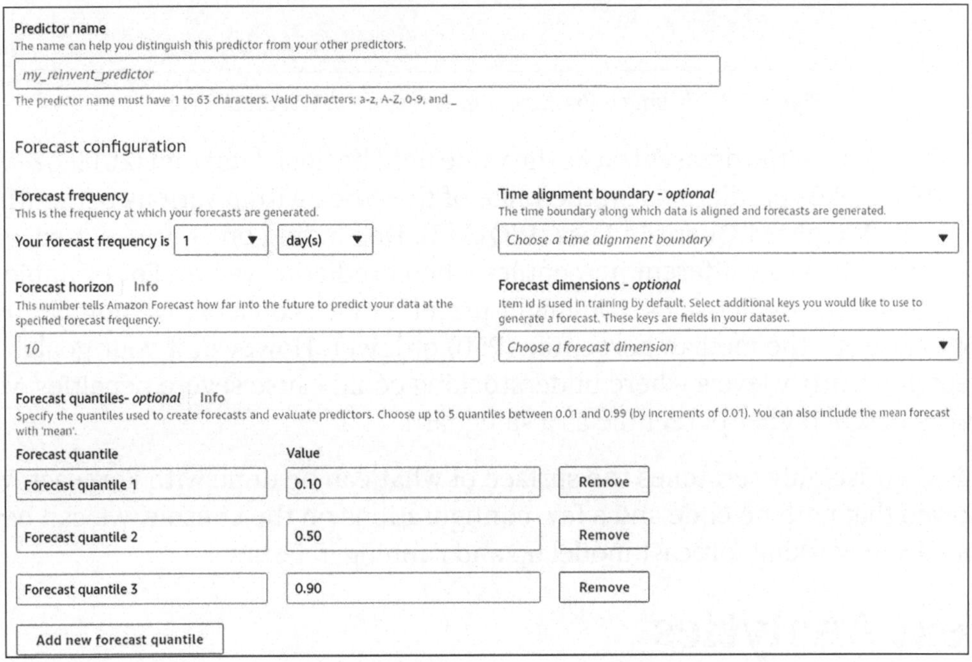

***Figure 7.5**: Creating a Predictor in Forecast*

3. Click **Create**, and Forecast will create the predictor for you. This may take a few hours as the model is trained.
4. Once complete, you can create a **forecast** that will take the trained model and make predictions. After creation is finished, you can then **query** the forecast with simple start/end times and an optional `item_id` filter to see the forecast in action:
   a. For this example, we will pick a start/end date range at the end of our dataset (2018-02-03 to 2018-02-12) and filter on `item_id = AAPL` to focus on one stock:

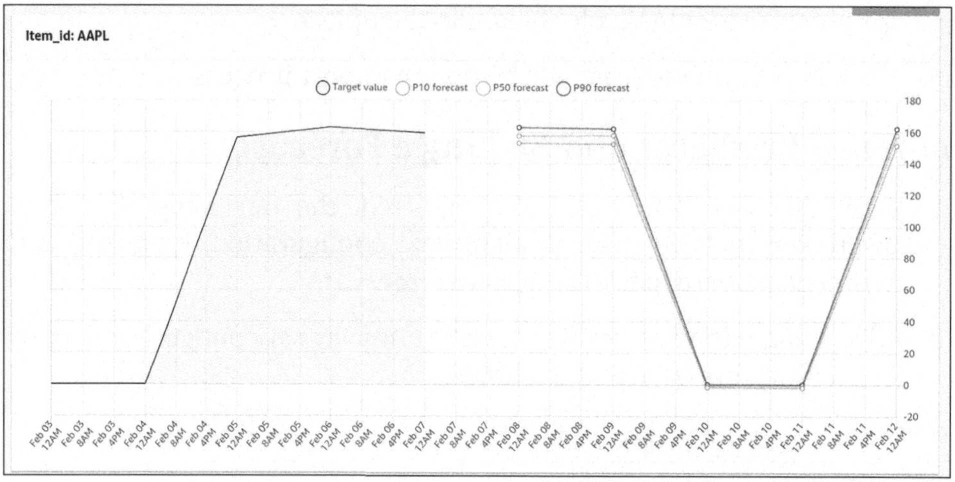

***Figure 7.6**: Viewing a Prediction in Forecast - AAPL Stock Prices*

You can see how the dataset tracks the value until its final datapoint (2018-02-07), and then makes predictions on the value of the stock within various percentiles using the **Weighted Quantile Loss** (**WQL**) [3]. Depending on your use case, you might prefer to use different percentiles when predicting values. For example, if your goal is to predict sales, you might prefer a more conservative number and stick closer to the median percentile (P50) or lower. However, if your goal is to predict inventory levels where understocking could cause severe penalties, you may choose a higher percentile as a safeguard.

This exercise only scratches the surface of what can be done with Forecast. We showed that with no code and a few configurations on the console, we can have a valid and working forecast model up and running in hours.

Text Analytics

Text analytics, a part of the larger field of **natural language processing** (**NLP**), is the process of extracting meaningful information from text. This effort combines elements of computer science, linguistics, and data analytics to understand and interpret human language in a structured and meaningful way. The primary goal of textual analytics is to enable computers to process, analyze, and understand textual data in a manner similar to human understanding. This capability opens up a myriad of applications, from sentiment analysis in customer feedback to topic extraction in large volumes of text.

One of the foundational elements of textual analytics is **text classification**. This involves categorizing text into predefined groups based on its content. For example, in **sentiment analysis**, text classification helps determine whether a piece of text expresses a positive, negative, or neutral sentiment. This application is particularly valuable in fields like marketing and customer service, where understanding customer sentiment is crucial.

"Your most unhappy customers are your greatest source of learning."

- Bill Gates

Another important aspect of textual analytics is **Named Entity Recognition (NER)**. NER seeks to identify and classify key information in text, such as names of people, organizations, locations, and even specific terms related to finance or medicine. This is particularly useful in data extraction processes, where specific information needs to be quickly and accurately extracted from large datasets, such as extracting company names and locations from news articles or identifying drug names and doses from medical documents.

Textual analytics also encompasses **topic modeling**, a technique that discovers abstract topics within a text corpus. This approach is essential for organizing, understanding, and summarizing large datasets. For instance, topic modeling can be used to sift through thousands of academic papers to find common themes or to analyze customer feedback to identify recurring topics. This not only helps in understanding the main themes in a large body of text but also aids in uncovering hidden patterns that might not be immediately apparent.

Furthermore, textual analytics is deeply intertwined with machine learning, particularly with the advent of deep learning techniques. Machine learning models, especially those based on neural networks, have significantly advanced the field of NLP. They have improved the accuracy and efficiency of language processing tasks, enabling more sophisticated applications like machine translation, automated summarization, and question-answering systems.

In conclusion, textual analytics plays a pivotal role in the field of NLP, providing tools and techniques to extract, analyze, and interpret human language. From text classification and named entity recognition to topic modeling, these methods help uncover insights in text data, driving applications across various domains. As technology continues to evolve, especially in the realm of machine learning, the capabilities and applications of textual analytics are set to expand, offering even more powerful ways to harness the wealth of information contained in the text.

Business Applications

Analyzing text has become a vital component in the business world, empowering organizations to derive meaningful insights from vast amounts of unstructured data. At the core of this field is the ability to analyze, understand, and interpret human language in a way that is both scalable and efficient. This is where AWS plays a pivotal role, offering a suite of cloud-based tools and services that enable businesses to harness the power of NLP without needing deep technical expertise.

One of the primary applications of NLP in business is sentiment analysis. This involves evaluating the sentiments expressed in textual data, such as customer feedback, social media comments, or product reviews. By utilizing AWS services like Amazon Comprehend, companies can automatically categorize these sentiments as positive, negative, or neutral. This insight is invaluable for understanding customer satisfaction, improving products and services, and tailoring marketing strategies. Moreover, it provides an agile way to respond to customer needs and market trends, as sentiment analysis can be performed in real time, offering almost immediate feedback.

Another significant application is text extraction and classification. Businesses deal with large volumes of documents like contracts, emails, and reports daily. Manually processing this information is time-consuming and prone to errors. AWS's machine learning services, such as Amazon Textract, enable the automatic extraction of text and data from documents. This capability not only accelerates the processing time but also enhances data accuracy and accessibility. Furthermore, it facilitates the categorization of documents, allowing for efficient organization and retrieval of information, crucial for decision-making processes:

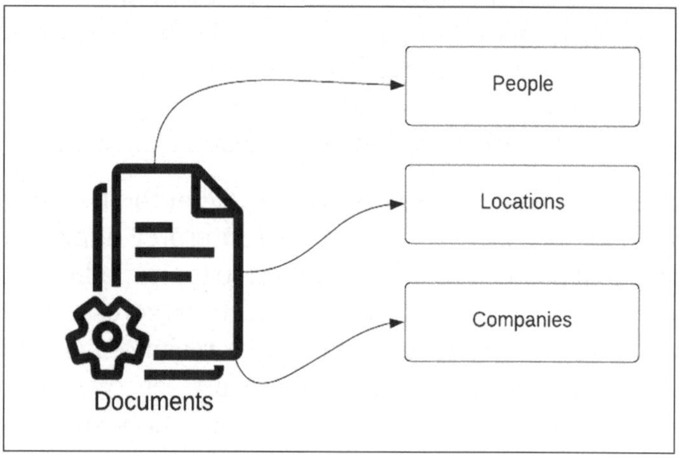

***Figure** 7.7: Sketch of Extracting Entities from a Document*

NLP also plays a crucial role in enhancing customer service. Chatbots and virtual assistants, powered by AWS's AI services, can understand and respond to customer inquiries in natural language. This technology not only improves the efficiency and availability of customer support but also provides a more engaging and personalized experience for the customer. The ability to analyze and respond to customer queries in real time helps businesses build stronger relationships with their customers, fostering loyalty and trust.

In conclusion, NLP and text analytics on AWS offer a powerful toolset for businesses looking to extract value from unstructured textual data. From sentiment analysis and text extraction to enhancing customer service, these technologies are reshaping how businesses interact with their data and customers. AWS democratizes access to these advanced capabilities, enabling businesses of all sizes to leverage the power of NLP without requiring extensive technical know-how, thus unlocking new opportunities for growth and innovation.

Introducing Amazon Comprehend

Amazon Comprehend is a robust NLP service provided by AWS that helps uncover valuable insights from textual data. This service leverages machine learning to analyze and interpret text, allowing users to perform complex NLP tasks without requiring extensive machine learning expertise. Amazon Comprehend provides a user-friendly platform, making it accessible for businesses and developers to integrate advanced text analytics into their applications and workflows.

The service offers a range of features that cater to various NLP needs. Key functionalities include sentiment analysis, entity recognition, key phrase extraction, language detection, and syntax analysis. Sentiment analysis allows businesses to understand the emotional tone behind text data, an invaluable tool for gauging customer feedback and market trends. Entity recognition identifies specific items in text such as locations, people, brands, or dates, providing deeper insights into the content. Key phrase extraction highlights important terms and concepts, offering a quick overview of the main points in large volumes of text. Language detection is useful for global businesses dealing with multilingual data, while syntax analysis helps in understanding the grammatical structure and composition of sentences.

Amazon Comprehend's integration with other AWS services enhances its capabilities. For instance, it can work seamlessly with Amazon S3 for storing and retrieving text data or with AWS Lambda for triggering analysis based on specific events. This level of integration ensures that Amazon Comprehend can easily fit into existing AWS-based architectures, providing a cohesive and efficient environment for text analysis.

In summary, Amazon Comprehend stands as a powerful and versatile tool in the realm of NLP. Its ability to deliver complex text analytics through a simple and intuitive interface makes it an excellent choice for businesses seeking to leverage data for strategic insights. Whether it's understanding customer sentiments, extracting relevant information from documents, or analyzing social media content, Amazon Comprehend offers the tools necessary to transform unstructured text data into actionable knowledge, enhancing decision-making and business strategies.

Analyzing Textual Data Using Comprehend

Let's review a practical example of taking a large block of text and extracting entities from it. While a production-ready model would require more setup, we can use the AWS Console to do some quick ad-hoc analysis using a block of text:

1. Log in to the AWS Console and navigate to Amazon Comprehend.
2. On the left sidebar, click Real-time analysis.
3. For the Input data section, keep the default selection of Built-in for the Analysis type. We will use this default and the default text to see how Comprehend works. The Custom analysis type allows you to train more advanced models of NLP detection and is a more advanced use case:

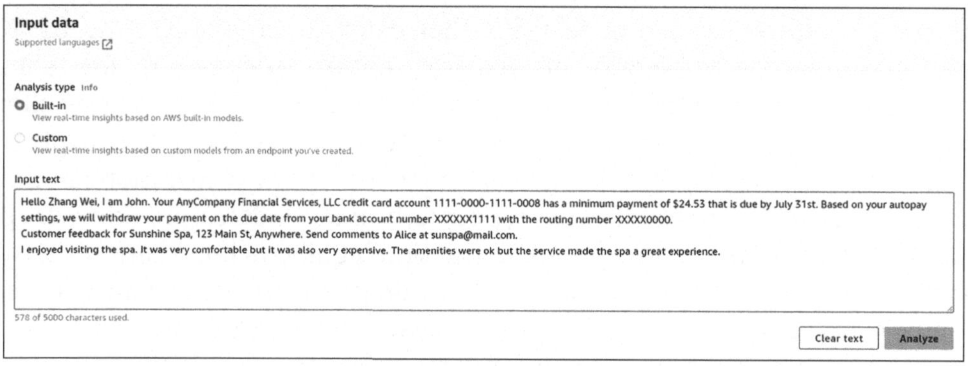

Figure 7.8: *Extracting Entities from the Amazon Comprehend Console*

4. Click **`Analyze`**, and you should see the following results of entities being extracted from the sample text. Note that Comprehend assigns the entities both a type and a confidence score indicating how confident the model feels about the entity type classification:

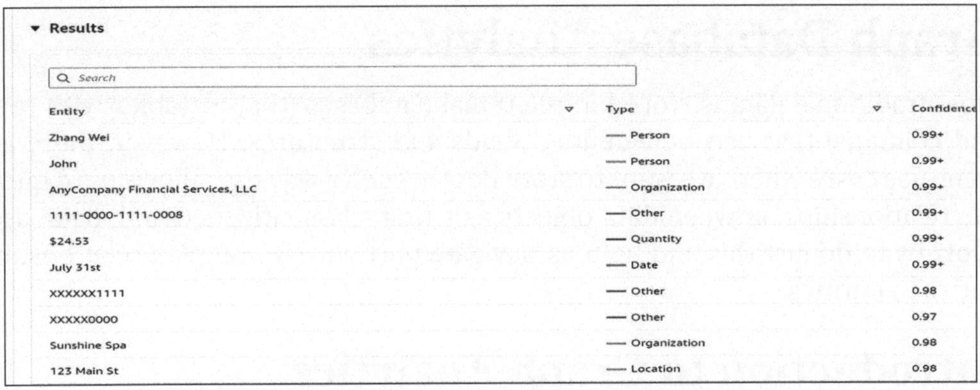

***Figure 7.9**: Entities Extracted From Sample Text*

In addition, note that the built-in model can also identify sentiment, key phrases, and even **Personally Identifiable Information** (**PII**), which can help assist you in compliance monitoring:

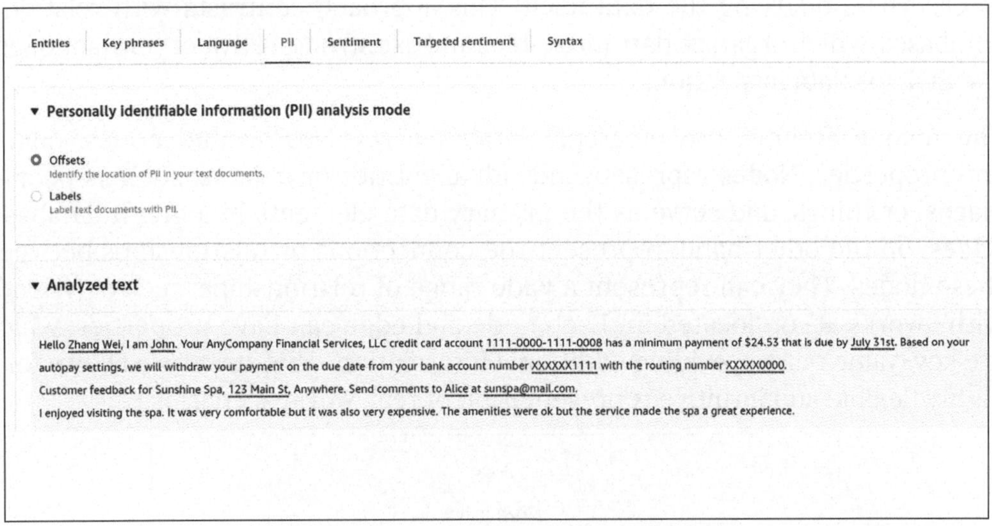

***Figure 7.10**: Additional Features of Comprehend*

Amazon Comprehend is a powerful tool, and experimenting with different features and types of analyses can help you better understand its capabilities to meet your use case.

Graph Database Analytics

Most traditional data is stored in relational databases (that is, tables with rows and columns) that use well-defined fields and structures. However, there are some use cases where we want to store data in such a way that allows us to query the relationships between data objects as a first-class citizen. Graph databases allow us to do just this and help us navigate particularly complex relationships between entities.

Introduction to Graph Analytics

Graph databases represent a fascinating and distinct approach to managing data, fundamentally different from traditional relational databases. At their core, graph databases focus on the **relationships** between data points, making them particularly well-suited for complex scenarios where querying relationships is as crucial as querying the data itself. This approach contrasts with relational databases, which organize data into tables and use structured querying languages like SQL for data inspection.

The unique architecture of graph databases revolves around nodes, edges, and properties. **Nodes** represent individual entities or objects, such as people, places, or things, and serve as the primary data elements in a graph database. **Edges**, on the other hand, represent the connections or relationships between these nodes. They can represent a wide range of relationships, such as 'friends with', 'works at', or 'located in'. Each node and edge can have properties, which are key-value pairs providing additional information. This structure allows for a highly flexible and intuitive representation of real-world scenarios:

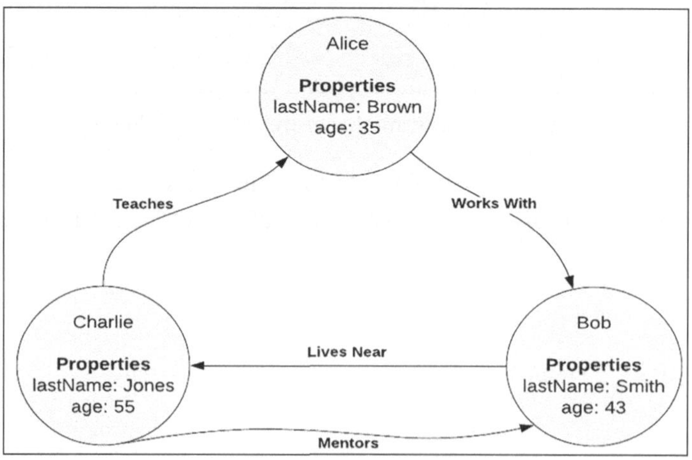

***Figure 7.11**: Simple Graph Database with Labeled Nodes and Edges*

One of the key strengths of graph databases is their ability to efficiently manage complex and interconnected data. In a relational database, complex joins and queries can become cumbersome and slow as the number and depth of relationships increase. Graph databases excel in this aspect, as they are designed to navigate and manage these relationships efficiently. This efficiency is particularly evident in use cases like social networks, recommendation systems, and fraud detection, where understanding the depth and nature of relationships is crucial.

Another significant advantage of graph databases is their **schema-less** nature. Unlike relational databases that require a predefined schema, graph databases allow for more flexibility in terms of data modeling. You can easily add new types of relationships, nodes, and properties without the need for extensive database redesign. This flexibility makes graph databases particularly appealing in scenarios where data structures are evolving or not fully known at the outset.

In summary, graph databases offer a powerful alternative to traditional relational databases, especially in scenarios involving complex, interrelated data. Their focus on relationships, efficient handling of interconnected data, and schema flexibility make them a valuable tool in the modern data landscape. Understanding the basics of graph databases opens up new possibilities for data management and analysis, particularly in fields where relationships and connections are key.

Business Applications

Graph databases offer a wide range of business applications across various industries. One of the most prominent applications is in the field of social network analysis. Social media platforms use graph databases to visualize the connections between users, enabling features such as friend suggestions, content recommendations, and community discovery. By analyzing the complex web of social interactions, businesses can tailor their marketing strategies, enhance user engagement, and identify influential network members.

Graph databases also play a pivotal role in managing recommendation systems. Retailers, streaming services, and content providers leverage them to understand customer preferences and behaviors. By analyzing the relationships between customers and products or content, these systems can make personalized recommendations. This capability not only improves customer satisfaction but also drives sales and content consumption. For instance, an e-commerce platform might use a graph database to recommend products based on a customer's browsing history, purchase history, and the behavior of similar customers.

Graph databases are also invaluable in fraud detection and cybersecurity. Financial institutions and online services utilize them to uncover patterns indicative of fraudulent activities. By analyzing the connections between accounts, transactions, and users, these systems can detect anomalies that might suggest fraudulent behavior, such as unusual transaction patterns or connections between known fraudsters and other accounts. This approach enables proactive measures to prevent fraud and enhances the security of financial transactions.

Supply chain management and logistics is another area where graph databases are increasingly applied. They help in optimizing routes, managing inventory, and analyzing supplier relationships. By mapping the entire supply chain as a graph, businesses can identify the most efficient paths for logistics, detect bottlenecks, and understand the impact of supply chain disruptions. This holistic view enables more effective decision-making and can lead to significant cost savings and efficiency improvements.

Lastly, in knowledge management and enterprise search, graph databases enable organizations to connect disparate pieces of information across the enterprise. This capability is crucial for large organizations dealing with vast amounts of unstructured data. By linking related documents, employee expertise, and project data, graph databases facilitate more efficient information retrieval and knowledge sharing. This interconnected approach to data management fosters innovation, improves productivity, and enhances decision-making processes.

Graph databases are a powerful tool for businesses dealing with complex and interconnected data. Their ability to efficiently map and analyze relationships provides actionable insights in areas such as social networking, personalized recommendations, fraud detection, supply chain optimization, and knowledge management. As data continues to grow in volume and complexity, the relevance and utility of graph databases in business contexts are likely to increase even further.

Introducing Amazon Neptune

Amazon Neptune is a fast, reliable, and fully-managed graph database service provided by AWS. It is designed to store and navigate highly connected data, making it an ideal choice for applications that require complex relationship queries. Neptune supports popular graph models such as Property Graph and W3C's **RDF (Resource Description Framework)**, along with their respective query languages, Apache TinkerPop Gremlin and SPARQL. This flexibility allows developers to choose the most suitable model and query language for their specific application needs.

One of the key strengths of Amazon Neptune is its high performance, especially when dealing with large datasets and complex queries. It is optimized for processing graph queries with high throughput and low latency. This makes Neptune an excellent choice for a variety of use cases, including knowledge graphs, fraud detection, recommendation engines, and network security. Its ability to efficiently navigate and analyze relationships in large datasets can unlock insights that would be challenging to derive using traditional relational databases.

Another notable feature of Neptune is its integration within the AWS ecosystem, offering high availability, scalability, and security. Neptune is designed to be highly available, with support for **multi-AZ (Availability Zone**) deployments, ensuring data redundancy and continuous operation even in the event of a data center failure. It can also scale automatically in response to the demands of your workload, both in terms of storage and query processing power. In terms of security, Neptune provides multiple levels of security, including network isolation using Amazon VPC, encryption at rest and in transit, and identity and access management through AWS IAM.

In addition to these core features, Neptune offers a user-friendly experience with its managed service attributes. It handles database management tasks such as hardware provisioning, software patching, setup, configuration, and backups. This management ease allows developers and database administrators to focus more on developing their applications rather than on the operational aspects of database maintenance.

Overall, Amazon Neptune offers a robust and versatile solution in the graph database domain. Its combination of performance, flexibility, and integration with the broader AWS ecosystem makes it a compelling option for businesses and developers looking to harness the power of graph databases. Whether it's exploring intricate data relationships, building interactive graph-based applications, or unlocking new insights from connected data, Neptune offers the tools and capabilities to achieve these objectives efficiently.

Analyzing Graph Data Using Neptune

We will start with a simple example by first creating our Neptune cluster and then using a Jupyter notebook to create a simple graph database and query it.

Creating a Custom VPC

To get started with Neptune, we first need to create a **Virtual Private Cloud (VPC)** with multiple subnets. This is a requirement for services like Neptune and

RDS, which require specific levels of redundancy not provided by the default VPC in your account.

To create a custom VPC, follow these steps:

1. Search for VPC from the AWS Console and click **`Create VPC`**.
2. Keep the default configuration, confirming there are at least two Availability Zones configured to allow for failover for your Neptune instance:
    a. For a full list of configuration options and instructions, refer to the **`Create a VPC`** documentation [4].

Creating a Neptune Database

1. From the AWS Console, navigate to Amazon Neptune and click **`Clusters`**.
2. Select **`Create database`**.
3. Choose an instance type and version:

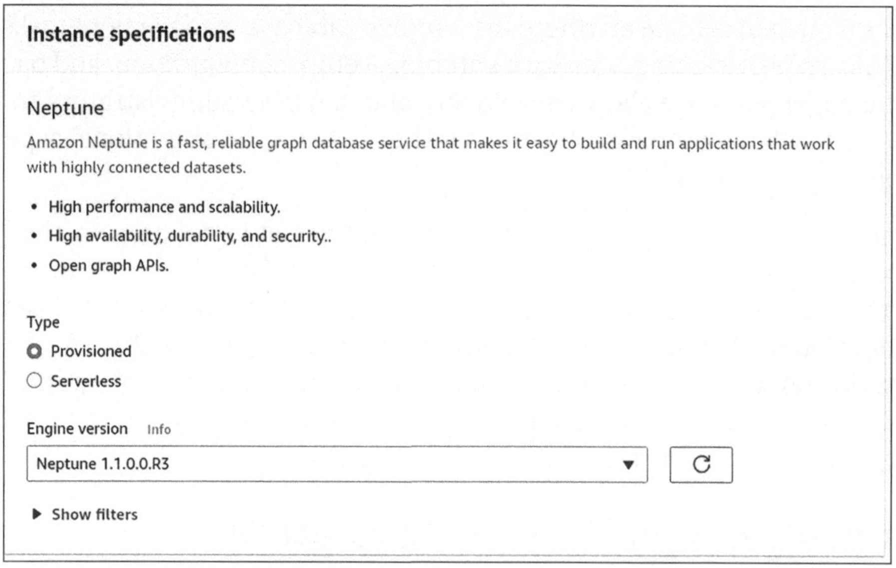

Figure 7.12: *Creating Your Neptune Cluster*

    a. Provisioned allows you to specify how much compute you need ahead of time. If your workload is variable (for example, a development instance), then choose Serverless so the instance can scale dynamically to meet your traffic needs.
    b. Use the default Engine version.

4. Choose a unique name for your Neptune database.
5. Choose the VPC that you created in the previous step.
6. Accept the default configurations for DB cluster and instance parameter groups:
    a. Customizing these parameters allows you to define things like logging configuration, authentication methods, and others.
7. Review all configurations and click **`Create database`** to launch your Neptune database.

Testing Your New Instance

To interact with your new database, the quickest way to get started is to create a notebook instance to execute Python code that can read and write data to the instance:

1. From the Neptune console, click **`Notebooks`** and click **`Create notebook`**.
2. Select your cluster and give a name to your notebook.
3. Choose an instance type for your notebook (the notebook runs on an underlying EC2 instance):

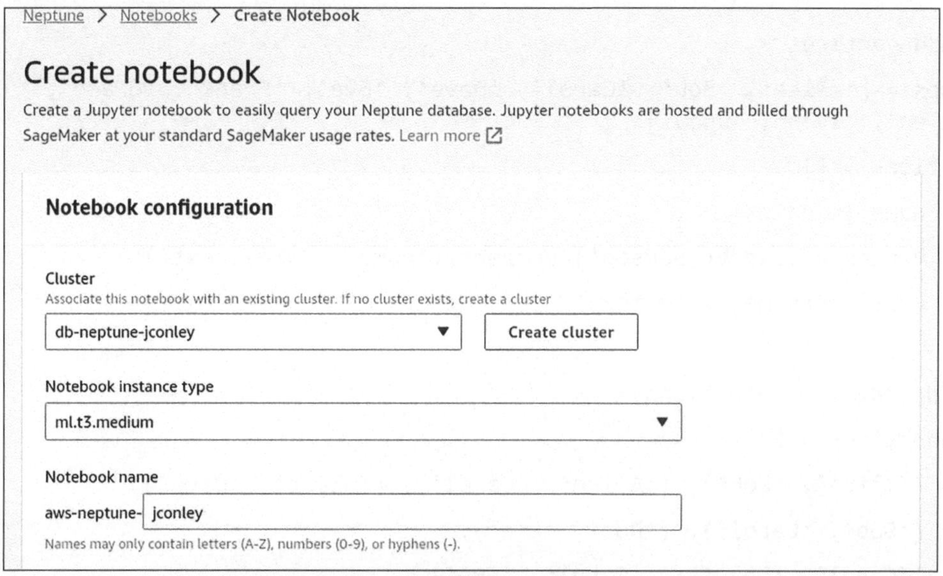

Figure 7.13: *Configuring Your Jupyter Notebook*

4. Create a new IAM role to use for these interactions.

5. Click **Create notebook** to create your notebook instance. It should take a few minutes for this process to finish.

Creating Graph Data

Using your new notebook instance, run the following code to initialize the graph database with initial data, representing a set of people and connections of who knows whom.

Here is the Python code in Jupyter to create sample graph data:

```
from gremlin_python import statics
from gremlin_python.structure.graph import Graph
from gremlin_python.driver.driver_remote_connection import Driver
RemoteConnection

# Connect to Neptune
graph = Graph()
remoteConn = DriverRemoteConnection('wss://your-neptune-endpoint:8182/
gremlin', 'g')
g = graph.traversal().withRemote(remoteConn)

# Add vertices
names = ['Alice', 'Bob', 'Carol', 'Dave', 'Eve', 'Frank', 'Grace',
'Helen', 'Ivan', 'Judy']
vertices = {}
for name in names:
    vertex = g.addV('person').property('name', name).next()
    vertices[name] = vertex

# Add edges (connections)
connections = [
    ('Alice', 'Bob'), ('Alice', 'Carol'), ('Alice', 'Dave'),
    ('Bob', 'Carol'), ('Bob', 'Eve'),
    ('Carol', 'Dave'), ('Carol', 'Eve'),
    ('Dave', 'Eve'),
    # less connected individuals
```

```
    ('Frank', 'Grace'), ('Helen', 'Ivan')
]


for (from_name, to_name) in connections:
    g.V(vertices[from_name]).addE('knows').to(g.V(vertices[to_name])).
next()


# Close the connection
remoteConn.close()
```

Querying Your Data

Now that your database has some basic graph data, you can use the following queries to figure out, for example, who is the most and least connected of the group of people.

Here are the sample queries:

```
# Well-Connected Nodes: Use Gremlin queries to find nodes with a high
number of outgoing or incoming edges.
# This query orders the 'person' nodes by the count of their edges, in
decreasing order, and limits the result to the top 3.
g.V().hasLabel('person').order().by(__.bothE().count(), decr).limit(3).
valueMap()

#Not Well-Connected Nodes: Find nodes with few or no connections.
# This query is similar to the above but orders by increasing edge
count, identifying the least connected nodes.
g.V().hasLabel('person').order().by(__.bothE().count(), incr).limit(3).
valueMap()
```

That's it! While setting up a graph database can be a bit more involved than standard SQL datasets, it does afford the unique advantage of being able to query the connectedness of data.

IoT Analytics

Processing Internet of Things (IoT) data involves a series of steps that transform raw data from IoT devices into actionable insights. IoT devices, ranging from simple sensors to complex machines, generate a massive amount of data.

This data can be temperature readings, location information, or even complex multimedia:

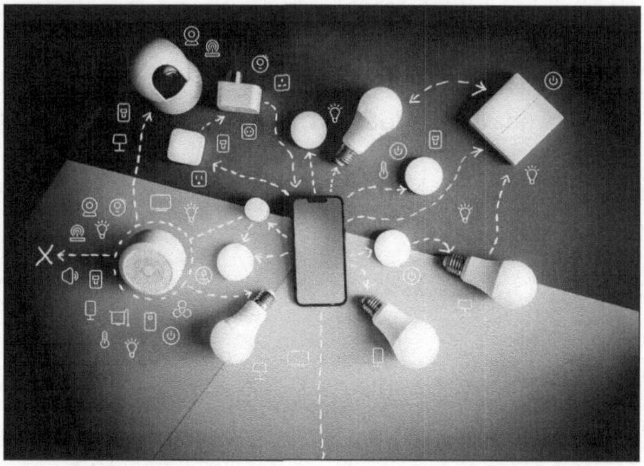

***Figure 7.14**: Example of IoT Devices Reporting Sensor Data*

The first step in processing this data is collection and ingestion. Once the data is collected, it's stored in a cloud-based repository (like Amazon S3). Storing this data effectively is crucial for efficient processing and analysis. It's important to choose the right storage solution based on the data type and the intended use.

The next step is data processing and analysis. This is where the raw data is transformed into meaningful information. Tools like Lambda can filter, sort, and aggregate the IoT data, preparing it for detailed analysis.

Finally, the processed data is presented in a user-friendly format. This involves using services like Amazon QuickSight, which provides visualization tools to create interactive dashboards. These dashboards make it easier to understand and interpret the processed data, enabling businesses to make informed decisions. Visualization is particularly important for non-technical users, as it translates complex data into easily digestible formats.

In summary, processing IoT data encompasses data collection, storage, processing, and visualization. Each step is facilitated by a range of AWS services designed to handle the scale and complexity of IoT data. This ecosystem allows even those with limited technical expertise to harness the power of IoT data, unlocking insights that drive smarter business decisions.

Business Applications

Analyzing IoT data opens a multitude of opportunities for businesses across various sectors. One of the primary applications is in predictive maintenance.

In industries such as manufacturing, IoT sensors placed on machinery can continuously monitor their status, predicting failures before they occur. By analyzing data like temperature, vibration, and sound, businesses can preemptively perform maintenance, thus reducing downtime and saving costs. This not only extends the life of the equipment but also ensures operational efficiency.

In the realm of customer experience, IoT data analysis plays a pivotal role in personalization. Retail businesses, for example, can use IoT devices like beacons to track customer behavior within stores. By analyzing this data, businesses can understand customer preferences and shopping patterns, enabling them to tailor marketing strategies and improve the customer experience. This level of personalization not only boosts sales but also enhances customer loyalty.

IoT data analysis is also transforming supply chain management. Sensors on shipping containers and vehicles provide real-time location and condition data, allowing businesses to track shipments more accurately. This data enables companies to optimize routes, predict delays, and manage inventory more efficiently. By analyzing historical data, businesses can identify trends and bottlenecks, leading to more informed decision-making and streamlined operations.

Energy management is another area where IoT data analysis is making a significant impact. Smart meters and sensors enable businesses to monitor energy usage patterns. Analyzing this data helps in identifying areas where energy consumption can be reduced, leading to significant cost savings and sustainability benefits. In sectors like real estate, this translates to smarter building management, where heating, lighting, and air conditioning are optimized for both comfort and efficiency.

Lastly, IoT data analysis plays a crucial role in enhancing safety and compliance. In sectors like construction or mining, sensors can monitor environmental conditions, alerting managers to potential safety hazards. Compliance with regulations can also be ensured by analyzing data to monitor adherence to environmental, health, and safety standards.

In summary, analyzing IoT data enables businesses to optimize operations, enhance customer experiences, manage supply chains efficiently, reduce energy costs, and ensure safety and compliance. These applications not only drive cost savings but also open new avenues for innovation and strategic growth in a data-driven business landscape.

Introducing AWS IoT Analytics

AWS IoT Analytics is a fully-managed service provided by AWS designed to simplify the analysis of data from IoT devices. This service is particularly tailored for businesses that accumulate large amounts of data from various IoT sources, such as sensors and devices, and seek to extract meaningful insights from this complex dataset. AWS IoT Analytics provides an integrated platform that handles the complexities of IoT data, such as its volume, variety, and velocity, enabling businesses to focus more on analysis and less on the underlying infrastructure.

One of the primary strengths of AWS IoT Analytics is its ability to process and enrich raw data. This service automatically filters, transforms, and enriches IoT data before storing it, making the data more accessible and meaningful for analysis. This preprocessing step is crucial for businesses as it helps in cleansing the data from inconsistencies and noise, which are common in raw IoT data. For instance, it can filter out irrelevant data points or convert raw sensor readings into usable formats. This significantly reduces the time and effort required for data preparation, a traditionally labor-intensive process.

Moreover, AWS IoT Analytics is equipped with robust analytical tools that allow businesses to run sophisticated analytics and queries on their data. Users can leverage SQL queries to easily perform ad-hoc analysis or use the service's integration with machine learning tools like Amazon SageMaker for more advanced analytics. This flexibility enables business users, regardless of their technical expertise, to derive actionable insights from their IoT data. For instance, a business could use the service to predict equipment failures, optimize operational processes, or understand customer usage patterns.

Finally, AWS IoT Analytics seamlessly integrates with other AWS services, such as AWS IoT Core for data ingestion and Amazon QuickSight for data visualization. This integration allows businesses to create a comprehensive IoT data pipeline, from data collection to visualization, under one roof. Users can build interactive dashboards in QuickSight to visualize their IoT data, making it easier to share insights across the organization. This end-to-end integration simplifies the architecture for IoT data analytics and accelerates the time to insight, making it an invaluable tool for businesses looking to leverage the power of IoT data.

Analyzing IoT Data Using AWS IoT Analytics

To get started, you should have an IoT-compatible device (for example, a smart thermostat) that has Internet access. However, you can also follow the instructions provided in [5] to create a virtual IoT device that simulates a smart thermostat:

1. **Create a Channel**: This channel will be used to collect data from your IoT devices.
    a. Upload your sample dataset here, or configure it to receive data from an IoT device.
2. **Create a Datastore**: Datastores are used to store your IoT data. Create a new datastore and link it to your channel.
3. **Create a Pipeline**: Pipelines allow you to process data. Create a pipeline that connects to your channel.
    a. Add activities to your pipeline, such as filtering or transforming data. For our example, you might add a filter to remove any records where the temperature is outside a reasonable range.
4. **Create a Dataset**: Datasets are used to retrieve and analyze your data. Create a new dataset that queries data from your datastore.
5. **Use SQL queries to select the data you want to analyze**. For example, `SELECT temperature, humidity FROM your_datastore WHERE timestamp > some_date`.

We now have a simple and scalable pipeline for real-time analysis of sensor data.

Conclusion

This chapter demonstrated the versatility of AWS's analytics capabilities in handling time series, text, graph, and IoT data. Through practical examples using Amazon Forecast, Comprehend, Neptune, and IoT Analytics, we saw how these specialized services can transform raw data into meaningful insights tailored to different business needs. The key takeaway is that AWS provides a vast array of analytics tools suited for diverse data types and use cases. Companies can pick and choose the appropriate services that align with their objectives and data landscape, rather than needing to build customized solutions from scratch.

In the next chapter, we will explore data visualization using Amazon QuickSight - a vital capability that makes data insights consumable and actionable across organizations. QuickSight complements the analytics services covered here by providing interactive dashboards and graphics that bring data stories to life in an intuitive, user-friendly fashion.

Points to Remember

- Amazon Forecast enables accurate time series forecasting and prediction without requiring machine learning expertise.
- Amazon Comprehend simplifies deriving insights from text using natural language processing for tasks like sentiment analysis and entity recognition.
- Graph databases like Amazon Neptune allow efficient modeling and querying complex real-world relationships between data.
- AWS IoT Analytics provides an end-to-end platform for collecting, processing, analyzing, and visualizing IoT device data at scale.
- AWS offers a diverse range of analytics services tailored to specific data types and use cases, eliminating the need for custom analytics infrastructure.

References

1. "S&P 500 stock data", https://www.kaggle.com/datasets/camnugent/sandp500
2. "all_stocks_5yr_forecast.csv", https://github.com/josephpconley/data-analytics-for-aws/blob/main/ch7/all_stocks_5yr_forecast.csv
3. "Evaluating Predictor Accuracy", https://docs.aws.amazon.com/forecast/latest/dg/metrics.html#metrics-wQL
4. "Create a VPC", https://docs.aws.amazon.com/vpc/latest/userguide/create-vpc.html
5. "Smart Thermostat", https://aws-iot-kit-docs.m5stack.com/en/smart-thermostat/

CHAPTER 8

Data Visualization and Interaction on AWS

Introduction

Visualizing data is the key to unlocking actionable insights. However, many find creating compelling visuals daunting. Have no fear - with the right tools, anyone can transform boring tables of numbers into vivid stories that inform decisions and drive growth. This chapter will guide you through the foundations of data visualization on AWS in a simple, step-by-step manner. We will explore services like QuickSight that make it easy for beginners to build stunning interactive reports fueled by real-time data. You will learn visualization best practices along the way - from choosing the right charts to fine-tuning colors and layouts that bring clarity to your data. You will gain the skills to create visualizations that not only look slick but also work, highlighting patterns, surfacing outliers, and giving you the power to impress stakeholders with data-driven insights using intuitive tools that do the heavy lifting for you. The future of business is data-rich, and mastering visual data exploration will be a crucial skill for you to learn.

Structure

In this chapter, we will cover the following topics:

- Basic Data Visualization Concepts
- Introducing Amazon QuickSight
- Building Visualizations on QuickSight
- Customizing Datasets
- Working with Dashboards in QuickSight
- Going Deeper with ML Insights
- Best Practices for Using QuickSight
- Advanced Visualizations with Grafana

Basic Data Visualization Concepts

Data visualization is the art and science of converting data into graphical form, making complex information more understandable and actionable. At its core, it's about storytelling, using visual elements like charts, graphs, and maps to reveal patterns, trends, and insights that might be missed in raw data. This chapter will guide you through the foundational concepts, helping you transform numbers and statistics into compelling visual narratives.

"We tell ourselves stories in order to live."

– Joan Didion

Understanding various chart types is crucial for effective data visualization. Bar charts are ideal for comparing discrete categories, while line charts excel in showing trends over time. Pie charts depict parts of a whole, and scatter plots are perfect for observing relationships between two variables. Each chart serves a distinct purpose, and selecting the right one depends on the story you want to tell and the data you are working with. We will explore these and other chart types, explaining the reasoning behind each visual display choice for your data:

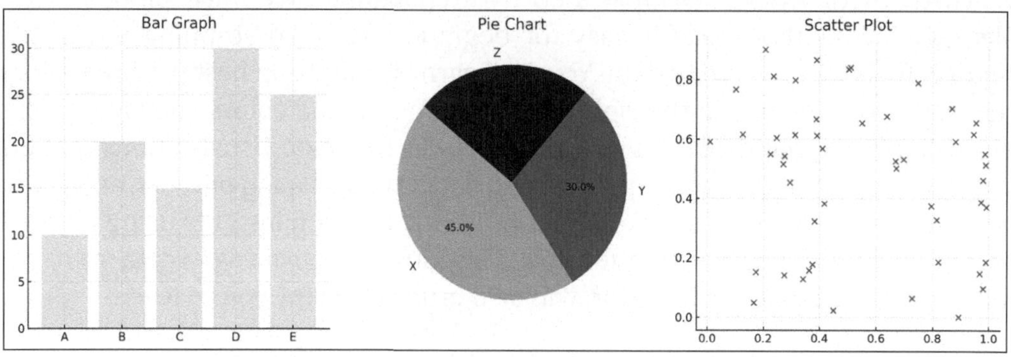

Figure 8.1: *Simple Examples of Bar Graph, Pie Chart, and Scatter Plot*

Color is a powerful tool in data visualization, which is used to differentiate data points, indicate categories, and direct the viewer's attention. However, it's not just about making graphs look attractive; color choices can significantly affect the readability and interpretation of data. We will delve into color theory, discussing how to use color effectively to enhance understanding and avoid common pitfalls, such as using colors that are hard to distinguish or that carry unintended cultural connotations.

The scale and axis on a graph might seem like minor details, but they are pivotal in accurately representing data. Scales can be linear or logarithmic, each with its own use depending on the nature of the data. Axes provide a reference frame for the viewer, helping them understand the size and direction of trends. Misrepresenting scales or axes can lead to misinterpretation of the data, so we will cover how to choose and implement them correctly.

Good design is about more than just aesthetics; it's about clarity and efficiency in communication. This involves choosing the right chart type, using color effectively, and eliminating unnecessary clutter. It also means adhering to best practices like labeling axes clearly, providing context with titles and legends, and ensuring that the visualization is accessible to all viewers, including those with color vision deficiencies.

In the digital age, static charts aren't the only option. Interactive visualizations allow users to explore data on their own, drilling down into details or zooming out for an overview. They can offer capabilities for creating dynamic visualizations where viewers can filter, sort, and manipulate data in real time. We will discuss the benefits and considerations of interactive visualizations and introduce you to the tools that can help you create them.

Ultimately, the goal of data visualization is to tell a story. Whether it's the story of a business's growth, the impact of a new policy, or trends in consumer behavior, the best visualizations convey a clear narrative. We will cover how to construct a narrative arc in your visualizations, choosing the right visuals to support your story, and tips for presenting your data in a way that engages and informs your audience.

Introducing Amazon QuickSight

Amazon QuickSight is a cloud-based service that seamlessly integrates with AWS services to provide advanced analytics and interactive data visualization capabilities. Its primary aim is to enable users to build and share rich visualizations and dashboards, drawing insights from various data sources with minimal technical know-how.

QuickSight operates on a serverless architecture, which means it requires no setup or management of infrastructure. This aspect is particularly beneficial for those looking to dive into data analytics without worrying about the underlying hardware or software. You simply log in, connect to a data source, and start creating visualizations. This ease of use doesn't compromise on power or scalability; QuickSight can handle everything from small datasets to large-scale enterprise analytics.

One of the key features of QuickSight is its "**SPICE**" engine – Super-fast, Parallel, In-memory Calculation Engine. SPICE underpins QuickSight's ability to perform advanced calculations and render visualizations quickly. It allows users to perform complex analyses and refresh datasets automatically, ensuring that dashboards and reports always reflect the most up-to-date information. This is crucial for making informed decisions in a fast-paced business environment.

QuickSight provides a wide array of visualization options – from bar and line charts to more advanced types like scatter plots and heat maps. Each visualization can be customized and tweaked to suit specific needs, allowing users to tell the most compelling story with their data. Furthermore, it offers machine learning-powered insights, which automatically uncover hidden trends and outliers, making it easier for users to identify significant patterns and relationships in their data.

Collaboration is another cornerstone of QuickSight. Users can easily share their dashboards and reports with others, facilitating a collaborative environment where insights and decisions are driven by shared data. This feature is especially useful for teams that need to work together on data-driven projects, as it allows for seamless sharing and communication of insights.

Recently, Amazon introduced **QuickSight Q**, which lets users simply type in questions about their data in plain English and receive visualizations and answers in real-time. This intuitive interface eliminates the steep learning curve typically associated with data analytics, making it accessible to recent graduates and business professionals alike. Whether you are looking to understand customer behavior trends, sales performance, or operational efficiencies, QuickSight Q acts as your personal data analyst, ready to uncover valuable insights with just a simple question.

By leveraging QuickSight, users can transform raw data into actionable insights, driving better business outcomes and fostering a culture of data-driven decision-making. Whether you are looking to create stunning visualizations, uncover hidden trends, or collaborate with team members, QuickSight provides the tools and capabilities to take your data analytics to the next level.

Core Concepts of QuickSight

Here is a review of the most basic concepts you will need to understand to get started with QuickSight:

- **Datasets** are the foundation of any analysis in QuickSight. They represent your source data and can be created from a variety of sources such as files (Excel, CSV), databases (SQL, PostgreSQL), or even big data (Redshift, S3). When you create a dataset in QuickSight, you have the option of importing your data into SPICE to allow for quicker analysis and the ability to refresh data periodically. Importing data is a straightforward process: select your source, define the data schema, and QuickSight does the rest, pulling in your data and preparing it for use in analyses.

- Once you have a dataset, you can create an **analysis**. An analysis is where you actually interact with your data, creating visualizations to uncover insights. QuickSight provides a variety of visualization types - from simple bar and line charts to more complex heat maps and scatter plots. The process is intuitive: drag and drop fields onto the visual canvas, and QuickSight generates the visualization. You can then customize and explore your data, adding filters, aggregations, and calculations as needed. The key to effective analysis in QuickSight is experimentation, trying different visualizations and configurations until you find the most compelling way to present your data.
- **Dashboards** are collections of visualizations that provide an at-a-glance view of your data and insights. In QuickSight, once you have created an analysis you are happy with, you can publish it as a dashboard. Dashboards are interactive, allowing end-users to drill down into the data, apply filters, and explore on their own. They are also shareable, making them a powerful tool for distributing insights across your team or organization. When creating a dashboard, consider your audience and the story you want to tell with your data - this will guide the selection and configuration of your visualizations.
- **Topics** refer to the main subjects or areas of interest within your data. Identifying topics helps to focus your analysis and dashboards on the areas most relevant to your audience. Topics could be anything from sales performance and customer behavior to inventory levels and operational efficiency. Once you have identified your topics, you can create tailored analyses and dashboards that provide insights into these specific areas, making your data exploration more targeted and effective.

Building Visualizations on QuickSight

Let's get started by creating basic data visualizations in QuickSight using a simple dataset. We will use a public dataset detailing the electric cars registered in the state of Washington [1]. Download the CSV associated with this dataset.

First, let's create an account for the QuickSight service, which will incur an additional monthly charge as QuickSight does not have a free tier at the time of this writing [2]. Do not sign up for the QuickSight Q service yet (that can be added later):

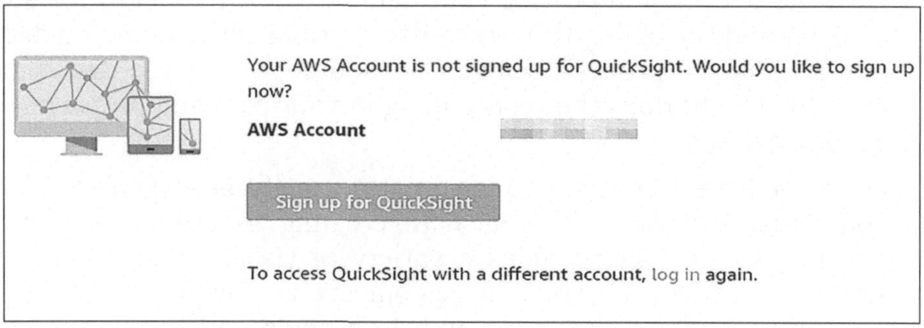

***Figure 8.2**: Sign-Up Process for Amazon QuickSight*

Follow the prompts to create your QuickSight account and configure authentication and access to the service.

Next, let's upload our CSV dataset for visualization:

1. Navigate to **`Datasets`** and click **`New dataset`**.
2. From the **`Create a Dataset`** screen, click **`Upload a file`** and choose the CSV file we downloaded. You should now see a preview of the file upload:

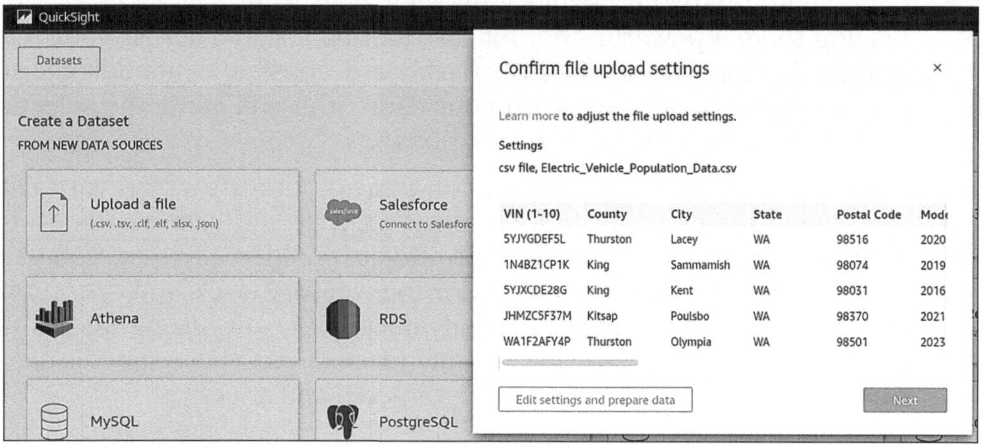

***Figure 8.3**: Upload a Custom CSV File to QuickSight Datasets*

   a. We could also upload this data in a variety of other data sources (for example, S3), but to keep our example simple, we will upload the data directly.

3. By default, your uploaded data should be uploaded to SPICE. As we discussed, SPICE allows for fast, optimized retrieval of data, and should

be used if there are no real-time requirements for data access. Note that there is a limit to how much SPICE capacity can be used on your account (typically around ~10GB).

4. Click **Visualize** to start building your first visualization:

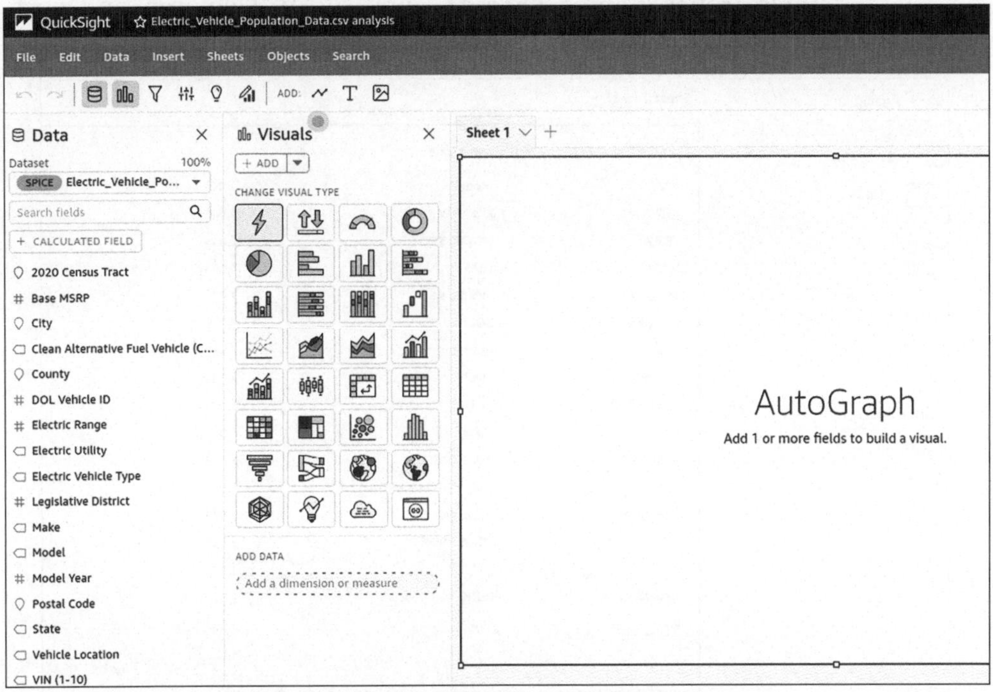

Figure 8.4: *Add a New Visual Analysis from a Dataset*

5. QuickSight will create a default analysis for you to start building a visualization.

Note that similar to spreadsheets, QuickSight uses the **sheet** terminology, so you can think of an analysis as a collection of one or more sheets that hold blocks of visuals.

Viewing Cars by Make and Model with a Table View

Let's build a simple table showing the counts of electric vehicles by make and model:

1. Drag the **Make** and **Model** fields into the Group By box.

2. Drag the **VIN** field into the Value box. By default, it will choose the measure of **Count** to do a simple count of vehicles across the unique dimensions of Make and Model. You can click on the field you added to customize the aggregation and other aspects of the visual.
3. In the table visual (named **Sheet1**), click the **VIN** column and sort it descending so we can see the most popular electric cars:

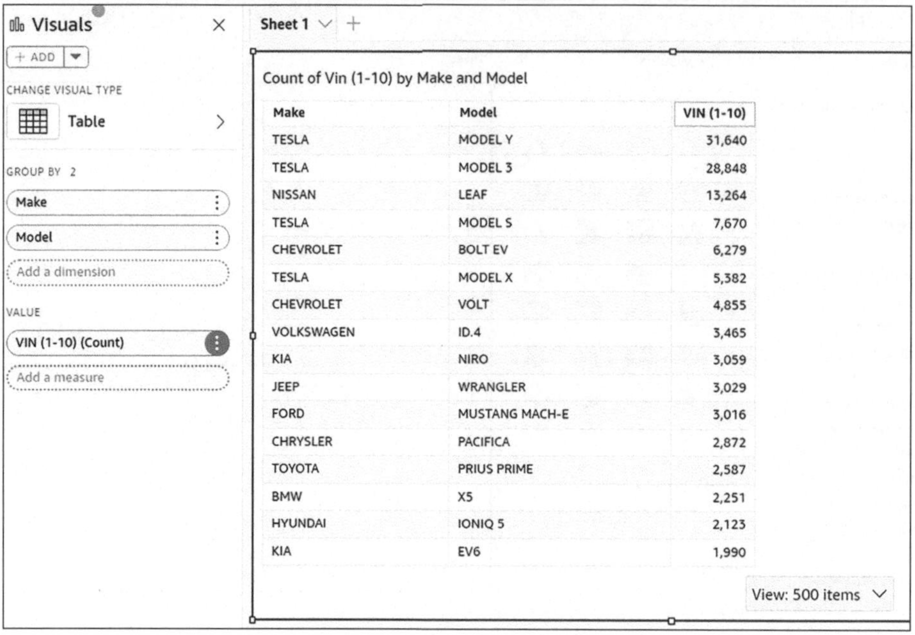

***Figure 8.5**: Simple Table View*

You can now see a simple view of the most popular electric cars by make and model in the state of Washington. Not surprisingly, Tesla occupies four of the top six places, which should match our expectations, given Tesla's market-leading status, confirming the quality of this dataset.

Seeing Car Ownership by Make: Pie Chart

Now let's look at a slightly more complex (and more visually appealing) view that can show us the composition of electric car producers in the state of Washington using a **Pie Chart**:

1. Create a new Sheet (by default, it will be called **Sheet 2**):
   a. We could also append another visual block to **Sheet 1**; however, for simplicity and rapid experimentation, it's typically easier to work on visuals in isolated sheets.

2. Click the **`Pie Chart`** visual icon.
3. Add the **`Make`** field to the **`Group By`** section.
4. Add the **`VIN`** field to the Value section (keeping the default aggregation of Count).
5. Click on the resulting chart, and use the **`Properties`** sidebar to customize the visualization:
    a. For example, you can turn the data label metric on so that the actual metric percentage shows next to each data label:

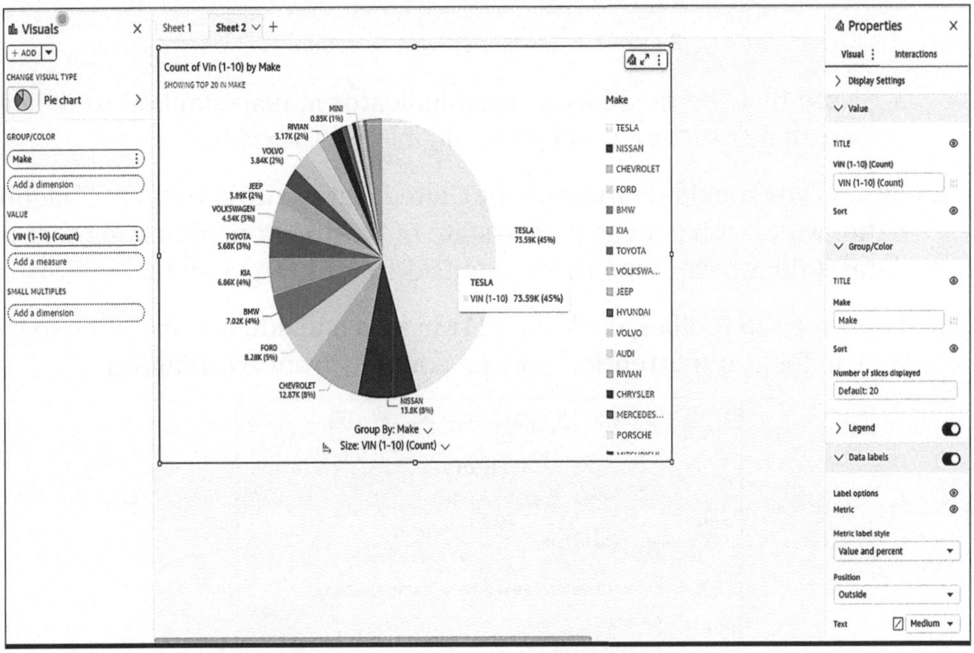

***Figure 8.6**: Simple Pie Chart of Vehicle Counts by Make*

Making Geospatial Visuals - Cars by County

Now that we have created some basic visuals, let's look at a more advanced example of using geospatial information to see electric car ownership by county:

1. Create a new sheet (**`Sheet 3`**) in the existing analysis.
2. Select the **`Filled Map`** visual, which requires that a **`Location`** dimension be added.
3. Drag the **`County`** field into the **`Location`** dimension and **`VIN`** as a measure:

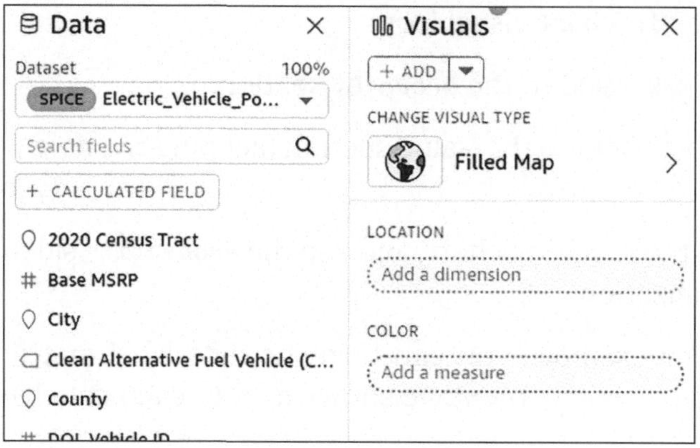

***Figure 8.7**: Geospatial Field Selection*

a. Note that the field has a visual indicator (a map symbol) to indicate which fields (**`City`**, **`County`**) are eligible for **`Location`**.

4. By now, you should see a map of the United States with counties highlighted nationwide, with a focus on the state of Washington, indicating that our dataset does have some records outside of our target state.

5. From the top toolbar, click the **`Filter`** icon and add a **`State`** filter so that we can focus our attention only on counties from Washington:

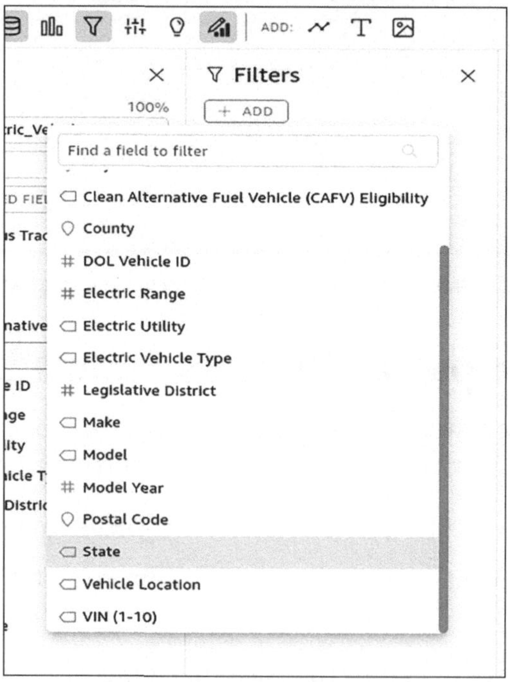

***Figure 8.8**: Visual Field Filters*

6. Once this filter is added, you should now see a focused view of just the counties in Washington State that reported electric car ownership. Zoom in to get a closer look at the counties, and use the hover functionality to get specific information on county names and counts:

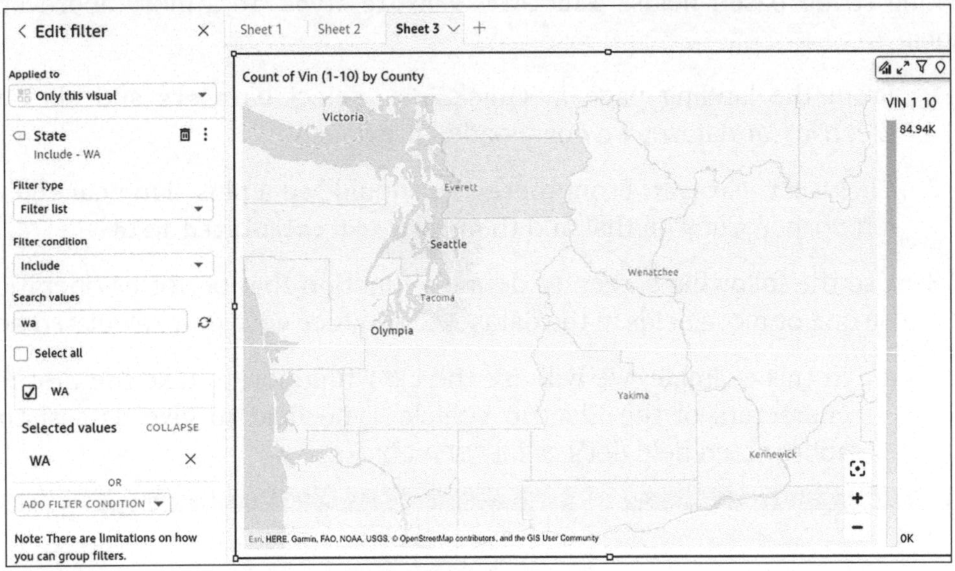

Figure 8.9: *Map Visual*

Customizing Datasets

We have been able to accomplish a lot by just importing our data as-is and using QuickSight visuals to inspect that data. Now we will review a few techniques to help us customize our data to improve the quality of our visuals.

Adding Calculated Fields

Calculated fields allow you to create new fields in your dataset using custom business logic. Similar to how you might create a new column in Excel and use a custom formula to populate that column, you can take the same approach working in QuickSight.

There are two main ways to add calculated fields to your dataset. You can define them at the level of the dataset itself (making the calculated fields available in all future analyses) or you can define calculated fields at the analysis level (restricting your customization to the scope of the analysis only). For this example, we will focus on adding a calculated field at the dataset level so that we can leverage it anywhere, but the same concept applies to the analysis level as well.

Defining a Calculated Field on a Dataset

Let's review the steps needed to create a calculated field on a dataset. We will continue with our electric car dataset, and this time we will map one of the existing string-based fields, "**`Electric Vehicle Type`**" to a more abbreviated value:

1. From the landing page in QuickSight, select **`Datasets`** and click the Electric Car dataset we downloaded previously.
2. Click **`Edit Dataset`**. From there you should see a plus sign near the top left corner. Click on that and then click **`Add calculated field`**.
3. Use the following screen to define a function that performs operations on one or more fields in the dataset to produce your new calculated field:
   a. In this example, we will use the `LEFT` function to take the first four characters of the Electric Vehicle Type field to give us a simpler abbreviated field (let's call it "`ETYPE`"):

***Figure 8.10**: Calculated Field Logic Definition*

   b. The right-side panel documents a wide range of functions covering operations such as mathematics, string, date, and conditional functions.

4. Confirm the function looks syntactically correct and save the new field. You should now see your new calculated field as part of your existing dataset.

5. Click **Save and Publish**. The `ETYPE` field can now be used just like any other field in analyses and dashboards.

Working with Dashboards in QuickSight

Now that we have finished building visuals as part of an analysis, we are ready to publish that analysis to a dashboard that is shareable with others.

From the analysis page, click the "**PUBLISH**" button in the top right corner. You will have the option to save this analysis to an existing dashboard or create a new one. Once done, you can use the controls in the top right corner to:

1. Schedule the dashboard to be sent at specific times.
2. Bookmark specific versions of the dashboard to act as a checkpoint.
3. Export the dashboard as a PDF/PNG.
4. Share the dashboard, either directly with named users or to generate embedding code to use as part of a web application.
5. Define custom alerts for dashboards with visuals that can track metrics (for example, KPI views) based on predefined thresholds.

Scheduling

Let's create a simple schedule that will automate the distribution of one of the sheets on our dashboard:

1. Click the clock icon in the upper right corner, and a right sidebar should open up.
2. Click **Add Schedule**.
3. Follow the prompts to define the content, frequency of the report, and target users of the scheduled report:

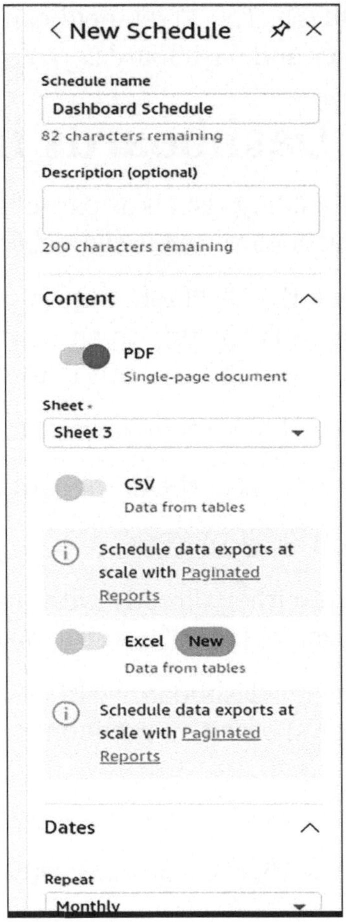

***Figure 8.11**: Custom Schedule Configuration*

4. After configuring your schedule, click **`Send Test`** to confirm the email is triggered properly.
5. Once confirmed, click **`Save`** to activate the schedule. You should now see regular emails sent to the intended recipients based on the date frequency you defined:

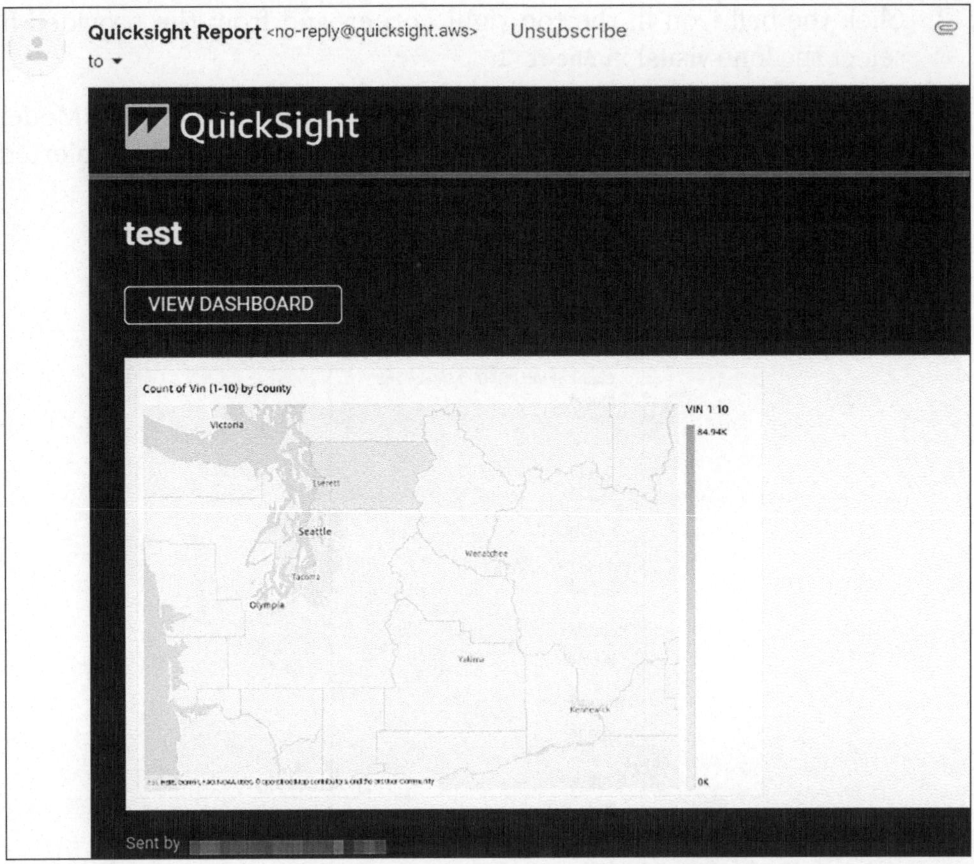

Figure 8.12: *Sample Email Report Sent from QuickSight*

The significance of this cannot be overstated! Before automations like this, software developers would have to cobble together several different frameworks to build and maintain custom code to create and email reports. Now, this capability is just a few clicks away!

Alerts

Certain visuals (Table, Pivot, KPI, and Gauge) [3] have additional capabilities wherein we can define thresholds that will trigger alerts. This is valuable if we are building operations dashboards linked to real-time data sources and need to be alerted if a certain number of servers become unhealthy.

For our example, let's add an alert to let us know if a specific electric car make/model has a drop in total ownership:

1. Click **Sheet 1**, which has a table view (one of the eligible visual types for alerts)

2. Click the bell icon in the top right corner, and from the provided list, select the lone visual in **`Sheet 1`**.

3. Select a specific cell (for example, the **`VIN`** field for the Tesla Model Y record) and configure the threshold for when you want to be alerted if this value drops:

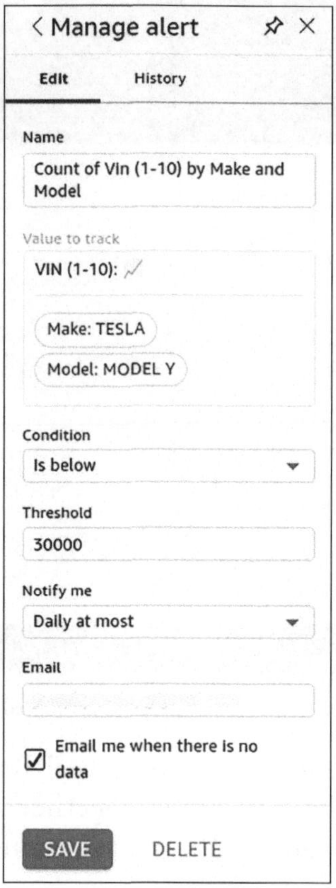

Figure 8.13: *Alert Configuration*

4. Finalize the configuration and click **`Save`**. You will now be alerted when the specified record value drops below the stated threshold.

Going Deeper with ML Insights

By now, you have likely noticed how manual the process of building visualizations can be. Fear not, for the makers of QuickSight have been continuously striving to automate as much of the insight generation process as possible. One such way is the use of **Machine Learning** (**ML**) to automatically generate insights on your data [4].

- The easiest QuickSight feature to use that leverages the benefits of machine learning is **QuickSight Q.** First, you create a **Topic** by navigating to the Topics section, selecting the dataset you want to analyze, and configuring fields (optionally renaming them or even adding calculated fields to fit your chosen topic). Once your Topic is configured, you can apply QuickSight Q to it by simply asking natural language questions related to the data fields you have included. QuickSight Q will use the structure and organization of your Topic to interpret these questions and generate insightful answers, visualizations, or analyses based on the underlying data.
- **Anomaly detection** is another ML-based feature. It employs sophisticated machine learning algorithms to identify irregularities in data that may otherwise go unnoticed. By continuously analyzing data, it alerts users to unexpected changes in patterns or behaviors, allowing for swift, informed decision-making. This is particularly valuable for businesses monitoring key metrics, as it helps pinpoint issues or opportunities early, guiding users to focus on the most impactful areas.
- **Forecasting** also uses machine learning, enabling users to predict future trends based on historical data. By leveraging advanced algorithms and a user-friendly interface, QuickSight allows users to generate forecasts with just a few clicks. This feature is invaluable for planning and decision-making, as it provides insights into future performance, helping users anticipate changes and adjust strategies accordingly.
- Finally, **autonarratives** offer a dynamic way to understand data through natural language summaries. This feature automatically generates narratives that describe data findings, trends, and patterns, making complex analyses understandable. Autonarratives bridge the gap between data and decision-making, enabling users to grasp the story behind the numbers quickly. This not only saves time but also ensures that insights are accessible to all users, regardless of their technical background, making data-driven decisions more inclusive and effective.

Best Practices for Using QuickSight

When building visuals in Amazon QuickSight, adhering to certain best practices can significantly enhance the clarity, impact, and usefulness of your data visualizations. These practices are not just about making charts look attractive; they are about making them functionally effective and insightful for your audience.

Prioritize clarity and simplicity. The primary goal of any visualization is to communicate information clearly and quickly. Start by selecting the right type of chart for your data. For instance, use bar charts to compare different groups, line charts for trends over time, and pie charts for showing proportions. Ensure that your visuals are not cluttered. Too much information can overwhelm the viewer and obscure the data's story. Use labels and legends judiciously, and always title your visuals clearly to convey the main insight at a glance. Avoid overly complex visualizations that require too much explanation, as they are likely to confuse rather than inform.

Colors play a crucial role in data visualization, helping to differentiate data points and guide the viewer's eye. Use a consistent color scheme across all visuals in a dashboard to maintain cohesion. Reserve bright or contrasting colors for highlighting key information or outliers. Additionally, be mindful of color blindness; avoid color combinations that are difficult for colorblind users to distinguish. In terms of layout, place the most important visuals in the top-left corner, as that is typically where viewers look first. Organize related visuals near each other to facilitate comparison and maintain a logical flow from one visualization to the next.

Use interactive features like filters and drop-downs to let your end-users explore the data themselves. Interactive elements can transform a static visualization into a dynamic tool, enabling users to uncover their own insights. However, ensure that the controls are intuitive and the changes they make to the visuals are clear. Besides interactivity, providing context is crucial. Always include axes labels, units of measurement, and time frames. Annotations can also be invaluable for pointing out specific data points, trends, or providing additional context. A visualization without context can be misleading or meaningless.

Finally, perform iterative testing with your end-users to gauge their feedback. Different audiences might interpret visuals differently, so gathering feedback is crucial to ensure your visualizations are effective. Check if the viewers understand the visuals quickly and if they can glean the intended insights without much explanation. Use this feedback to iterate and improve your visuals. Remember, the best visualizations are those that are refined over time based on user interaction and feedback.

Advanced Visualizations with Grafana

QuickSight provides a wealth of tools to help you visualize bespoke datasets geared towards end-users and executives. However, there are more powerful visualization tools that can be even more powerful for more customized cases like operations monitoring and alerting. Enter Grafana.

Grafana is an open-source platform known for its extensive customization capabilities and flexibility [5]. It allows users to integrate with a wide range of data sources, not just those within the AWS ecosystem. Grafana is particularly favored for its advanced real-time monitoring features, making it ideal for operations teams and developers who need to keep a close eye on their systems and infrastructure. Its alerting system is robust, enabling users to quickly respond to any anomalies or issues. Grafana's detailed dashboards and rich visualization options make it a go-to choice for users who require deep technical insights and the ability to customize every aspect of their data analysis and reporting:

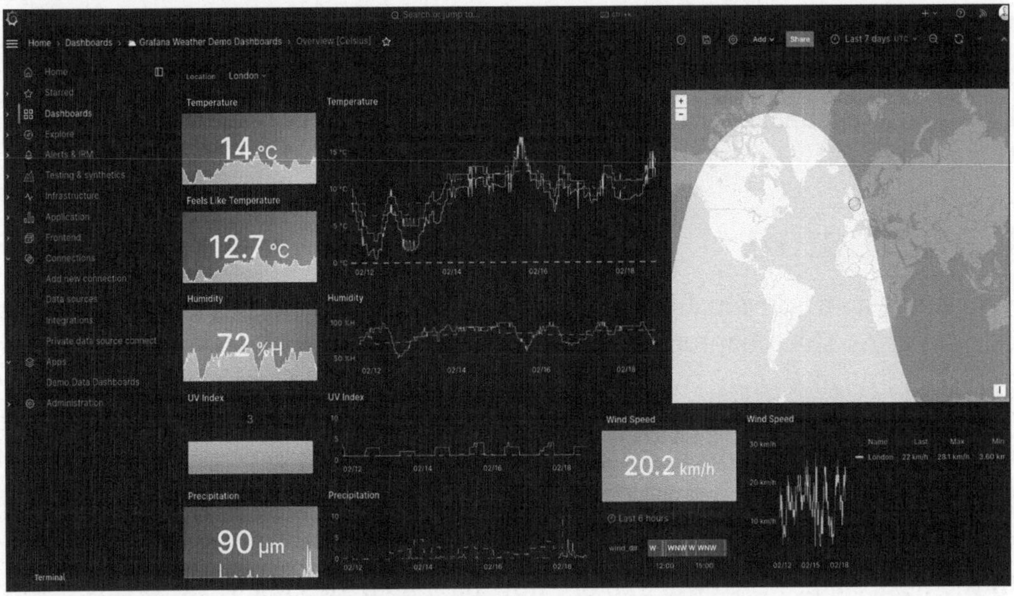

Figure 8.14: *Sample Grafana Dashboard*

Grafana's advanced visualization features are another key aspect of its value. With a wide variety of charts, graphs, and tables, users can create detailed and intricate dashboards that provide deep insights at a glance. The platform's visualization tools are highly customizable, allowing users to tailor their dashboards to meet specific monitoring and analysis needs. From setting up simple gauge panels to crafting complex time-series predictions, Grafana provides the flexibility to represent data in the most insightful way.

Moreover, Grafana excels in its alerting and notification system. The platform can continuously monitor data for any condition defined by the user and send alerts via various channels like email, Slack, or PagerDuty. This real-time awareness is crucial for maintaining system performance, ensuring uptime, and quickly reacting to potential issues before they escalate. It's a feature that adds significant value for IT teams, DevOps, and businesses relying on continuous monitoring for operational excellence.

Finally, Grafana's vibrant community and ecosystem significantly enhance its value. Being open-source, it benefits from contributions that continuously extend its capabilities, from new data source plugins to visualization types. The community also provides a wealth of resources, including pre-configured dashboards and extensive documentation, which helps new users get up to speed quickly and allows advanced users to push their analytics further. This collaborative environment ensures that Grafana isn't just a tool but a platform that evolves with the changing needs and technologies of its users.

As with other open-source frameworks like Redis or Postgres, Grafana can be launched as a managed service in AWS. Managed services like this make it easier to maintain software and facilitate integration with other AWS services as well.

Conclusion

Visualizing data is invaluable for discovering insights, telling stories, and guiding decisions. As this chapter demonstrated, with the right tools and strategic approach, anyone can transform raw datasets into compelling, interactive dashboards that bring clarity to complex information. The key is to let the data speak for itself through thoughtful visual design choices guided by best practices. Armed with services like QuickSight and Grafana, you now have the power to turn data into insights with just a few clicks.

In the next chapter, we will explore how data analytics itself is evolving - with innovative capabilities like ML and automation promising to reshape business capabilities. We will discuss the future data landscape, so you can prepare for new opportunities to harness the power of data.

Points to Remember

- Visualizations transform raw data into impactful stories and insights that guide better decisions.
- Tools like Amazon QuickSight make it easy for beginners to visualize data and build interactive dashboards.
- Choosing the right chart type (bar, line, pie, and more) is crucial for accurately representing different kinds of data.
- Following best practices around clarity, use of color, layout, interactivity, and iterative testing ensures effective visualizations.

- Advanced tools like Grafana provide greater customization and real-time monitoring capabilities for more technical users.

References

1. "Electric Vehicle Population Data", https://catalog.data.gov/dataset/electric-vehicle-population-data
2. "Amazon QuickSight Pricing", https://aws.amazon.com/quicksight/pricing/
3. "Working with threshold alerts in Amazon QuickSight", https://docs.aws.amazon.com/quicksight/latest/user/threshold-alerts.html
4. "Gaining insights with machine learning (ML) in Amazon QuickSight", https://docs.aws.amazon.com/quicksight/latest/user/making-data-driven-decisions-with-ml-in-quicksight.html
5. "Grafana", https://grafana.com

CHAPTER 9
The Future of Data Analytics

Introduction

The field of data analytics is advancing at a breathtaking pace, with new technologies and techniques emerging that promise to revolutionize how we gather, process, and glean value from data. In this chapter, we explore several innovations on the horizon that are set to shape the next generation of data analytics on AWS. We dive into trends such as generative AI, which brings unprecedented natural language capabilities; blockchain networks, enabling decentralized analytics; edge computing, supporting real-time insights; and quantum computing, unlocking orders of magnitude greater processing power. While these innovations bring vast opportunities, we also outline strategies such as continuous skill-building, community participation, and developing versatile skillsets to help you stay ahead of the curve. By the end, you will have not just knowledge of trailblazing data analytics technologies, but also perspectives and practices to keep pace with changes on the horizon. The ideas presented serve as both an inspiration for what may be possible and as a compass for navigating the exhilarating changes ahead in this fast-moving field.

Structure

In this chapter, we will cover the following topics:

- Generative AI and Amazon Bedrock
- Blockchain and Amazon Managed Blockchain
- Edge Computing and AWS IoT Greengrass
- Quantum Computing and Amazon Braket
- Sustainability and Green Data Analytics
- Keeping Up with the Pace of Innovation

Generative AI

Generative AI (GenAI), popularized by ChatGPT, has taken the world by storm. OpenAI's revolutionary product set a record by amassing over 100 million monthly active users just two months after its release [1]. One year later, it is difficult to find a popular SaaS product that does not have some form of GenAI-based "CoPilot" to answer user questions and perform basic tasks.

Large Language Models

The heart of innovation powering ChatGPT and other generative AI chatbots are **large language models (LLMs)**. LLMs are trained on massively large datasets of text (for example, the entire public text on the Internet), resulting in neural networks composed of billions of parameters. These models then respond to plaintext instructions by attempting to predict the next word of a response based on its trained data. The result is a remarkably powerful generation engine that appears to have the ability to reason and interact with users, and in most cases can produce meaningful responses to answers.

However, it's important to note that since this is a probability-based engine, there are edge cases where the LLM will make up ("hallucinate") responses that might seem factual but in essence are fabricated. This should not be entirely surprising, given that LLMs like ChatGPT are trained on Internet-facing public documents, which likely contain a significant percentage of false material and commentary.

Despite this inherent risk of inaccuracy, these tools provide powerful generation capabilities and can perform many useful tasks including summarizing large documents, performing simple coding tasks, and doing research.

Using Generative AI for Data Analytics

As of early 2024, the ability to perform extensive data analytics using LLMs is limited. Recent papers, such as "*Retrieval-Augmented Generation for Large Language Models*: A *Survey*" [2], highlight the challenge of LLMs in performing reasoning and calculations across structured datasets. While LLMs shine when analyzing unstructured data like large blocks of text, they currently fall short when tasked with generating SQL queries or performing rigorous algorithms.

However, it can prove useful for tasks related to data analytics. One possible use case is the ability to simulate scenarios. Imagine being able to forecast market trends or customer behavior with a high degree of accuracy. This capability stems from the AI's ability to learn from existing data and generate predictive models. This is not just about making predictions based on past trends; it's about understanding the underlying patterns and behaviors that drive those trends. Such insights could prove invaluable in fields ranging from finance to healthcare, enabling analysts to make more informed decisions

Figure 9.1: *Fictional Depiction of the Power of Generative AI, Generated using ChatGPT*

Another application is data augmentation. Often, analysts face the challenge of incomplete or biased datasets, which can skew results and lead to inaccurate conclusions. Generative AI can mitigate this by generating synthetic data that reflects a wider range of scenarios and possibilities. This not only enhances the quality of analysis but also helps in training machine learning models more effectively, leading to more accurate and reliable predictive analytics.

Generative AI can also help supercharge your data visualization powers. Traditional methods of visualizing data can be limited, especially when dealing with complex, multidimensional datasets. Generative AI can create more dynamic, intuitive, and interactive visualizations, making it easier for analysts to identify patterns and insights that might otherwise go unnoticed. These advanced visualizations can be particularly beneficial for those who may not have a deep technical background, allowing them to understand and engage with the data more effectively.

Generative AI is poised to democratize data analytics. With its ability to simplify complex data patterns and generate user-friendly reports and visualizations, it lowers the barrier to entry for non-technical users. This democratization means that more people can participate in data-driven decision-making, leading to more diverse perspectives and potentially more innovative solutions to business challenges.

"I for one welcome our new computer overlords."

- Ken Jennings (paraphrasing The Simpsons) after losing to IBM Watson

The best part is that the development of LLMs is accelerating at a rapid pace. As it continues to evolve, it promises to unlock exciting new use cases and abilities, making the field of data analytics more accessible, accurate, and insightful than ever before.

Generative AI with Amazon Bedrock

Amazon Bedrock offers a comprehensive solution for working with large language models. This platform stands out for its ability to simplify the complexities typically associated with managing and deploying these models. Large language models, like GPT-4, are at the forefront of AI, offering capabilities ranging from text generation to complex data analysis. However, their size and complexity demand significant computational resources and expertise. Amazon Bedrock addresses these challenges, making advanced AI accessible to a wider range of users.

One of the key features of Amazon Bedrock is its scalable infrastructure. Large language models require substantial processing power, and Bedrock's cloud-based architecture provides the necessary computational resources on demand. This scalability is crucial for handling varying workloads, from small-scale experiments to large deployments. Users can easily adjust the resources allocated to their projects, ensuring efficient use of the platform without needing deep technical knowledge of cloud computing.

Data security and privacy are paramount in the field of data analytics, and Amazon Bedrock offers robust mechanisms in this regard. The platform incorporates advanced security protocols to protect sensitive data. It allows users to work with confidential datasets while ensuring that all information remains secure and compliant with data protection regulations. Bedrock's security framework is further reinforced by continuous monitoring and regular audits, designed to detect and respond to potential threats in real-time. This security aspect is especially vital for business users who handle sensitive customer or proprietary data.

Amazon Bedrock also simplifies the integration of large language models with other AWS services. This integration capability is a significant advantage, as it allows users to seamlessly connect their language model-based applications with other cloud services such as data storage, analytics, and machine learning tools. For instance, users can easily store and retrieve vast datasets using Amazon S3, or process data using AWS Lambda, enhancing the functionality and efficiency of their projects.

Moreover, Amazon Bedrock provides a user-friendly interface that abstracts much of the technical complexity. Users can deploy, manage, and interact with large language models through intuitive graphical interfaces. This ease of use is particularly beneficial for recent graduates and business professionals with limited technical expertise. They can focus on the application of the technology in their domain, rather than the underlying technical intricacies.

In summary, Amazon Bedrock emerges as a powerful platform for users looking to leverage the capabilities of large language models. Its scalable infrastructure, robust security features, seamless integration with AWS services, and user-friendly interface make it an ideal choice for both beginners and professionals in the field of data analytics. With Amazon Bedrock, users can harness the power of advanced AI to gain insights, enhance decision-making, and innovate in their respective fields.

Simple Analytics Example with Bedrock

Let's try a simple example of using a foundation model to perform a simple analytics task:

1. From the AWS Console, search for Bedrock.
2. Before proceeding, it is necessary to request access to use one or more models. Be sure to read the **End User License Agreement** (**EULA**) for each model you request to ensure compliance with its usage:
    a. For this example, select `Titan Text G1 - Express`, as it is one of the simpler models currently available with minimal restrictions on usage. You should be granted access immediately:

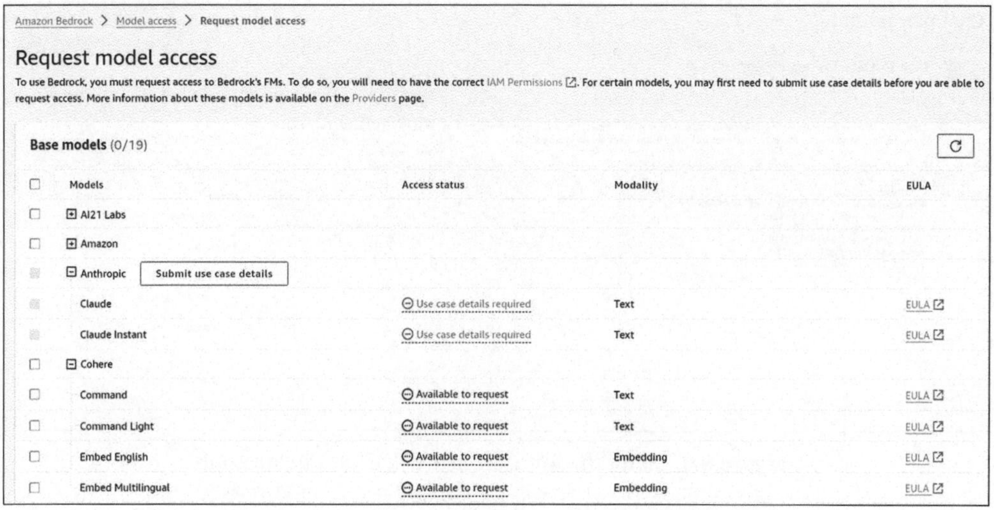

***Figure 9.2**: Requesting Model Access in Amazon Bedrock*

3. From the Bedrock sidebar, go to **Playground** > **Chat** to start testing out this model.
4. Note the **Load examples** button on the top right, which allows us to test out common scenarios with our model. Search for **synthetic data** to show examples of how to use this LLM to generate synthetic data.
5. You should now see a prompt in your chat that looks like the following. Update the example prompt to return data in CSV format instead of JSON:

```
Generate synthetic data for daily product sales in various categories - include row number, product name, category, date of sale and price. Produce output in CSV format. Count records and ensure there are no more than 5.
```

6. Run this prompt to see some example data generated for you:

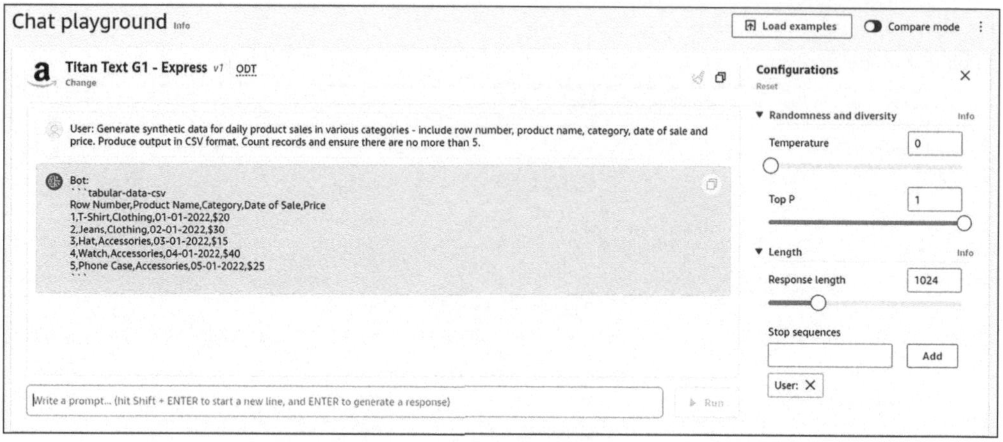

Figure 9.3: *Using the Amazon Bedrock Chat Playground*

7. From here, you can copy and paste the output in your favorite text editor (saving it as a *.csv file), or copy and paste the content into an Excel/ Google Sheet workbook and use the `Split Text to Columns` feature to load this as a proper dataset.

LLM Configuration

Note that in our aforementioned example, we have several configuration settings that can refine how the LLM generates output. Let's review what each of these means. However, keep in mind that the best way to optimize the configuration is to experiment with different settings, as these will likely vary across specific use cases:

- **Temperature** specifies the level of randomness (on a 0 to 1 scale) that the model uses to generate output. A value of 0 should be used when you want the output to focus on accuracy, while a higher value closer to 1 should be used when you are experimenting with more creative outputs like composing a poem or writing a piece of fiction and you want the model to incorporate more variety in its responses.
- **Top P** limits the number of options an LLM should consider when looking at predicting the next token probabilistically. This could be used to remove low-quality options from consideration. However, it's likely you won't need to alter this value as recent LLMs typically do a good job of focusing on high-probability tokens, and thereby will naturally exclude low-quality options.
- **Response length** ensures the LLM output is constrained to a specific length. While this might not be critical for cheaper open-source LLMs, you might want to consider constraining output when using more powerful and expensive models.

Blockchain

The integration of blockchain technology into data analytics marks a significant shift in how data is managed, secured, and analyzed. Blockchain, most commonly known for its role in cryptocurrencies, is essentially a **distributed ledger technology** (**DLT**) that allows for secure, transparent, and tamper-proof record-keeping. The implications of this technology for data analytics are profound and multifaceted, promising to reshape the landscape of data-driven decision-making.

First and foremost, blockchain introduces an unprecedented level of security and integrity to data analytics. In a blockchain, data is stored in blocks that are cryptographically linked and distributed across a network of nodes, making it nearly impossible to alter or tamper with the data. This inherent security feature is invaluable for data analytics, particularly in fields where data integrity is paramount, such as financial services, healthcare, and government operations. Analysts can trust the data's authenticity, leading to more accurate and reliable analytical outcomes.

Another key impact of blockchain on data analytics is the enhancement of data provenance and traceability. With blockchain, each transaction or data entry is recorded with a timestamp and a unique cryptographic signature. This creates an immutable audit trail, allowing analysts to trace the origins and history of any data piece easily. This level of transparency is crucial for compliance, auditing, and verifying the legitimacy of data, especially in sectors where regulatory compliance and data provenance are critical concerns.

Blockchain also opens up new possibilities in decentralized analytics. Traditional data analytics often relies on centralized data storage, which can be a bottleneck in terms of accessibility and a single point of failure. Blockchain enables a decentralized approach, where data is stored and processed across a distributed network. This not only enhances data security and accessibility but also allows for more collaborative and inclusive data analysis, as various stakeholders can contribute to and access the data without the need for a central intermediary:

Figure 9.4: *Fictional Depiction of the Blockchain, Generated Using ChatGPT*

In addition to these benefits, blockchain facilitates the creation of smart contracts - self-executing contracts with the terms of the agreement directly written into code. In the realm of data analytics, smart contracts can automate various processes, such as data access permissions, compliance checks, and even certain analytical tasks. This automation can streamline operations, reduce the potential for human error, and ensure consistency and efficiency in data processing.

Lastly, the integration of blockchain with emerging technologies such as the **Internet of Things** (**IoT**) and **Artificial Intelligence** (**AI**) presents exciting opportunities for advanced analytics. IoT devices can record vast amounts of data directly onto a blockchain, ensuring secure and reliable data for analysis. When combined with AI, this data can be used to derive deeper insights, predict trends, and make more informed decisions. The synergy of blockchain with these technologies not only enhances the scope and accuracy of data analytics but also paves the way for innovative applications across various industries.

In conclusion, blockchain technology is set to have a profound impact on the future of data analytics. Its capabilities in ensuring data security, enhancing transparency, facilitating decentralized analytics, enabling smart contracts, and integrating with other advanced technologies position it as a key driver of innovation in the data analytics domain. As blockchain continues to evolve, it will undoubtedly unlock new potentials and opportunities, transforming how data is analyzed and utilized in decision-making processes.

Introducing Amazon Managed Blockchain

Amazon Managed Blockchain is a comprehensive service provided by AWS that significantly simplifies the process of setting up, managing, and scaling a blockchain network. It offers robust support for popular blockchain frameworks like Hyperledger Fabric and Ethereum, catering to a variety of use cases ranging from supply chain management to financial transactions. The service is designed to overcome the traditional complexities associated with creating and maintaining a blockchain network, such as ensuring network security, scaling infrastructure, and managing software.

One of the key features of Amazon Managed Blockchain is its fully managed nature. It automates many of the time-consuming tasks typically involved in running a blockchain network, such as hardware provisioning, software installation, and network setup. This allows businesses to focus on developing their blockchain applications rather than on the underlying infrastructure. The service scales automatically to accommodate the needs of thousands of applications running millions of transactions, making it highly suitable for enterprises that require robust and reliable blockchain solutions.

In addition to simplifying blockchain network management, Amazon Managed Blockchain ensures secure and reliable transactions across a distributed network. It facilitates easy addition and management of network members, each with specific permissions, enhancing collaboration while maintaining privacy and security. Moreover, it integrates seamlessly with other AWS services, enabling users to enhance their blockchain networks with additional capabilities such as data analytics, machine learning, and secure data storage. This comprehensive integration positions Amazon Managed Blockchain as a versatile tool for organizations looking to harness the potential of blockchain technology in a cloud environment.

Using Amazon Managed Blockchain

Let's outline how to use Amazon Managed Blockchain and perform basic analytics on it:

1. Navigate to the Amazon Managed Blockchain service and review the **`Dedicated public networks`** available from the Networks tab. Ethereum is a popular choice for public use cases, so we will choose **`Ethereum Testnet Goerli`** to create our nodes.

2. Click **`Create node`** and keep the default configuration to create a node on the Ethereum network. Note that it may take at least 30 minutes to create this node:

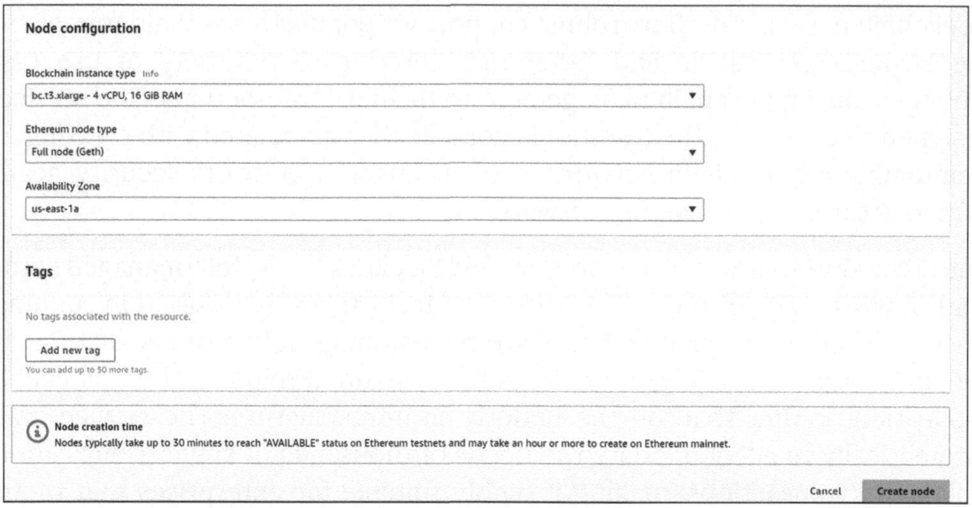

***Figure 9.5**: Configuring a Blockchain Node in Amazon Managed Blockchain*

3. Once created, you can interact with this node to manage ledger transactions and query them.
4. Use the APIs provided by Amazon Managed Blockchain to query the ledger for transaction data, block information, and other relevant data points. In Hyperledger Fabric, you can use tools like CouchDB to facilitate data queries.
5. For efficient analysis, it's often practical to store the extracted data in a database. Amazon S3 or Amazon RDS can be used to store this data. Ensure that the data is stored securely and is compliant with data governance policies.
6. Use further analysis tools like Athena or QuickSight to perform analytics on the ledger data.

This example shows how Amazon Managed Blockchain facilitates not just the creation and management of blockchain networks but also makes it easier to perform analytics on blockchain data. By utilizing a combination of AWS services, you can extract meaningful insights from your blockchain transactions, aiding in decision-making and strategy formulation for your business.

Edge Computing

Edge computing, a paradigm that brings computation and data storage closer to the location where it is needed, is set to play a crucial role in the future of data analytics. This shift toward processing data at the edge of the network, as opposed to a centralized data-processing warehouse, has significant implications for how data is analyzed, processed, and leveraged for decision-making.

One of the primary impacts of edge computing on data analytics is the reduction in latency. In traditional cloud computing models, data must travel to a central server for processing, which can cause delays. Edge computing, by processing data locally or at nearby edge nodes, significantly reduces this travel time, leading to faster data processing and real-time analytics. This is especially critical in applications requiring immediate insights, such as autonomous vehicles, real-time traffic management, and industrial automation.

Another key benefit of edge computing in data analytics is bandwidth conservation. By processing data locally and only sending relevant or processed data back to the cloud, edge computing greatly reduces the amount of data that need to traverse the network. This is increasingly important as the volume of data generated by IoT devices continues to grow exponentially. Reducing bandwidth usage not only saves costs but also ensures that networks are not overwhelmed by the sheer volume of data.

Edge computing also enhances privacy and security. By processing sensitive data locally, rather than sending it over the network to a central server, there is less exposure to potential security breaches. This local processing approach is particularly beneficial for industries handling sensitive information, such as healthcare, finance, and government operations. Moreover, with the implementation of advanced encryption and localized security protocols, edge computing provides a more secure framework for data analytics.

The integration of edge computing with AI and machine learning offers another transformative potential for data analytics. Edge devices, equipped with AI capabilities, can analyze data on the spot and make intelligent decisions without the need for constant back-and-forth communication with a central server. This leads to more autonomous and efficient systems, where real-time data analysis can lead to immediate actions, adjustments, or predictions.

Furthermore, edge computing enables more scalable and flexible data analytics solutions. Instead of being constrained by the processing power and storage capacity of a central server, edge computing allows for a distributed approach, where multiple edge devices can work in tandem to process large datasets. This scalability is essential as the amount and variety of data continue to grow, ensuring that analytical systems can adapt and expand as needed.

In conclusion, edge computing is set to revolutionize the field of data analytics. By enabling real-time data processing, conserving bandwidth, enhancing security, integrating with AI, and offering scalable solutions, edge computing addresses many of the limitations of traditional cloud-based analytics. As technology continues to evolve, the role of edge computing in enabling faster, more efficient, and more secure data analytics will become increasingly vital, shaping the future of how we leverage data for decision-making and innovation.

Living on the Edge with AWS IoT Greengrass

AWS IoT Greengrass is a service offered by Amazon Web Services that extends cloud capabilities to local devices, enabling them to perform data processing and decision-making at the edge. This service is particularly crucial in Internet of Things (IoT) environments where devices often need to respond quickly to local events, operate with intermittent connectivity, and securely handle data. By bringing cloud functionality closer to IoT devices, Greengrass plays a vital role in reducing latency and bandwidth usage, ensuring more efficient and responsive IoT applications.

One of the key features of AWS IoT Greengrass is its ability to run AWS Lambda functions locally on IoT devices. This feature allows the same code that runs in the AWS cloud to be deployed and executed on devices in the field. As a result, developers can apply the same programming model both in the cloud and at the edge, streamlining the development process. Additionally, IoT Greengrass facilitates local data caching, message routing between devices, and secure connections to AWS services, even when devices are offline. Once the connection is re-established, the data can be synced with the cloud for further processing and storage.

IoT Greengrass also emphasizes security at the edge. It incorporates secure, local encryption of data and offers secure and authenticated communications within local networks and with the cloud. This is critical in ensuring that sensitive data generated by IoT devices is handled securely, maintaining data integrity and privacy. Moreover, Greengrass seamlessly integrates with AWS IoT Core, allowing for easy device management and configuration, including secure, over-the-air (OTA) software updates.

In summary, AWS IoT Greengrass is a powerful service for businesses looking to harness the potential of IoT by bringing cloud capabilities closer to where data is generated. With its ability to run local compute, messaging, data caching, sync, and ML inference capabilities, IoT Greengrass enhances IoT applications' efficiency and responsiveness. Its integration with other AWS services and emphasis on security make it an essential tool for developing advanced, scalable, and secure IoT solutions.

Performing Basic Analytics at the Edge

Setting up a basic AWS IoT Greengrass project and performing basic analytics involves several steps, from configuring the Greengrass environment to deploying and executing Lambda functions. Here is an outline to guide you through this process:

1. Secure a device that can act as a Greengrass Core, like a Raspberry Pi or an EC2 instance.
2. Confirm your device is connected to the internet.
4. From the AWS IoT Greengrass console, connect this device by clicking **`Set up one core device`**.
5. Give a name to your device, add to an existing group (or create a new one), and then follow the instructions to install the Greengrass Core software onto your device (instructions vary depending on the operating system):

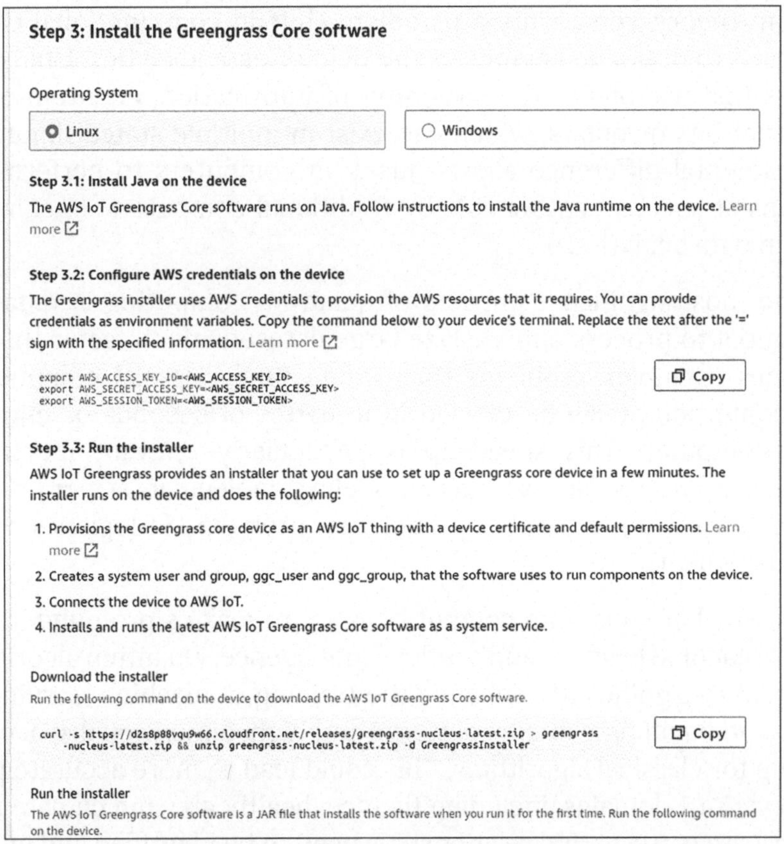

Figure 9.6: *Installing a Greengrass Core Device*

6. Write a Lambda function for a desired analytics task. This could be data processing, aggregation, or any other computation.
7. Deploy the Lambda Function to Greengrass. You can do this by associating the Lambda function with your Greengrass Group and then deploying it. The function will now run locally on the Greengrass Core device.
8. Configure your device data sources by setting up sensors or other data collection devices. This data can be stored locally or sent to the cloud for further analysis in a separate system such as S3, Glue, or QuickSight.
9. Use the deployed Lambda function to process the data collected from your IoT devices. This could involve filtering, aggregating, or transforming data.

Quantum Computing

Quantum computing, a groundbreaking technology based on the principles of quantum theory, represents a paradigm shift in computational capabilities and is poised to dramatically impact the field of data analytics. Unlike classical computers that use bits as the basic unit of information, quantum computers use quantum bits or qubits, which can exist in multiple states simultaneously. This fundamental difference allows quantum computers to perform complex calculations at speeds unattainable by traditional computers, opening up new frontiers in data analytics.

One of the most significant impacts of quantum computing in data analytics is its potential to process and analyze large datasets much faster than current technologies. Complex problems that would take classical computers years to solve could potentially be tackled in a matter of seconds or minutes on a quantum computer. This speed-up is particularly relevant for tasks such as optimizing large-scale systems, modeling molecular structures in drug discovery, and solving intricate optimization problems in logistics and supply chain management.

Another area where quantum computing is set to make a profound impact is in the field of machine learning and artificial intelligence. Quantum algorithms have the potential to significantly enhance the training of machine learning models, particularly in handling complex patterns and high-dimensional spaces that are challenging for classical algorithms. This could lead to more accurate predictive models in various domains, including finance, healthcare, and climate modeling, where intricate patterns and relationships need to be identified and understood.

Quantum computing also promises advancements in cryptography and data security, areas crucial to data analytics. With its ability to efficiently perform calculations that are infeasible for classical computers, quantum computing can both pose a threat to traditional encryption methods and offer new, more secure cryptographic techniques. This dual aspect underscores the need for quantum-safe cryptography to protect data in a future where quantum computing is ubiquitous.

The integration of quantum computing with big data analytics could revolutionize how we approach complex, data-intensive problems. For instance, quantum algorithms are well-suited for searching through vast databases and performing complex optimization tasks, making them ideal for applications in sectors such as finance, where real-time market analysis and risk assessment are crucial.

Recently, the team at Atom Computing was able to build the largest quantum computer using 1000 qubits, over twice as many as the previous record holder by IBM [3]. However, despite these great strides, quantum computing is still in its nascent stages, and practical and widespread applications in data analytics are yet to be fully realized. Current quantum computers face challenges such as error rates and maintaining qubits in a stable state (quantum coherence). Despite these challenges, ongoing research and development in quantum computing promises to overcome these hurdles, paving the way for its transformative integration into data analytics.

In conclusion, quantum computing holds immense potential for the future of data analytics. Its ability to process vast amounts of data at unprecedented speeds, enhance machine learning models, advance cryptography, and tackle complex optimization problems could revolutionize various sectors. As the technology matures, it is poised to unlock new capabilities and insights in data analytics, leading to more informed decision-making and innovation across numerous fields.

Introducing Amazon Braket

Amazon Braket is a fully-managed AWS service that provides scientists, researchers, and developers with a development environment to explore and build quantum computing algorithms and applications. This service is designed to facilitate access to quantum computing technology, making it more accessible to a broader audience. With Amazon Braket, users can design quantum algorithms, test them on simulated quantum computers, and run them on a variety of quantum hardware technologies.

A key feature of Amazon Braket is its hardware-agnostic approach. The service offers access to different types of quantum computing devices from multiple providers, including gate-based superconducting systems and quantum annealers. This variety allows users to select the hardware that best fits their specific application needs. Users can experiment with and compare results across different quantum technologies, providing valuable insights into the strengths and limitations of each approach. This flexibility is crucial in a field that is still in its exploratory stages, where different quantum technologies are being developed and assessed for various applications.

Amazon Braket also includes a high-performance, fully-managed quantum circuit simulator, which enables users to test and refine their quantum algorithms in a simulated environment. This feature is especially important for optimizing algorithms before running them on actual quantum hardware, which can be costly and limited in availability. The integrated development environment, based on Jupyter notebooks, offers a familiar and interactive interface for coding, making it accessible for users who are new to quantum computing as well as experienced practitioners.

Moreover, Amazon Braket supports the development of hybrid algorithms that combine classical and quantum computing techniques. Such hybrid algorithms are particularly relevant in the current stage of quantum technology development, known as the **Noisy Intermediate-Scale Quantum** (**NISQ**) era, where quantum systems are not yet fully error-corrected and can benefit from classical optimization techniques. Amazon Braket, therefore, serves as a comprehensive platform for exploring the potential of quantum computing, offering a bridge between classical computing infrastructure and the emerging world of quantum technology.

Simple Analytics Using Amazon Braket

Using Amazon Braket for a simple analytics use case requires a basic knowledge of Python programming and quantum mechanics concepts. Let's create a Braket environment, write a basic quantum algorithm, and analyze the results:

1. Navigate to the Amazon Braket console and complete the onboarding process to give your account access to Braket hardware. This involves creating a service role and optionally enabling third-party service access, and creating a notebook to run a basic simulation.

2. Once your notebook instance has been created, navigate to the notebook instance and open the Jupyter notebook.

3. Create a new notebook titled **`Bell_State.ipynb`**
4. Use the following script to create a simple quantum circuit (for example, Bell State) [4]:

```
from braket.circuits import Circuit
from braket.devices import LocalSimulator

bell_circuit = Circuit().h(0).cnot(control=0, target=1)
print(bell_circuit)
```

5. You can use a local simulator provided by Braket to execute the circuit (in this case, 1000 times):

```
device = LocalSimulator()
result = device.run(bell_circuit, shots=1000).result()
counts = result.measurement_counts
print(counts)
```

6. The output **`counts`** show how many times each bitstring was measured. For a Bell State, you should see roughly equal counts for 00 and 11, indicating entanglement.
7. As this is effectively just like any other Jupyter notebook, you can use libraries like `Matplotlib` to visualize the results:

```
import matplotlib.pyplot as plt

plt.bar(counts.keys(), counts.values())
plt.xlabel('States')
plt.ylabel('Counts')
plt.show()
```

8. The resulting graph should also confirm roughly equal counts for 00 and 11:

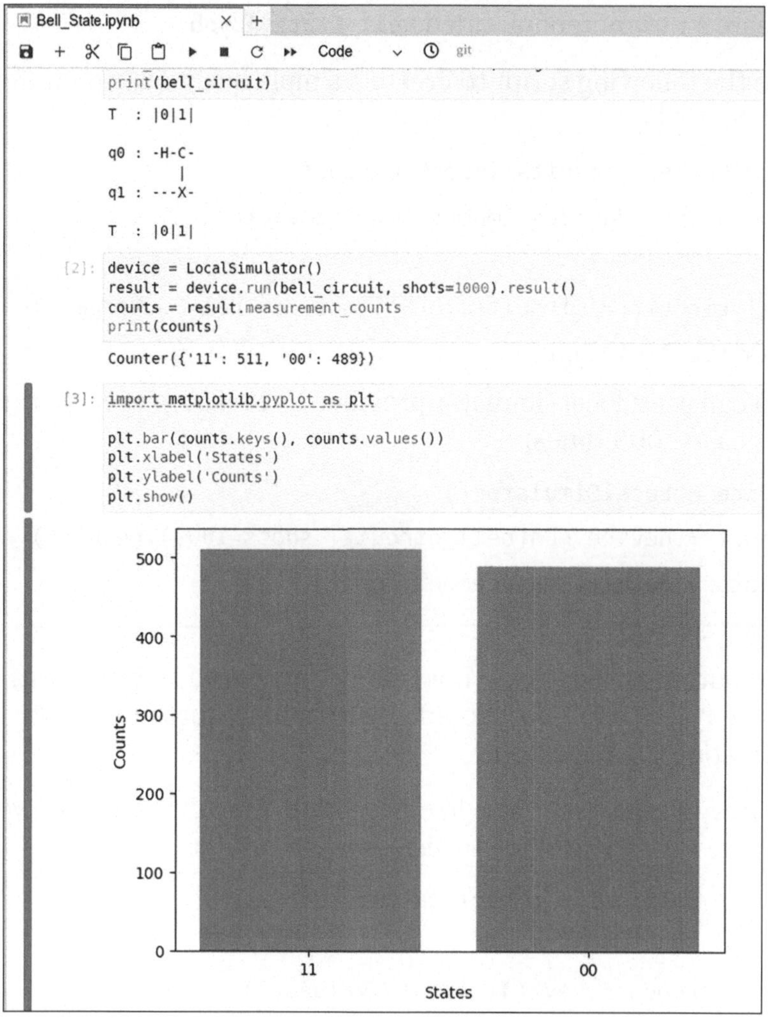

***Figure 9.7**: Running Quantum Computing Algorithms on a Jupyter Notebook*

Sustainability and Green Data Analytics

As the world increasingly focuses on environmental responsibility, data analytics on AWS offers a unique opportunity to drive advancements in green technology and sustainable practices. One of the key areas of focus is data center efficiency, a crucial aspect of reducing the environmental footprint of technology.

Data centers, which are the backbone of cloud services like AWS, consume a significant amount of energy. To address this, there is a growing trend towards making these data centers more energy-efficient and environmentally friendly. AWS, for instance, has been investing heavily in green data center designs that maximize energy efficiency. This includes using advanced cooling techniques, optimizing server utilization, and incorporating renewable energy sources. These efforts not only reduce carbon emissions but also lower operational costs, making it an attractive proposition for businesses.

In addition to improving data center infrastructure, there is a push towards developing analytics tools that specifically focus on sustainability. These tools enable businesses to analyze their carbon footprint, energy usage, and other environmental metrics. By leveraging big data and machine learning algorithms, companies can identify patterns and inefficiencies in their operations, leading to more sustainable practices. For instance, predictive analytics can forecast energy demands, allowing for better integration of renewable energy sources into the grid.

The integration of clean tech with data analytics is another exciting frontier. Technologies like IoT sensors and smart grids collect vast amounts of data that can be analyzed to optimize energy usage and support sustainable practices. For example, IoT sensors in agriculture can provide data on soil moisture and nutrient levels, enabling precise irrigation and fertilization, which conserves resources and reduces environmental impact.

Moreover, there is an increasing emphasis on the concept of 'circular data centers.' This concept revolves around the idea of creating a circular economy for data center resources. It includes recycling waste heat for community heating, repurposing old equipment, and using recycled materials in construction. By analyzing data related to resource utilization and lifecycle management, AWS can play a pivotal role in advancing circular economy practices in the tech industry.

In conclusion, the intersection of data analytics and sustainability on platforms like AWS is not just a trend but a necessary evolution in our approach to technology. By harnessing the power of data to drive efficiency and embracing innovative green technologies, we can pave the way for a more sustainable future. This evolution is crucial not only for the health of our planet but also for the long-term viability of businesses in a world increasingly conscious of its environmental impact.

Viewing Your Carbon Footprint on AWS

As you may have seen by now, the AWS Billing and Cost Management Console provides very useful, up-to-the-minute data on your overall account usage by service and type of usage. From this console, click the **`Cost and Usage Reports`** section and scroll down to see a summary of the carbon footprint resulting from your infrastructure usage on AWS:

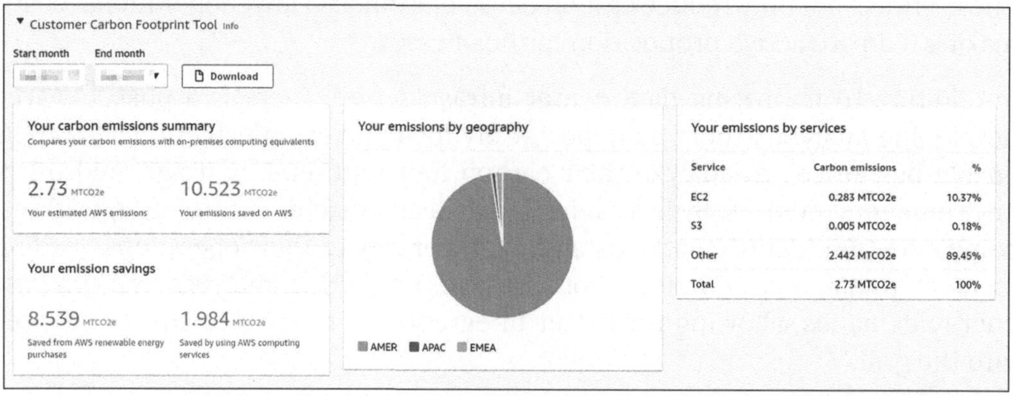

Figure 9.8: *Carbon Footprint Tool from the AWS Billing and Cost Management Console*

You can click **Download** to export this information as a CSV file if ever needed for compliance or other reporting reasons. Scroll down to see your emission usage over time and projections on future emissions as AWS works to optimize its own usage.

Keeping Up with the Pace of Innovation

At this stage, you might feel overwhelmed, and who could blame you? You probably feel a bit like Alice:

'Well, in our country,' said Alice, still panting a little, 'you'd generally get to somewhere else – if you ran very fast for a long time, as we've been doing.'

'A slow sort of country!' said the Queen. 'Now, here, you see, it takes all the running you can do, to keep in the same place.

If you want to get somewhere else, you must run at least twice as fast as that!'

- Lewis Carroll, "Through the Looking Glass" (1871)

That's why it's important to stay grounded in the fundamentals of your business. You could chase shiny objects until you are out of breath, but ultimately finding the one or two right tools for your analytics project should carry most of the freight for you as you continue your journey in data analytics.

Here are some additional ideas to keep in mind as you think about the future.

Always Be Learning

Embracing a mindset of lifelong learning can help you in all walks of life. The field of data analytics, more than ever, is one where the learning never stops. Graduates should stay abreast of emerging trends and technologies through online courses, workshops, and industry conferences. Platforms like Coursera, edX, and Udacity offer courses in cutting-edge topics like AI, blockchain, and quantum computing, often developed in collaboration with leading universities and companies. Engaging with these resources not only builds technical competence but also helps in understanding how these technologies are applied in various industries.

By now, you might have noticed a recurring theme here, namely that while we have many different ways to generate data, we have a core set of tools that we rely on (SQL, notebooks) that carry most of the freight for us. Finding interesting ways to keep using these core tools should help you gain further familiarity and have their use feel like second nature.

Finally, developing a strong foundational knowledge in data analytics is also essential. While it's important to stay updated with the latest technologies, having a solid understanding of core principles in data science, statistics, and programming provides a stable base upon which to build new skills. This foundational knowledge enables graduates to better adapt and understand how emerging technologies fit into the broader context of data analytics.

Show Your Work

Networking and community involvement play a significant role in keeping pace with changes. Joining professional organizations, attending meetups, and participating in forums can provide insights into industry trends and best practices. Engagements like these offer opportunities to connect with experienced professionals and thought leaders who can provide guidance and mentorship. Additionally, contributing to open-source projects or online communities can be a practical way to gain hands-on experience with new technologies and methodologies.

Another key aspect is to focus on developing soft skills alongside technical abilities. Skills like problem-solving, critical thinking, and effective communication are invaluable in an environment where collaboration and rapid adaptation are the norms. These skills are crucial for translating complex data insights into actionable business strategies, a core competency in the realm of data analytics.

Staying relevant in the face of rapid technological advancements involves a combination of continuous learning, community engagement, building a strong foundational knowledge, honing soft skills, and being proactive in career development. By embracing these strategies, you can not only keep pace with the changes but also leverage them to build a successful and fulfilling career in data analytics.

Conclusion

As we reach the end of our exploration into the future of data analytics, the main takeaway is that while the pace of innovation may seem dizzying, the fundamentals remain our guiding stars. Amidst all the groundbreaking technologies discussed, our core tools like SQL, statistical knowledge, and computational skills continue to serve as the bedrock. By honing these fundamentals while judiciously integrating the right new innovations for our use case, we position ourselves for success even in periods of rapid change. In our concluding chapter, we will provide guidance on officially validating your AWS data analytics skills through certification, securing roles in this high-demand field, and highlighting additional learning sources to level up as new advances emerge. With the perspectives, examples, and tips covered in this book, you now have a comprehensive playbook both for delivering impactful data insights today and staying ahead of the curve in this dynamic domain tomorrow.

Points to Remember

1. Generative AI and LLMs like ChatGPT are gaining tremendous momentum and have promising applications for data augmentation and simulation, though accuracy issues remain.

2. Blockchain technology brings unprecedented data integrity, provenance tracking, decentralization, and automation via smart contracts that are set to transform data analytics.

3. Edge computing reduces latency, conserves bandwidth, enhances privacy, and enables real-time localized decision making critical for data analytics.

4. Quantum computing offers exponential leaps in processing power to analyze immense datasets, enhance machine learning, and transform cryptography and security.

5. Sustainability is becoming integral to data analytics through improving data center efficiency, developing analytics for tracking environmental impact, integrating clean technologies, and transitioning to circular data center designs.

References

1. "ChatGPT sets record for fastest-growing user base", https://www.reuters.com/technology/chatgpt-sets-record-fastest-growing-user-base-analyst-note-2023-02-01/
2. "Retrieval-Augmented Generation for Large Language Models: A Survey", Jan 2024, Yunfan Gao, et. al. https://arxiv.org/pdf/2312.10997.pdf
3. "Record-breaking quantum computer has more than 1000 qubits", https://www.newscientist.com/article/2399246-record-breaking-quantum-computer-has-more-than-1000-qubits/
4. https://github.com/ava-orange-education/Data-Analytics-on-AWS-Joseph-Conley/blob/main/ch9/Bell_State.ipynb

CHAPTER 10

Conclusion and Next Steps

Introduction

The exponential growth of data in the digital age has opened up exciting new possibilities for businesses to gain valuable insights and drive strategic decisions. In this chapter, we will review the reasons why data analytics is important in business operations, discuss how to approach a career path in data analytics, and explore other frameworks outside the AWS ecosystem that would be useful as you continue your journey in data analytics. We will also explore the AWS certification process and consider additional resources for learning.

Structure

In this chapter, we will cover the following topics:

- Why Data Analytics is Important?
- Career Paths in Data Analytics
- Data Frameworks Compatible with AWS
- AWS Certifications
- Additional Resources for Learning

Importance of Data Analytics

We have seen the power of consuming, transforming, and visualizing data to generate insights for our business. Let's review why that's important.

Innovate or Die

Innovation and speed stand as twin pillars in the realm of Data Analytics, driving organizations towards unprecedented levels of efficiency and competitive edge. In an era where data burgeons at an explosive pace, the ability to innovate in how we collect, analyze, and interpret this data becomes paramount. Innovation is not just about adopting new technologies; it's about reimagining business processes, models, and strategies through the lens of data-driven insights. This relentless pursuit of innovation enables businesses to uncover novel opportunities, tailor their services to meet evolving customer needs, and navigate the complexities of an ever-changing market landscape:

Figure 10.1: *Futuristic Race Car, Generated by GPT-4*

Speed, on the other hand, is the lifeline that sustains innovation in the fast-paced digital economy. The agility to process and analyze data swiftly allows organizations to make informed decisions in real time, transforming how they respond to market dynamics, customer behaviors, and operational challenges. Speed in Data Analytics means being able to stream, process, and analyze data as it's generated, turning the tide from reactive decision-making to a proactive and predictive stance. This rapid pace is crucial not only for seizing fleeting opportunities but also for identifying and mitigating risks before they escalate.

Together, innovation and speed in data analytics forge a formidable duo that propels businesses forward. They enable a culture of continuous improvement and adaptation, where insights derived from data analytics become the driving force behind strategic decisions. In such a landscape, businesses that harness these twin forces effectively stand to gain a significant advantage, carving out niches for themselves and setting new benchmarks in operational excellence and customer satisfaction.

Data Moats Help Defend the Castle

The renowned investor Warren Buffett often uses the analogy of a moat when discussing the strength of a business in a capitalist society [1]. Marauders try to attack from all angles, and he looks for good business owners and CEOs who focus not on quarterly stats but on widening the moat (making his investments stronger and safer). Data moats serve a similar function:

Figure 10.2: *Data Castle Protected by a Digital Moat, Generated by GPT-4*

Data platforms collect many different types of data from their users and can wield that data as a competitive advantage to build unique features, predict consumer sentiment, and even sell data-driven insights to third parties. Unlocking these advantages requires a solid understanding of the basics of data analytics, especially as data volumes grow and become more complex. It also comes with the responsibility to respect your users' wishes in terms of data usage and protect that data from marauders as well.

What Gets Measured Gets Managed

To effectively operate any business at scale, you need to have a firm grasp on your operating metrics and KPIs. Most startups learn this lesson the hard way, as growing from a small band of close-knit teammates to a larger army preparing for battle creates organizational burdens that can be solved with simple data analytics tools and pipelines.

The challenge is building internal controls that are lightweight, don't slow progress, but still meaningfully focus on the most important insights and not vanity metrics. For example, measuring **lines of code** (**LoC**) is tricky, as there are often times when it's better to remove lines of code rather than add lines, which leads to bloat and technical debt.

Measuring internal operations can also help identify bottlenecks and improve operational efficiency. Using analytics to manage throughput, work-in-progress, and cycle time metrics can identify stages with unusually high delays or resource constraints, as outlined in the Theory of Constraints [2]. This discipline can help your business operate effectively and provide peace of mind to executives.

Career Paths in Data Analytics

Data analytics has rapidly evolved into a crucial aspect of modern business, driven by the growing importance of data-driven decision-making in various industries. As organizations increasingly rely on data to guide their strategies and operations, the demand for skilled data analysts has surged.

All that is gold does not glitter; not all those who wander are lost...

- *J.R.R. Tolkien, The Lord of the Rings*

These professionals, adept at interpreting complex datasets, provide valuable insights that can significantly influence business outcomes. The role of a data analyst encompasses a broad range of responsibilities, from gathering and processing raw data to conducting advanced analysis and presenting findings in an understandable format. This field offers diverse career paths, ranging from specialized roles like business intelligence analysts and data engineers to more strategic positions like data scientists and analytics consultants.

As we have shown, platforms like AWS have become instrumental in the data analytics landscape. Proficiency in AWS has become a valuable skill for data analysts, opening doors to numerous opportunities in industries that are increasingly migrating to cloud-based infrastructure services like AWS.

The future of data analytics promises even more exciting prospects. The field is rapidly evolving, with advancements in areas like artificial intelligence (AI) and machine learning (ML), both of which are integrally supported by AWS. These technologies are revolutionizing the way data is analyzed and interpreted, allowing for more accurate predictions and deeper insights. As these technologies become more mainstream, the role of the data analyst will likely shift towards leveraging AI and ML to drive decision-making. This progression signifies a shift from traditional data analysis to a more dynamic role where analysts not only interpret data but also contribute to the development of intelligent systems.

For those aspiring to enter the field of data analytics, AWS offers a robust platform to develop and hone their skills. Its extensive range of services and resources, such as AWS Analytics and AWS Machine Learning, provides a practical learning environment. Engaging with AWS can help build a solid foundation in cloud-based analytics, a skill that is increasingly in demand. Additionally, AWS certifications are recognized globally and can significantly enhance a candidate's professional profile, making them more attractive to employers seeking skilled analysts.

Building out a Portfolio

Building a portfolio of practical work is a crucial step for anyone looking to showcase and develop their data analytics skills. Start by selecting projects that demonstrate a range of abilities, from data cleaning and preprocessing to advanced statistical analysis and predictive modeling. Each project should ideally highlight a different aspect of data analytics, such as data visualization, machine learning, or big data processing. Consider including projects that involve real-world datasets, which can be found on platforms like Kaggle or GitHub, to show your ability to derive meaningful insights from complex data.

When presenting your projects, clarity and context are key. For each project, provide a concise overview that outlines the problem you aimed to solve, the datasets used, the analytical methods and tools applied, and the insights or solutions you discovered. This narrative approach not only showcases your technical skills but also your ability to communicate complex information effectively, a vital skill in data analytics. Including visual elements like charts, graphs, and dashboards can make your portfolio more engaging and demonstrate your proficiency in data visualization tools.

To further enhance your portfolio, consider incorporating feedback loops and continuous improvement into your projects. Documenting the iterations of your analysis and the rationale behind each decision can offer insight into your problem-solving process. Additionally, engaging with the data analytics community by sharing your projects on social media platforms, blogs, or forums can provide valuable feedback and new perspectives. This not only enriches your learning experience but also expands your professional network.

Lastly, don't overlook the importance of technical documentation and code quality. Ensure your code is well-commented and organized, making it easy for others to understand your workflow and thought process. Using version control systems like Git can also demonstrate your familiarity with industry-standard practices. By carefully curating a diverse and well-documented portfolio, you not only prove your data analytics prowess but also showcase your commitment to professional development and continuous learning.

Finding Your Niche

As we have seen, there is a wide set of skills and applications to cover in data analytics. While it can be useful to learn the full toolbox, focusing on a specific niche within data analytics offers several significant advantages, particularly in an era where the breadth and depth of data being analyzed are expanding rapidly. Specializing in a niche allows professionals to develop deep expertise and nuanced understanding in a particular area, setting them apart in a competitive job market. This depth of knowledge not only makes them more attractive to employers seeking specific skill sets but also enables them to provide more insightful, high-value analysis that can drive targeted business outcomes.

Moreover, as industries increasingly rely on data-driven decision-making, the demand for analysts who not only understand data but also the unique challenges and opportunities within specific sectors (such as healthcare, finance, marketing, or e-commerce) continues to rise. Specialists who can navigate the specific regulatory environments, data types, and business processes of these industries can offer tailored solutions that generalists might overlook. This level of expertise allows for more effective problem-solving, innovation, and the ability to predict industry trends, thereby offering a strategic advantage to employers and clients.

Additionally, carving out a niche in data analytics fosters professional identity and personal branding, making networking and career advancement efforts more focused and effective. It opens up opportunities for thought leadership, such as speaking engagements, specialized consulting roles, and contributions to professional publications, further enhancing one's career trajectory. Ultimately, focusing on a niche not only enhances job satisfaction by allowing professionals to work in areas they are passionate about but also accelerates career growth through the development of highly sought-after expertise.

Managing Data Teams

Managing teams composed of data analysts, data engineers, and machine learning engineers requires a nuanced approach that balances technical expertise with collaborative synergy. The key is to foster an environment where each role's unique skills and perspectives contribute to the team's overall objectives. Begin by clearly defining each team member's responsibilities, ensuring that there is a mutual understanding of how their roles intersect and complement each other. Data analysts, for example, focus on extracting insights from data, while data engineers build the infrastructure for data ingestion and processing, and machine learning engineers develop predictive models. By delineating these roles, team members can collaborate more effectively, reducing overlaps and gaps in the workflow:

***Figure 10.3**: Managing a Data Team, Generated by GPT-4*

Communication is the linchpin of effective team management, especially in technically diverse teams. Encourage regular team meetings and open channels of communication to facilitate knowledge-sharing and problem-solving. It's crucial to establish a common language or set of terminologies that all team members understand, regardless of their technical background. This shared language enhances collaboration and ensures that insights and strategies are communicated clearly across the team. Moreover, leveraging collaborative tools and platforms that integrate well with data analytics and engineering workflows can streamline project management and keep everyone aligned on project goals and progress.

To further enhance team performance, invest in continuous learning and professional development opportunities. The fields of data analysis, engineering, and machine learning are rapidly evolving, and staying abreast of the latest technologies, tools, and methodologies is essential. Encourage team members to attend workshops, conferences, and training sessions, and to share their learnings with the team. This not only boosts individual skill sets but also fosters a culture of innovation and continuous improvement within the team. Additionally, recognizing and leveraging the unique strengths of each team member can lead to more innovative solutions and a more engaged and motivated team. By fostering a culture of respect, collaboration, and continuous learning, you can effectively manage a team of data professionals and drive your projects to success.

Data Frameworks Compatible with AWS

We have reviewed the major AWS services that can help us on our analytics journey. Let's now review some other prominent frameworks outside of the AWS ecosystem that complement these services and give us valuable tools to add to our analytics toolbox.

Apache Spark

Apache Spark stands as a powerful open-source unified analytics engine, renowned for its ability to process large-scale data analytics pipelines efficiently. Its core advantage lies in its in-memory computing capabilities, which significantly speed up data processing tasks compared to traditional disk-based processing. Spark supports a wide array of data analytics tasks, from simple data transformations and aggregations to complex machine learning algorithms, making it a versatile tool for data scientists and analysts.

One of Spark's key features is its resilience. It achieves fault tolerance through its advanced **Directed Acyclic Graph (DAG)** execution engine that optimizes workflow execution. This ensures that even if part of the process fails, Spark can recover quickly without needing to restart the entire workflow from scratch. Furthermore, Spark's ability to handle real-time data streaming, in addition to batch processing, allows for the development of robust, real-time analytics applications. Its ecosystem includes powerful libraries like Spark SQL for structured data processing, MLib for machine learning, GraphX for graph processing, and Structured Streaming for stream processing, offering a comprehensive toolkit for data analytics.

dbt

dbt (Data Build Tool) has emerged as a powerful tool in the realm of data analytics, particularly for transforming data within a data warehouse [3]. This tool enables analysts to transform data using SQL, a familiar language to most in the data field. dbt simplifies the process of cleaning, testing, and preparing data for analysis, making it an invaluable asset for teams seeking to streamline their data pipelines.

One of the key strengths of dbt is its ability to bring software engineering practices into the data analytics workflow. It leverages version control, modular code, and testing - practices that are staples in software development but were previously less common in data analytics. This approach ensures better data quality and reliability, as well as more efficient collaboration among team members. With dbt, data transformations are defined in simple and reusable SQL models. These models can be version-controlled, peer-reviewed, and tested just like any other piece of software, leading to a more maintainable and scalable analytics codebase.

Integrating dbt with AWS enhances its capabilities significantly. AWS offers a wide array of data warehousing and analytics services like Amazon Redshift, which work seamlessly with dbt. By using dbt in conjunction with AWS, teams can leverage the scalability and performance of AWS services while maintaining the simplicity and efficiency of dbt for data transformation tasks. For instance, data can be extracted and loaded into Amazon Redshift using any ETL tool, and then dbt can be used to perform complex transformations within Redshift. This integration allows teams to build robust, scalable, and efficient data pipelines that are essential for today's data-driven decision making.

Furthermore, dbt's compatibility with the AWS ecosystem empowers analytics engineers to interact with data and transform it wherever it resides within the AWS cloud. This flexibility is crucial for organizations that manage large volumes of data across different storage solutions. dbt's ability to plug into these systems reduces the time and effort required to prepare data for analysis, allowing analysts to focus more on deriving insights rather than managing data infrastructure.

dbt represents a significant advancement in the way data teams approach analytics. Its emphasis on software engineering best practices brings a new level of efficiency and reliability to data transformations. When combined with the power and scalability of AWS, dbt becomes an even more potent tool. It enables organizations to build sophisticated, efficient, and reliable data pipelines, paving the way for more effective and insightful data analytics. For businesses looking to optimize their data operations, embracing dbt within the AWS ecosystem offers a pathway to achieving these goals.

Snowflake

Snowflake, a cloud-based data warehousing platform, has revolutionized the world of data analytics by providing a highly efficient, scalable, and easy-to-use solution for managing and analyzing large volumes of data. Its unique architecture, separate compute and storage capabilities, and support for multi-cloud environments make it an attractive choice for businesses seeking to leverage their data for strategic insights.

One of Snowflake's most compelling features is its ability to handle diverse data workloads. It supports both structured and semi-structured data, such as JSON, Avro, or XML, directly. This flexibility allows businesses to analyze various data types without the need for extensive transformation or integration processes. Additionally, Snowflake's architecture is designed to scale effortlessly. Users can scale up or down the computational resources (compute clusters) independently of the storage, ensuring they only pay for the compute power they use. This elasticity is particularly beneficial for businesses with fluctuating data analytics needs.

Integrating Snowflake with AWS enhances its capabilities. AWS provides robust infrastructure and a wide array of complementary services that Snowflake can leverage. For example, data stored in AWS S3 can be seamlessly integrated and analyzed using Snowflake. This integration allows businesses to take advantage of Snowflake's powerful analytics capabilities while keeping their data within the AWS ecosystem, benefiting from AWS's security, reliability, and extensive network.

Snowflake on AWS also simplifies the data sharing and collaboration process. Snowflake's unique data-sharing capabilities allow real-time sharing of datasets without the need for data movement or copying, facilitating secure and efficient collaboration both within and between organizations. When combined with AWS's global reach and network, this enables a highly effective and collaborative environment for data analytics, regardless of geographical location.

Snowflake stands out as a powerful tool for data analytics, particularly when integrated with AWS. Its ability to handle diverse data types and workloads, combined with its scalable architecture, makes it an ideal solution for businesses of all sizes. The integration with AWS further enhances its capabilities, providing businesses with a robust, secure, and efficient platform for data analytics. As data continues to be a critical asset for businesses, tools like Snowflake, especially in conjunction with cloud services like AWS, become indispensable for driving insights and strategic decisions.

Reverse ETL

Reverse ETL (**Extract, Transform, Load**) represents a relatively new, yet rapidly evolving concept in the field of data engineering. Traditional ETL processes involve extracting data from various sources, transforming it to fit operational needs, and loading it into a data warehouse for analysis. Reverse ETL, on the other hand, flips this process. It starts with the data that is already processed and stored in a data warehouse and pushes it back into operational systems and applications. The primary purpose of reverse ETL is to operationalize the insights gained from data analytics, making them directly actionable within business applications like CRMs, marketing platforms, or customer service tools.

The power of reverse ETL lies in its ability to enhance operational systems with rich, analytical insights. By integrating data from a centralized warehouse into daily business applications, organizations can make data-driven decisions in real time, personalize customer interactions, and streamline various business processes. For instance, customer service teams can receive updated customer segmentation information directly in their CRM systems, enabling more personalized interactions. Marketing teams can use detailed customer profiles to tailor campaigns more effectively, all thanks to the insights fed from the data warehouse through reverse ETL.

Several reverse ETL tools have gained popularity for their effectiveness and compatibility with AWS. One such tool is Census, which allows users to synchronize their customer data from a data warehouse like Snowflake, BigQuery, or Amazon Redshift directly into various business applications. Another notable tool is Hightouch, which operates similarly, offering robust features for syncing data warehouse insights back into operational tools. These tools are designed to be user-friendly, often requiring minimal coding expertise, thus making them accessible to a wider range of professionals, including those in marketing, sales, and customer support.

The integration of these reverse ETL tools with AWS enhances their capabilities. AWS's extensive cloud infrastructure, coupled with its powerful data warehousing services like Amazon Redshift, provides a solid foundation for reverse ETL processes. These tools can leverage the scalability, performance, and security of AWS to ensure seamless and efficient data synchronization. As data continues to drive business strategy, the role of reverse ETL becomes increasingly significant, offering a direct bridge between analytical insights and everyday business operations.

In-process Analytics with DuckDB

DuckDB has recently emerged as a compelling analytics SQL database that can actually run in the same process as your application, providing optimal performance and ease-of-use. At its core, DuckDB is an in-memory, columnar storage engine designed to provide fast ad-hoc analytical workloads. It works on any platform and offers a lightweight alternative to other bulkier analytics database solutions.

One of DuckDB's standout features is its ease of integration with popular data science tools and programming languages such as Python and R. This seamless integration means that users can directly query data within their preferred coding environment without the need for extensive data migration or transformation processes. For users working in cloud environments like AWS, this translates to a more streamlined workflow, as they can quickly move from data storage to analysis within the same ecosystem.

DuckDB also brings a unique capability to the table with its support for SQL, a widely used language for database management and data manipulation. This feature enables users, even those with minimal technical skills, to leverage the power of SQL for data querying and analysis. The familiarity of SQL can significantly lower the learning curve for new users, allowing them to quickly gain insights from their data.

Moreover, DuckDB's architecture is designed to efficiently handle large datasets, a common challenge in the data analytics field. Its columnar storage format allows for optimized data compression and faster query execution, particularly for aggregate functions, which are essential in data analytics. This efficiency makes DuckDB an attractive option for performing complex analyses on large volumes of data, a typical scenario in cloud environments like AWS.

Finally, DuckDB's lightweight nature and ability to run as an embedded database make it highly versatile for various applications. Users can easily set up DuckDB on their local machines for development and testing, and then scale their solutions to cloud platforms such as AWS for production workloads. This flexibility, combined with its powerful analytical capabilities, positions DuckDB as a valuable tool for anyone looking to harness the power of data analytics, regardless of their technical background.

AWS Certifications

AWS offers a range of certifications across different levels, including Foundational, Associate, Professional, and Specialty, each catering to various roles such as Cloud Practitioner, Solutions Architect, Developer, and SysOps Administrator. These certifications are highly regarded in the tech industry, serving as a benchmark for professionals to demonstrate their cloud skills and advance their careers.

The AWS Certified Data Analytics - Specialty certification [4] underwent significant changes recently and has been retired in favor of the new AWS Certified Data Engineer - Associate certificate, which focuses more on the earlier stages of our pipeline (integrating and transforming data) and requires more programming. If this doesn't pique your interest, take a look at other possible certifications [5], as earning these provides a good learning opportunity and can show potential employers what you are capable of.

Preparing for AWS Certification exams requires a strategic approach. First, it's essential to choose the right certification that aligns with your career goals and current skill level. AWS provides detailed exam guides and sample questions for each certification, which are invaluable resources for understanding the scope and format of the exam. Engaging in hands-on practice is crucial; AWS offers a free tier and practical labs to gain real-world experience working with AWS services. Additionally, leveraging online courses and training materials from reputable sources, participating in study groups, and utilizing practice exams can significantly enhance your readiness for the test.

It's also beneficial to immerse yourself in the AWS ecosystem by exploring AWS whitepapers, FAQs, and case studies, which provide deeper insights into how AWS services are used in various scenarios. Time management and stress reduction techniques should not be overlooked in your preparation strategy, ensuring you can navigate the exam efficiently and effectively. By combining these resources and strategies, candidates can build a solid foundation of knowledge and practical experience, positioning themselves for success in the AWS Certification process.

Additional Resources for Learning

AWS provides a bevy of documentation, training, and a generous free tier that allows us to experiment and build smaller-scale proof-of-concept projects. Here are some additional useful sources to advance your learning and give you ideas for future projects:

Figure 10.4: *Learning about Data Analytics, Generated by GPT-4*

Coursera

Coursera offers a comprehensive range of data analytics courses and specializations that combine video lectures from university professors and industry experts with hands-on projects, allowing learners to gain both theoretical knowledge and practical experience in data analytics.

Kaggle

Kaggle serves as a unique platform where learners can immerse themselves in the practical aspects of data analytics through participating in data science competitions, working on real datasets, and engaging with a community of data professionals to solve complex problems.

DataCamp

DataCamp provides an interactive learning experience focused on data analytics by offering bite-sized video lessons and hands-on coding exercises in R, Python, and SQL, enabling learners to apply concepts immediately in a real coding environment.

Conclusion

As we have seen, AWS provides a robust and versatile platform for realizing the full potential of data analytics. Its wide range of storage, processing, and analytics services empower teams to build scalable and efficient data solutions. However, technology is only one piece of the puzzle. Success ultimately depends on having skilled professionals who can leverage these technologies optimally. Therefore, the most vital takeaway from this chapter is the importance of continuous learning and skill development in data analytics. Whether it's pursuing AWS certifications, contributing to open-source projects, taking online courses, or experimenting with new tools, making a habit of upskilling is crucial. As technologies and methodologies evolve rapidly, staying current with the latest concepts and capabilities will determine who extracts the deepest insights from data. Commit to lifelong learning, and you will find yourself ahead of the curve, delivering greater value to organizations seeking to harness the power of data analytics.

Points to Remember

- Data analytics plays a crucial role in enabling data-driven decision making to gain a competitive advantage. Mastering data analytics unlocks growth opportunities.
- Building effective data pipelines, architectures, and teams is key to unlocking the true value from data analytics. This requires continuous skill development.
- AWS provides a versatile toolkit of services to ingest, store, process, analyze, and visualize data at scale. Becoming fluent in these services is a valuable skill.
- Complementary open-source tools like dbt, Spark, and DuckDB integrate well with AWS and add useful capabilities for data transformation, processing, and analysis.
- Specializing in a niche analytics domain allows you to build deep expertise needed to deliver targeted, high-value analysis and solutions. Finding your niche accelerates career growth.

References

1. "Buffett's Moat: Google's Competitive Advantage", https://www.investopedia.com/articles/insights/051316/buffetts-moat-how-sustainable-googles-competitive-advantage-googl.asp
2. "Theory of Constraints", https://www.leanproduction.com/theory-of-constraints
3. "dbt Labs", https://www.getdbt.com/
4. "AWS Certified Data Analytics Specialty", https://aws.amazon.com/certification/certified-data-analytics-specialty/
5. "AWS Certification - Validate AWS Cloud Skills", https://aws.amazon.com/certification/

Index

E

G

I

J

M

P

Q